D1523270

Jessie Redmon Fauset

Jessie Redmon Fauset
Reproduced from the Harmon Foundation Collection
By Permission of the Library of Congress

Jessie Redmon Fauset,

Black American Writer

by

Carolyn Wedin Sylvander

Whitston Publishing Company, Inc.
Albany, New York

For my mother, Ruth Hane Wedin

Jessie Redmon Fauset
circa 1935-1943?
Reproduced from the Farm Security Administration Collection
By Permission of the Library of Congress

Preface

Jessie Redmon Fauset, Black American novelist and journalist, has not been fairly or completely enough studied by critics and historians of Black literature. Erroneous or misleading information about her 19th century family origins and social class has frequently served as an inadequate basis for summarizing her work. In fact her early life was not easy or socially established, but in many ways struggling and full of hard work. Her high school and college records and her early involvement with the National Association for the Advancement of Colored People in the first decades of the 20th century indicate her efforts and wide interests in social issues. Fauset also deserves more credit for the literary importance of *The Crisis* and the *Brownies' Book* during the Harlem Renaissance period, primarily 1919-1926, than she has generally been given.

In her own writing, particularly in her essays and novels, Fauset demonstrates an awareness of the world-wide implications of the Black struggle in the United States and an understanding of the unique situation of the American Black woman. Her discussions of racial and sexual matters are disguised in novels with romantic and entertaining plots. Nevertheless, her exposure of the Black woman's confrontation with race and sex stereotyping is quietly thorough. Contrary to the repeated critical claim that Fauset wrote to promote respectable middle class Black life, she in fact emphasizes individual morality which is at variance with society's codes. In works more exploratory than dogmatic, more searching than protesting, she presents alternatives in defining "Black American woman."

Jessie Fauset and her novels have been much maligned. She deserves an accurate presentation of the achievements of her life. She defied habits and expectations and norms for Black and white women alike by her college career, her subsequent professional career, her financial independence. In her writing, she sensitively and unobtrusively examined the difficulties and the achievements of an understudied group in her portrayal of Black women. I hope that this study of her life and work, using letters and office memos and interviews as well as published sources, and concentrating on the whole of her work as editor and writer, will enhance the fuller and fairer reconsideration of Fauset's contributions to American literature which has begun here and there with a few critics.

This study of Jessie Fauset was originally undertaken in 1975-76 as a Ph.D. dissertation at the University of Wisconsin-Madison under a Woodrow Wilson Dissertation Fellowship in Women's Studies. My advisor, Dr. Annis Pratt of the English Department, and my readers, Dr. Walter Rideout, English, and Dr. William Van Deburg, Afro-American Studies, were unfailingly helpful to me in my early work on Fauset. I thank them very much, and I thank the Woodrow Wilson Fellowship Foundation for enabling me to spend a year on leave from teaching to do the first research and writing.

In revising and updating the Fauset manuscript for publication, I have been enormously assisted by a State of Wisconsin Research Grant, and I would like here to express thanks to the many people who made the grant possible. The assistance and support of many other people is also greatly appreciated; I will mention only a few of them here. I thank Ms. Donna Lewis for her enviable typing skills; Dr. Ruth Schauer for her proofreading; Ms. Judy McGuigan for her secretarial assistance; Dr. Harry Krouse, Chairperson of the English Department at the University of Wisconsin-Whitewater for his consistent and enthusiastic support of my combining writing and teaching roles.

Finally, I am personally indebted to Dr. Arthur Huff Fauset for his thoughtful, thorough generosity in sharing memories and information with me; to my husband, Stefan and my children, Monika, Mario, and Brendan for their patience, kindness, and enthusiasm.

Acknowledgements

Grateful acknowledgement is made for the use quotations from the following works, publishers, archives, letters; as well as for the research assistance given by many of the following libraries and people: Countee Cullen Papers, Amistad Research Center, Dillard University; Lee R. Edwards and Arlyn Diamond, *American Voices: American Women.* New York: Avon Books, 1973; Bryn Mawr College Archives, M. Carey Thomas Office Files, letterbooks 1897-1925; Herbert Aptheker, ed. *A Documentary History of the Negro People of the United States, The Reconstruction Era to 1918.* Secaucus, New Jersey: Citadel Press, 1951; Jean Fagan Yellin, "An Index of Literary Materials in *The Crisis,* 1910-1934; Articles, Belles-Lettres, and Book Reviews," *CLA Journal,* 1971; Manuscripts and University Archives, Olin Library, Cornell University Libraries, Ithaca, New York; *The Crisis,* New York; *The Way of the New World: The Black Novel in America.* Copyright © 1965 by Addison Gayle, Jr. Used by permission of Doubleday & Company, Inc.; Langston Hughes and Arna Bontemps, eds. *The Poetry of the Negro: 1746-1949,* New York: Doubleday & Co., Inc., Quotations from Jessie Redmon Fauset, "Enigma," "Dead Fires," "Oblivion"; A selection from *The Big Sea* by Langston Hughes. Copyright © 1940 by Langston Hughes. Reprinted with the permission of Hill and Wang (now a division of Farrar, Straus & Giroux, Inc.); Letters to the author and an interview with Arthur Huff Fauset; Elinor Sinnette, "The *Brownies' Book:* A Pioneer Publication for Children," 1965, and Paule Marshall, "The Negro Woman in Literature," 1960, *Freedomways* Magazine, 799 Broadway, New York; Claude McKay. *A Long Way From Home.* New York: Harcourt Brace Jovanovich, Inc., 1937, rpt. 1970; Excerpts from Jessie Fauset's poetry from *Caroling Dusk: An Anthology of Verse by Negro Poets,* ed. Countee Cullen. Copyright © 1927, Harper & Row Publishers, Inc. Copyright renewed 1955 by Ida M. Cullen. By permission of the Pub-

lisher; Letter to the author from David A. Lane; The Library of
Congress, Manuscript Division; Jessie Fauset. *Plum Bun*, 1929. By
permission of J. B. Lippincott Co., New York. Jessie Fauset. *The
Chinaberry Tree*, 1931, *Comedy: American Style*, 1933, New York:
J. P. Lippincott Co.; Jessie Fauset. *There Is Confusion.* Liveright &
Publishing Corporation, New York Copyright 1924 by Boni &
Liveright, Inc. Copyright Renewed 1952 by Jessie Redmon Fauset;
W. W. Norton Co., Inc.; E. Franklin Frazier, *The Negro in the United
States.* Rev. ed. New York: Macmillan Publishing Co., Inc. Copy-
right © 1957, 1971; The Joel Spingarn, Arthur Spingarn, Archibald
Grimke, Alain Locke Papers, Moorland-Spingarn Research Center,
Manuscript Division, Howard University, Washington, D.C.; Gerald
Sykes. "Amber-Tinted Elegance," *Nation*, 27 July 1932; "The
Reminiscences of George Schuyler," "The Reminiscences of W. E.
B. DuBois," in the Oral History Collection of Columbia University;
Pittsburgh Courier; Letters of Jessie Fauset to Zona Gale, Portage
Public Library, Portage, Wisconsin; Carl Van Vechten, *Nigger Hea-
ven.* Copyright © Alfred A. Knopf, Inc., New York; Hugh Morris
Gloster. *Negro Voices in American Fiction,* Copyright © 1948,
1976 by Hugh M. Gloster. Chapel Hill: University of North Carolina
Press, 1948. Rpt. New York: Russell & Russell, 1965; Letter to the
author from Elsie B. Smith; Frances Gaines, "The Racial Bar Sinister
in American Romance." October 1926, *South Atlantic Quarterly.*
Copyright © 1926 by Duke University Press; Letters of Jessie Fauset
to Zona Gale, Zona Gale Papers, The State Historical Society of
Wisconsin; James Weldon Johnson, *Along This Way,* New York:
Viking Penguin, Inc. Copyright © 1933, by James Weldon Johnson.
Renewed 1961 by Grace Nail Johnson, rpt. 1967; The James Weldon
Johnson Memorial Collection, Collection of American Literature,
Beinecke Rare Book and Manuscript Library, Yale University.

Contents

1

Historical, Literary, and Critical Context

Jessie Redmon Fauset, Black female novelist, poet, essayist, journalist, has been most frequently referred to in American literature or Black American literature anthologies and histories as a representative of the Black middle class, upper middle class, or intelligentsia. Her work has been said to reflect the respectable, proper, educated, imitation-white values and goals of the elite Black American, divorced from the Black masses and from the wealth of folk art which is nourished by and nourishes those masses. These commonly held views of Fauset's life and work are selective, incomplete, and unfair.

Fauset's four novels—*There Is Confusion*, 1924; *Plum Bun*, 1929; *The Chinaberry Tree*, 1931; *Comedy, American Style*, 1933—are often quoted out of context, are often inaccurately and incompletely summarized, and are rarely considered as deliberately constructed, subtle works of literature apart from incomplete and often inaccurate information about Fauset's own family background and upbringing. Her work as Literary Editor of the National Association for the Advancement of Colored People's publication, *The Crisis* from 1919 to 1926, her journalistic writing for that magazine from 1911 on, and her poetry and essays have not been critically summarized or evaluated as they deserve.[1] Although Langston Hughes and a few other writers and historians have mentioned the importance of her background work in the 1920's as a "midwife" to the Harlem Renaissance—that ferment of artistic and literary endeavor centering around the new Black metropolis created by migration from rural South to urban North—her work and influence during the period have been overlooked because of the attention paid to W. E. B. DuBois, longtime *Crisis* editor and influential author, sociologist, historian. That Jessie Fauset herself was "unduly modest," as her step-brother Arthur Huff Fauset has said, is clear when one compares the quantity, quality and range of her literary endeavors to her reputation as a minor figure in Black literature. Her work needs exposure, consideration, re-consideration.

A study of Fauset at this time must begin with a biography. Many errors about the facts of her life, originating perhaps partially in her own modesty in self-promotion, persist in printed materials about her. Even her birthdate is variously reported, usually in error. Her family background and childhood are made to appear wealthy and influential and comfortable when clearly they were in many ways struggling and difficult. Errors are compounded by omission, as in the many writers on DuBois who give him credit for important *Crisis* literary work which clearly belongs to Fauset. Since so much interpretive comment on Fauset's novels unfortunately depends on relating them to her background, her upbringing, her Harlem social position, the errors and omissions in facts about her life lead to errors and omissions and simplifications in interpreting her written work.

The necessary facts of Fauset's biography must be allowed to play against a background of the history and sociology of the Black American, the Black American woman, between 1882, Fauset's birth date, and 1961, the year of her death. Many slight biographical facts only attain significance against such a background; that Fauset was a Phi Beta Kappa graduate of Cornell University in 1905, for example, grows in significance when one discovers the number of Black women at Cornell at the time, the number of Black men and women there, the number of Black Phi Beta Kappas at that date, and, finally, the number of Black women Phi Beta Kappas at that date. This background information points out the exceptional nature of her achievement.

Even more important as an indicator of need for beginning a study of Fauset with a biography-history is the fact that the events and achievements of Fauset's life are amazingly representative of changes taking place in that portion of the United States—Black America—that feels and reflects changes of the larger culture in a

kind of distilled, intensified fashion. Fauset's first contacts, by letter, with W. E. B. DuBois were in 1903, when DuBois was the only
significant challenge to Black America's social, cultural, educational,
political and economic dominance by Booker T. Washington and his
"Tuskegee Machine." From that time can be dated the demand for
equal political and educational rights for Black Americans, given up
or deferred by Washington in favor of an oftentimes fictitious
economic advance, and the serious treatment of elements of Black
culture in the United States in DuBois' powerful *The Souls of Black
Folk* (1903), which Fauset praises enthusiastically in her 26 December 1903 letter to him.[2] Works like DuBois' *The Philadelphia Negro*
(1899), *The Suppression of the African Slave-Trade in the United
States of America: 1838-1870* (1896) had shortly before instituted
the scientific and historical study of Black America. John Lash, in
a 1949 article in *Social Forces*, "The Race Consciousness of the
American Negro Author," goes even further in defining the significance of the 1903 date in judging that Negro race consciousness
itself dates from these early DuBois publications and from DuBois'
challenge to Washington in the 1903 book.

   Jessie Fauset's early involvement with the activities of the
NAACP, founded in 1909, in its early integration cases as well as
in its publication, *The Crisis*, put her in a leadership position in the
first wide-reaching Black-white radical attempt to influence post
Civil War United States policies and practices in regard to Blacks.
Her moving to New York City and her position as Literary Editor of
The Crisis spanned the most controversial, struggling, free-wheeling,
exciting development of Harlem social and intellectual life and gave
her inter-racial social and professional contacts with many of the
major literary figures of the day: from publisher Horace Liveright
to Carl Van Vechten, to Sherwood Anderson, Sinclair Lewis, Eugene
O'Neill, Zona Gale among the whites; Claude McKay, Langston
Hughes, Jean Toomer, Countee Cullen, James Weldon Johnson
among the Blacks. Her several trips to France and trips to Africa,
and her training in languages, especially French, gave her a world-
wide perspective on Black issues at a time, after World War I, when
such "Pan-African" vision was of growing importance and need, and
when the flood of Spanish and French-speaking Black immigrants
into Harlem was of increasing account. Facts of history and

sociology, in other words, not only make clear the distinction of Fauset's life and work, but are themselves newly perceived and highlighted by a tracing of her path through them.

The lack of full biographical information on Jessie Fauset and the use of erroneous or misleading selected biographical information are not the only reasons for inadequate critical treatment of her work. Being Black in America, being Black woman in America, and being Black writer in America are all experiences historically fraught with pressures, conflicts, frustration, irony, and exploratory creativity. Critical attempts to categorize and thereby understand the flux of events, the range of the literature, the nature of Black authors, particularly in the Harlem Renaissance period, have leaned toward a dichotomizing which is of little value in looking descriptively at the work of a single author, and often toward a politicizing which simplifies the work of a single author to the point of misreading and misrepresentation. It would seem to be of value here to look at some of the peculiar questions the Black writer has been forced to deal with and use in American life and literature, and to look as well at some of the critical approaches to the Harlem Renaissance period which have created slightly varying, yet insufficient, summations and judgements of Jessie Fauset's writing and literary activities.

Black authors, and thereby Black literature, have been a vocal part of the distilled American experience which is Black life, impacted by and impacting upon it. Yet the role of the Black author is filled with unresolved and perhaps unresolvable questions. Is his/her art to be judged specially because it is Black? Is he/she an American author or a Negro American author? Do peculiarly Black themes have the potential of universality? Is any theme Black if a Black writer is using it? Is Black the color of one's head or one's skin? Is there a perceptible difference between Black themes written on by Blacks and written on by whites? Is a Black writer denying identity by writing of white characters? Is there such a thing as a Black aesthetic? If there is, can it be used by a white critic? If there isn't, should it be created? Can a Black writer be truly Black if supported, published, read and praised by whites? The distance readers and critics are in 1979 from wide agreement on answers to these and many more questions like them makes one humble when faced with struggles with the same questions in 1910, 1920, 1930. The beat goes on.

The American Black woman has had, of course, all the strictures of "woman" added to Black American identity, and without either the compensation of idealized femininity or the unity with white women in feminist and suffragist causes. Perhaps the more obvious and spectacular race prejudice has forced the Black woman to fight the racial battle before the sexual one. Perhaps simply because of white woman prejudice against the Black woman there has been little historical joining of white and Black hands to combat sexism. The Black woman has, for the most part, made a clear and forced choice of priorities—fight racism first, sexism will wait.

Examples of this choice of priorities on the part of Black women go back to 1866, when the proposed 14th Amendment to the Constitution, assuring freedmen the vote, introduced the word "male" into that document for the first time, and raised the questions as to whether or not women were actually citizens by its specific reference to "male inhabitants" and "male citizens." Despite the horror of Elizabeth Cady Stanton and Susan Anthony, staunch women's suffrage supporter Frederick Douglass supported the amendment.[3] A Black woman, author, speaker, Francis E. W. Harper, made the same ordering of priorities. "When it was a question of race, she let the lesser question of sex go. But the white women all go for sex, letting race occupy a minor position. . . . If the nation could handle only one question, she would not have the black women put a single straw in the way, if only the men of the race could obtain what they wanted."[4] White women's race prejudice also led to the same priorities. The formation of the National Association of Colored Women, in 1896, was clearly a result of Black women having been excluded from white women's organizations and activities, and of the persistent notion that the Black woman was particularly immoral.

Despite the double burden of racism and sexism; the thoroughgoing sexual use made of the Black woman by the white man since slave times; and the marginal economic position of the Black woman, she often became the strength and mainstay of the Black family. In 1908, Blacks interviewed by journalist Ray Stannard Baker agreed that, especially among the poor, the Black woman was the saviour of her race. "A Negro woman of the lower class rarely expects her husband to support her. She takes the whole burden herself."[5] Mary White Ovington, in a chapter entitled "The Colored Woman as Bread Winner" in *Half a Man: The Status of the Negro in New York* (New York: Longmans, Green and Company, 1911), reaches the same conclusions. "Self-sustaining work" for the Black woman begins at about age 15, does not stop with marriage, and does not ease up when children begin to earn a wage, as is likely with white women, Ovington reports. New York census figures in 1900 showed only 4.2% white married women employed, but 31.4% Black married women employed outside the home. The Black woman is consequently less fearful of leaving her husband, and the Black grandmother is a respected asset to the working mother (pp. 138, 140). At the same time, since 90% of the work available to the Black woman is "the job that the white girl does not want"— personal and domestic work—the temptation of prostitution is ever-present for those who can't or won't do housework, and the frustration of lack of employment opportunity is a great hindrance to education and skills training (pp. 141, 158). The combination of necessary independent strength and exclusion from the privileges allotted the white woman explains some of the distance between white women's groups, goals and actions and those of Black women's groups.

Jessie Fauset's American experiences with racism and sexism make less than surprising her own quite obvious ordering of social concerns: combat racism first. She was denied a teaching job in Philadelphia not because of her sex but because of her race. Girls in the dormitory at Cornell were discriminated against not because they were female, but because they were Black. She was involved in an early NAACP battle with Smith College, a women's school, because of its refusal to house a Black woman.

In 1922 she wrote of the denial of any special privileges she might have had as a white woman. While not in danger of beating or lynching, she felt instead, "only the reflex of those things. Perhaps it is mere nervousness, perhaps it is something more justifiable. Often when I am sitting in a crowded assembly I think, I wish I had taken a seat near the door. If there should be an accident, a fire, none of these men around here would help me."[6]

Yet even though Fauset's social concerns, most evident in her journalistic work, place questions of race before those of sex, in her fiction she does explore the psychology of not just the Black, but of the Black woman. Understanding the double discrimination suffered by the Black woman as well as her particular strengths and particular longings lends a helpful insight into some of Fauset's plots and themes. The happy marriage at the end of *There Is Confusion*, in which the theatrically successful Joanna Marshall will stay home and raise a family; the great urge toward respectability in Laurentine of *The Chinaberry Tree*; the influence of the mother and the temptation of the rich white lover to Angela of *Plum Bun*, all reverberate with the distinctive history of the Black American woman.

Just as the difficult question "What is an American?" is transformed into an intense quandry in "What is a Black American?" or "What is a Black American Woman?" so do the more concrete inspirations and problems of authoring in America intensify with a focusing in on the Black writer. The period of writing with which this study is most concerned, 1910 to 1935, is of course one of great innovation and productivity in all of American literature. The literature grows of and responds to the social and political and intellectual ferment of the first modern war, the United States Civil War; rapid uncontrolled industrialization; increasing speed in transportation; corrupt government, writings of Sigmund Freud, John Dewey, Thorstein Veblen, William James, G. B. Shaw, H. G. Wells, Arnold Bennett, Fĕdor Dostoevski, Henrik Ibsen; economic and behavioral entrapment of women; intellectual and political struggle of feminists; growing political agitation by radical groups— progressives, socialists, anarchists. When one centers on the ferment for a Black person or author leading to the period of literature in question, one finds additional burdens to thought and creativity.

There were 3,513 known lynchings between 1882 and 1927 (105 in 1901 alone). Jim Crow railroad cars, boats, waiting rooms, sections of jury boxes, Bible to kiss, drinking fountains were in place all across the South. Discriminatory disenfranchisement was accomplished in all eleven former Confederate States by 1910 (in 1896 130,334 Negroes were registered to vote in Louisiana; by 1904, after a literacy test, property test, and poll-tax were adopted, the total had shrunk to 1,342). Expenditures for Black education dwindled to trifling amounts (in Wilcox County, Alabama, in 1891, $4,397 was spent on teacher salaries for 2,482 white school age children and $6,545 on teacher salaries for 9,931 Negro children. By 1907-08, sixteen years after the law was changed to make distribution of monies at the discretion of local authorities, $23,108 was spent on teacher salaries for 2,285 white children; $3,940 was spent on teacher salaries for 10,745 Negro children). These Southern actions received national support in Supreme Court decisions such as *Plessy vs. Ferguson*, in 1896, which legitimatized "separate but equal" facilities. Between 1900 and 1910 alone, there were six major riots, four of them in the North. Southerners were quick to point out in 1898 that Northern support for United States acts in the Philippines, Hawaii and Cuba on the basis of inferiority of colored peoples was not much different than what the South was doing with the Negro.

It is no wonder that the scene was set for writers' calling attention to "failings and inadequacies of capitalistic democracy in America." *Main Street*, 1920; *Babbitt*, 1922; *An American Tragedy*, 1925—"American writers interested themselves in numerous social and economic problems. Labor problems received considerable attention, as did housing, crime, social planning, and disarmament. Novelists, dramatists, publicists, and other writers also turned to the American race problem."[7] White writers led the way to a surge of interest in Black life. Ridgely Torrence in 1917 wrote and Emile Hapgood produced three all-Black cast plays, *Simon the Cyrenian, Granny Maumee, The Rider of Dreams*. Eugene O'Neill wrote *Emperor Jones*, 1920; *All God's Chillun Got Wings*, 1924. Paul Green won the Pulitzer Prize with *In Abraham's Bosom* in 1926, produced with an all-Black cast. Carl Van Vechten, Victor Calverton, H. L. Mencken, Joel Spingarn encouraged Black writers. Finally, after the earlier need for a hiding of racial identity, as Charles Chesnutt's was hidden when he first published in the *Atlantic Monthly*, or need for white patron sponsorship, as in Paul Lawrence Dunbar's sponsorship by William Dean Howells, now "a market was created for stories of the dispossessed, and the Negro storyteller had an opportunity to tell his tale."[8]

While this new receptivity to Black authors on Black life was a real impetus to writing, it also created some evaluative problems that are still with us. The concern with content, with social issues or social exposure and protest in American literature in the 1920's was balanced with a concomitant concern with form. Frederick Hoffman in *The Twenties: American Writing in the Postwar Decade* makes the point emphatically that formal experiment and concern with form were major and necessary values for the 1920s novelists. of manners. In this balancing concern with form, which is able to retrieve an artist's concern with social issues from blatant (and often ineffective) protest and propaganda, the Black writer was at a dis-. advantage. First of all, from the social, educational, political conditions cited as special burdens which were inherited by Black America from the nineteenth century, comes a lag in simple technical competency, basic to innovative departures. Edward Bland spells it out in a 1942 *Negro Quarterly* article called "Social Forces Shaping the Negro Novel." Supporting his thesis that the 1920s produced only technically incompetent novels by Blacks, he sees the inadequacy in such skills as manipulation of foreshadowing, foreshortening, flashback, point-of-view, dialogue, tone, understatement and characterization as stemming from both biographical and social conditions for the Black author. Biographically, Bland suggests, the Black author did not have enough valued material, or enough participation in "the literary currents" of the day; socially he/she inherited an attitude toward literature as a tool, where "how" something is done is not nearly as important as "what" is done.

Others have made much the same observation about a differential in form in Black literature and the "main currents" of literature, at least up to 1935. St. Clair Drake in his Introduction to the 1970 republication of Claude McKay's autobiography, *A Long Way From Home*, finds that in Black autobiography, intimate personal experience is frequently subordinated to social considerations of oppression. "The traumatic effects of the black experience seem to have made confessional writing an intellectual luxury black writers cannot afford."9 Gary De Cordova Wintz sees "Negro thought" before 1920 as "primarily outer-directed," directed toward survival in a "hostile environment." The change in the Harlem Renaissance period is then a turning inward to search for the meaning of existence. Prior exposure of racism becomes search for racial identity through description and explanation of the life of Blacks.10 Carl Van Doren, writing "The Roving Critic: The Negro Renaissance" in *Century* in March of 1926, sees Black art in the 20s in relation to white American literature at the stage of American art in relation to England in the early nineteenth century. Harlem, a growing Black metropolis, was the key to the change from a people bound by a common condition to a people bound by a common consciousness. The turning from protest to search and from obscurity to exposure began in the 1920s but was not completed then. Through the 1920s an unfamiliarity with literary form and a lack of longstanding concern with matters of form proved to be technical handicaps to the Black writer. In Carl Van Vechten's *Nigger Heaven*, when would-be Black author Byron brings his manuscript to a white publisher, the latter asks him if he has ever been to a cabaret. "Many times," says Byron. "Well, that I can't believe!" replies the publisher. "Jean Cocteau could have done a cabaret better without ever having heard of such a dive."11

It has been exceedingly difficult for the Black writer to answer the questions of at what stage how one says something gets in the way of what one is saying, and of how far one must be emotionally detached from one's material in order to mold it into an emotionally and intellectually engaging experience for one's reader. Even when one agrees with W. E. B. DuBois that "all art is propaganda . . . ; the apostle of Beauty . . . becomes the apostle of Truth and Right not by choice but by inner and outer compulsion,"12 and with Sterling Brown that "the truth of Negro experience in America is strong enough propaganda,"13 the task of translating experience and history into effective literary form is ever present. In parts of her novels, Jessie Fauset was quite successful in reconciling the form-content difficulty; in other parts she overwrote or preached. Her problem was not unique.

Nor was a form-content struggle the only problem created with the new receptivity to Black authors on Black life in the late teens and early 1920s. Earlier well-known Black writers, such as Charles Chesnutt, while in a sense forced into an unnatural and unfortunate publishing position, were at least sure of their audience—it was white. But moving into the twentieth century there were two audiences, white and Black, with different knowledge, expectation, and sophistication. White readers, inheriting the stereotypes of the Black character in American literature which Sterling Brown lists in "Negro Character as Seen by White Authors"—the contented slave, the wretched freeman, the comic, the brute, the tragic mulatto, the local color Negro, and the exotic primitive—expected more of the same, and, as DuBois wrote in 1926, would buy nothing else. The popular and lucrative 1920s tale of the exotic Harlem primitive was, in Brown's estimation, just "a 'jazzed-up' version" of the contented slave, "with cabarets supplanting cabins."[14] Breaking out of the stereotypes the white audience expected was seen as fatal to opportunity. "The more truthfully we write about ourselves, the more limited our market becomes. . . . when we cease to be exotic, we do not sell well."[15]

But while Brown, DuBois, James Weldon Johnson in "The Dilemma of the Negro Author," and other Black critics point out the racial prejudgement demanded by the white audience, it is with the limitations of expectation and sophistication in the Black audience that they especially struggle. Johnson writes of the taboos and group-leveling operating on the Black writer, who arouses "bitter resentment" with certain phases of life, subjects, or manners of treatment.[16] DuBois, after describing what he sees as distorted white expectation, writes that "the young and slowly growing black public still wants its prophets almost equally unfree." In the 1920s, when breaking the bounds of conventional literary expression is almost *de rigueur* for the American author, DuBois sees the limits the Black audience seeks to impose on the Black author. "We are bound by all sorts of customs that have come down as second-hand clothes of white patrons. We are ashamed of sex and lower our eyes when people talk of it. Our religion holds us in superstition. Our worst side has been so shamelessly emphasized that we are denying we have or ever had a worst side."[17] The reaction is understandable, as DuBois suggests, because of the vitriolic anti-Negro propaganda coming from the pens of writers like Thomas Dixon in the pre-Renaissance period. One of the Harlem Renaissance novelists, Wallace Thurman, writes in 1927 that, "The American Negro feels that he has been mistreated and misinterpreted so long by insincere artists that once a Negro gains the ear of the public he should expend his spiritual energy feeding the public honeyed manna on a silver spoon."[18] Redding says that Negro readers "clamor to glorify the race, to increase the race's pride in itself, to speak only honor of it."[19] Benjamin Brawley also explains the desire of the Negro "that his case be properly presented to the American public." He concludes that "In some ways this stimulus was a good thing, but it clearly meant that the black man had constantly to be on dress parade."[20] Again, the reaction is understandable as counter-information to existent anti-Negro white literature. But the understandability of the pressure of course makes it no less bothersome for the artist who wants and needs to express personal vision without stultifying group pressure to conform to a limiting notion of acceptability. When one adds this Black group pressure to the mainstream American literature problems of censorship at the time of Fauset's first novels and to the similar group pressures on the woman writer, one begins to recognize the difficult publishing context of Fauset's work.

In addition to the limits the Black reading audience has often in effect imposed on material and treatment in Black literature, the audience has also lacked a reading sophistication and this lack has in turn hindered the Black writer. Sterling Brown writes of this problem, too, in *Opportunity* in 1930 (*Opportunity*, published by the National Urban League, is the Black magazine which, with *The Crisis*, is credited by most writers on the Harlem Renaissance with discovering, inspiring, and supporting new Black artists in the 1920s). Blacks, he writes, do not read much in the first place, but when they do, they are too quick to judge a Black writer as an apologist for the race, assuming that every character is meant to be representative. In a later, 1942, article, Brown adds to the indictment by seeing among Negroes "a dislike for books about Negroes and books by Negroes." Some have a "caste-ridden disdain of Negro life and character"; others "still condemn without reading, because they do not approve of the way of life portrayed."[21] Super-sensitivity to negative pictures of members of the race extends even to jacket covers of books, if one may judge by a 1942 article in *Negro Quarterly* by L. D. Reddick, "Publishers are Awful," in which he bemoans the "derogatory stereotypes" and "racial slander" of jacket drawings on Langston Hughes' *Shakespeare in Harlem*, published by Knopf (one of the publishers which had gone out of its way to foster Negro talent), and Arna Bontemps' children's book, *Golden Slippers*, published by Harper and Brothers. Reddick does place the blame on the publishers in these instances, but makes a clear ultimatum to the authors—they'd better not let it happen again.

Criticism of the Harlem Renaissance period, including Jessie Fauset's novels, from a later, retrospective position, has added its own elements of clarification and confusion to the problems of audience and of evaluation of Black literature. The 1960s and 1970s have brought forth reconsideration of the evaluative standards of "the white man's achievement" in the development of methods or perspectives of criticism called the "Black aesthetic" and "feminist criticism." Of exceeding helpfulness in jarring reader and critic into looking at what is there in a work of literature rather than at what one expects to be there based on traditional white male academic training, these two revisionist modes of criticism, in all their diverse and debated natures, share some features clearly of use in a study of Fauset.

Implicit to both the Black aesthetic and feminist criticism are attempts to define and document a subculture through more thorough looks at the cultural history of Blacks and women, through resurrection of forgotten writers, new consideration of minor figures, and reconsideration of major ones. Fauset's work, as has already been briefly seen, contains much untapped insight into the Black American woman's world. Relationships between writing and living, weight put on experience as well as artifact are common principles of feminist literary criticism and the Black aesthetic. They exemplify philosophy of criticism particularly suited to a study of Jessie Fauset, whose own attempts to unify writing and living have been frequently misunderstood. Both forms of criticism have called new and needed attention to the disguised forms which protest and discussion of forbidden topics are likely to take in minority art. The spiritual, the folk tale, jazz, blues, are seen as coded concealment of impulses or messages not allowed to surface directly; women's novels disguise "feminist critiques of the patriarchy by feints, ploys, and punishing denouements"—the "drowning effect."[22] As Gary De Cordova Wintz has pointed out, Fauset, "in spite of her conservative, almost Victorian literary habits, . . . introduced several subjects into her novels that were hardly typical drawing room conversation topics in the mid-1920s. Promiscuity, exploitative sexual affairs, miscegenation, and even incest appear in her novels. In fact prim and proper Jessie Fauset included a far greater range of sexual activity than did most of DuBois' debauched tenth."[23] The "drowning" theory enables one to look at this phenomenon as deliberate disguise on Fauset's part, rather than as a kind of unwitting accident, as Wintz seems to see it.

The lack of technical training and concern with form, the split or double audience of Black writers, and the closely attached question of proper and fair evaluation assumptions have been described as problems developed for the Black writer during the very growth of demand for his/her work. While the Black writer has had these problems superimposed upon the normal problems of artistry in America—such as the censorship abounding from 1917 to 1925—adding to the possible or probable stifling of the potentially great writer, it must also be pointed out that there are experiences of being a Black writer in America with potential benefit to literary creation. Two of these have particular relevance to Fauset's work: the intense ironic mode of Black life and the mulatto as the character embodying that irony; and the superiority which may come from suffering.

It is a commonplace that to be Black in America has been to live an irony. Whether patriotic rhetoric be compared with historical action, the Declaration of Independence with slavery and lynching, or the "American Dream" with the "American nightmare," the continuous awareness of barriers imposed simply by race as against the American promise of individual liberty and justice for all, makes of Blacks ironists. It also makes ironists of Black fictional characters.

It is not at all surprising that much Black American literature has used race mixture and passing to express the irony of American life, and that these topics have been used differently by Black than by white writers. Trying to define "Negro" in the United States has long been difficult, whether it be done by Southern state statute, where one-sixteenth Negro blood made one a "Negro," or by the train conductor examining hands and feet to see which Jim Crow car to send a person to. Instances of struggle with the question attain an ironic humor in their most simple factual outlines. Ray Stannard Baker, muck-racking journalist, spends pages in his 1908 book, *Following the Color Line*, in the chapter "The Mulatto: The Problem of Race Mixture," coming up against the question, "What is a Negro?" After seeing blond, blue-eyed and red-haired "Negroes" all across the country, and learning of whites being Jim-Crowed and kicked out of town for supposedly being Negro, he is no longer sure of the subject of his book. The 1900 United States census, Baker reports, gave up counting mulattoes, and simply counted as Negro all those who were thought of as such in their community. When Arthur B. Spingarn set out in the early days of the NAACP to collect everything written by Negroes (the collection which is now at Howard University), he ended up defining "Negro" as anyone who would be classified that way in the United States, broadening his number of foreign writers considerably. Even that definition becomes difficult in the self-defined case of Jean Toomer, certainly one of the most highly respected "Black" writers in America, who refused in the late 1920s to be included in James Weldon Johnson's anthology of Negro verse, maintaining that he was no more colored than white. The incident, Langston Hughes says, created critical consternation—how should Toomer be classified in lists and summaries?[24]

The use of the mulatto in American literature has for the most part differed between white and Black authors. The white writer has been much more likely to use "the hypothesis that white-Negro hybrids have acumen and attractiveness because of their white ancestry; that they deserve pity because the blood of Caucasian fathers flows in their veins, and that their misery, bitterness, defiance, and ambition are traceable to proud paternal forbears."[25] This suggestion of white credit for all the good points in a mulatto is present even in a sympathetic look like T. S. Stribling's *Birthright*, which, interestingly, inspired Fauset to write her first novel, *There is Confusion*.

The Black writer has been more likely to see in the mulatto character (and in "passing for white," which logically follows), a rich literary material which can encompass the intense irony of racial identity in America, and which has complex psychological implications for the individual character as well as the racial representative. Charles Chesnutt in June 1931 wrote in *The Crisis* as to why substantially all his writing except *Conjure Woman* dealt with problems of people of mixed blood. The problems, while "in the main the same as those of the true Negro," he says, "are in some instances and some respects much more complex and difficult of treatment in fiction as in life" ("Post-Bellum—Pre-Harlem"). Nora Waring makes the same point, though by comparing the mulatto to the white, in reviewing Walter White's *Flight* in 1926. "In fact the life of the cultured mulatto provides a far richer field for artistic literary development than the Nordic. A greater variety of complexes, due to his mixed blood, creates an involved psychology often misunderstood" ("Books," *The Crisis*, July 1926). It must be repeated that the mulatto as vessel for the ironies of American Black life has, in Black literature (as has the theme of superiority) the *potential* for literary creation, and that there are numerous examples of unfortunate use of the material. When a Black writer uses the cultured mulatto woman, for example, as a counter-stereotype to the unflattering image of the Black woman depicted by white writers, in an attempt to show "that there was another kind of life, that of the colored elite, a world of refinement, education, and respectability, culture and second, that there was another kind of Negro woman, the genteel mulatto, who except for her few drops of black blood was almost as good as her white sister,"[26] then the richness of the material is reduced to formula. But some of the negative reaction when all books dealing with mulattoes are lumped together is certainly in the reader and not in the books themselves. The best of the mulatto and passing novels explore the psychology and struggle of the mixed-blood character. James Weldon Johnson's *Autobiography of an Ex-Colored Man*, Walter White's *Flight*, Nella Larsen's *Quicksand* and *Passing*, and Fauset's *Plum Bun* and *Comedy: American Style* are especially strong in this important exploration.

In a 1971 article, Herbert Aptheker, student and historian of Black life and work in the United States, points out a theme often found in the work of Black writers, but quite thoroughly ignored, he says, by white writers on Black life, and white critics on Black literature, a theme he calls "Afro-American Superiority."27 The article serves as an excellent reminder of the possibility for new creation always contained in embryo form in a minority liberation movement. Black liberation does not mean making all Blacks like whites; it can nudge examination of white life and create a new humanness. Women's liberation does not mean making women as much like men as possible; it can encourage examination of positives and negatives in a male-dominated world, build on the former, eliminate the latter.

The Black artist, the writer, shares in the possibility of creating not just something the same, or something different, but something better than what exists. Carl Van Doren, writing "The Younger Generation of Negro Writers" in *Opportunity* in May 1924, predicted a valuable Black contribution to American literature because the Black author would have a happy balance between rage and complacency, passion and humor, the ideal balance for creative artists. "They will be artists while being critics." Though not freed from the social necessity of being propagandist, the Black artist would find that "the facts about Negroes in the United States are themselves propaganda—devastating and unanswerable."

This sense of capacity for something new and better in American life and American literature, a theme, as Aptheker says, that has been ignored for the most part by white writers and critics, helps to explain both some of the Black critical reaction to white authors who are clearly sympathetic to Black problems, and the generally up-beat nature of books like Fauset's *There Is Confusion, Plum Bun*, and *Chinaberry Tree*. Benjamin Brawley in 1929 writes that there is "just one thing to say" about white portrayers of Negro life: "there is undue emphasis on futility and fatalism. . . . The upstanding, industrious, self-respecting Negro who actually succeeds in the battle of life is not mentioned."28 DuBois, in a March 1927 *Crisis* review of Paul Green's *In Abraham's Bosom*, expresses essentially the same reservation. He approves of Green's sympathy—"he feels with his black folk"—but then goes on to deride so much horror, the "defeatist genre of Negro art, which is so common and at the present apparently inescapable." An honest white, he thinks, looks at the Negro situation and can't consider it bearable, "and therefore his stories and plays must end in lynching, suicide or degeneracy." or if he is a producer, he refuses a play in which a Black hero wins over difficulties. "The time has come," DuBois concludes, "for the Negro to be treated humanly on the stage, not only as to his suffering, but as to his plain and unquestionable triumphs."

There is a thin line between honestly depicting "plain and unquestionable triumphs" and showing only the good side of a people or a culture. One can readily see how Black novels with happy endings, such as Fauset's first three, can be read, as they have often been, as middle-class cover-up jobs, seeking to show only the good side of Black experience or Black character. One must look carefully at Fauset's work, however, to discover that support for such negative reading is often highly selective and incomplete. When one seeks and analyzes the ignored theme of superiority in the literature, the victories of Fauset's female characters over white and male oppression and over self-doubt and self-deprecation appear as much less the romantic dreams of a middle-aged prim and proper society woman and as much more the thoughtful and wise searchings of a widely-read social activist. Fauset does not underplay the difficulties of Black life, nor does she create characters who are always defeated by those difficulties.

Aptheker makes clear that the superiority he is describing in the literature is not superficial, Pollyanna-ish, is not racist, and is not to be credited to oppression itself. It is a moral and ethical superiority that "does not affirm, and often explicitly denies, anything smacking of the biological or genetic, and so, in that sense, ... it is the negation of racism." As with an ethical, moral, or aesthetic superiority to be sometimes found in Jews and women, this Afro-American superiority, he says, comes not from oppression, but from struggle against oppression.[29] Aptheker's insight into a theme she clearly made use of is especially helpful in a fresh look at Jessie Fauset's fiction.

When one turns from the questions and materials faced and used by the Black writer in the United States to a closer look at critical attempts to summarize or analyze the "Harlem Renaissance," used here to mean the period from 1918 to 1933, the clearest conclusion reached is that these summaries and analyses are more misleading than helpful in a study of Jessie Fauset. Because of the wide range of the literature of the period; the intensity of the critical debates; the change or growth in thought of people who experienced much before and after 1919, such as Alain Locke, W. E. B. DuBois, Jessie Fauset, and those who were very young in 1919 but who lived long after, such as Langston Hughes, Sterling Brown, Arna Bontemps; the criticism which attempts to classify writers of the Renaissance into two camps—conservative and radical, or middle class and folk, or "old guard" and "Harlem School," nearly always rings false when one moves to it from extensive study of the work of a single author.

Together with dichotomizing and politicizing, dividing up what is and deciding what should be, the tendencies to create "Schools" out of Harlem Renaissance writers or to find heroes and villains in personages with whose sentiments at any one time one agrees or disagrees, are unfortunate hindrances to clear study of the work of a single writer. Fauset's work is in some ways seen more clearly by comparing it to the work of Nella Larsen and Walter White, but to do the comparison beneath the assumption that these three form a "School of Passing Literature" is less than helpful. In fact, comparisons with other Harlem Renaissance novelists contain just as much potential insight into Fauset's work.

This study of Jessie Fauset will neither assume conscious overall aim in the period under primary study, nor will it assume that diversity is a weakness or a failure, either in the work of a single author or in the productivity of the entire Harlem Renaissance. Jessie Fauset's work was a literature of search more than a literature of protest; the appropriate critical approach to her work at this time, an approach lacking heretofore, is one of descriptive analysis, not one of prescriptive judgment. The period in which she did her primary work, the Harlem Renaissance period, is creative, fluctuating, diverse, not stagnant or frozen. Even critical description must be constantly aware of what such fluid movement and diversity implies for use of terms like "integrationist," "racist," "assimilationist," "conservative," "radical," "middle class," "folk." To be used accurately, such terms must be carefully defined in relation to a statement, a passage, a work, not attached indiscriminately to a novel, a person, a life. To keep in mind events of Fauset's life, and the historical context of those events, is to be constantly aware of the complexity of human life and human creation, and to be constantly humbled before the critic's task.

Notes

[1] A delightful exception to the general lack of full consideration of all of Fauset's work, journalistic as well as literary, is Abby Arthur Johnson's recent *Phylon* article: "Literary Midwife: Jessie Redmon Fauset and the Harlem Renaissance" (June 1978, pp. 143-153). In a balanced, fair and informed manner, Dr. Johnson confirms the need for full reconsideration of Fauset's contributions to Black literature.

[2] Herbert Aptheker, ed., *The Correspondence of W. E. B. DuBois, I: Selections, 1877-1934* (Amherst: University of Massachusetts, 1973), p. 66.

[3] Eleanor Flexner, *Century of Struggle: The Woman's Rights Movement in the United States* (1959; rpt. New York: Atheneum, 1973), p. 143.

[4] Elizabeth Cady Stanton, Susan Anthony and Mathilda Joslyn Gage, eds., *History of Women's Suffrage*, 2 (Rochester, New York: 1881), 391-92. Quoted by Flexner, *Ibid.*, p. 144.

[5] Ray Stannard Baker, *Following the Color Line: American Negro Citizenship in the Progressive Era* (1903; rpt. New York: Harper and Row, 1964), pp. 140-41.

[6] Jessie Fauset, "Some Notes on Color," *The World Tomorrow* (March, 1922), pp. 76-77, rpt. in *A Documentary History of the Negro People of the United States, 1910-1932*, ed. Herbert Aptheker (Secaucus, New Jersey: Citadel Press, 1973), p. 357.

[7]John Hope Franklin, *From Slavery to Freedom*, 4th ed. (New York: Knopf, 1974), pp. 372-73.

[8]Kenny Williams, *They Also Spoke: An Essay on Negro Literature in America, 1787-1930* (Nashville, Tennessee: Townsend Press, 1970), p. 225.

[9]St. Claire Drake, "Introduction," *A Long Way From Home*, by Claude McKay (1937; rpt. New York: Harcourt, Brace and World, 1970), p. x.

[10]Gary DeCordova Wintz, "Black Writers in 'Nigger Heaven': The Harlem Renaissance," Diss. Kansas State University 1974, pp. 72, 78.

[11]Carl Van Vechten, *Nigger Heaven* (1926; rpt. New York: Harper Colophon, 1971), p. 225.

[12]W. E. B. DuBois, "Criteria for Negro Art," *The Crisis*, 32 (October 1926), 297.

[13]Sterling Brown, "The Negro Author and His Publisher," *Negro Quarterly*, 1 (Spring, 1942), 19.

[14]Sterling Brown, "Negro Character as Seen by White Authors," *Journal of Negro Education*, 2 (January 1933), 180-201, rpt. in *Dark Symphony*, eds. Emanuel and Gross (New York: Free Press, 1968), pp. 140-164.

[15]Brown, "The Negro Author and His Publisher," pp. 14-15.

[16]James Weldon Johnson, "The Dilemma of the Negro Author," *American Mercury* (December 1928), p. 480.

[17]DuBois, "Criteria for Negro Art," p. 297.

[18]Wallace Thurman, "Negro Artists and the Negro," *New Republic*, 31 August 1927, p. 38.

[19]Saunders Redding, "The Negro Author: His Publisher, His Public, and His Purse," *Publisher's Weekly*, 24 March 1945, p. 1288.

[20]Benjamin Brawley, "Negro Contemporary Literature," *English Journal*, 18 (March 1929), 194.

[21]Brown, "The Negro Author and His Publisher," p. 18.

22Annis Pratt, "Archetypal Theory and Women's Fiction: 1688-1975," Paper for Women's Caucus for the Modern Languages Panel: "The Theory of Feminist Literary Critics," San Francisco, California, 27 December 1975, p. 4.

23Wintz, "Black Writers in 'Nigger Heaven' . . . ," p. 236.

24Langston Hughes, *The Big Sea* (New York: Hill and Wang, 1940), p. 242.

25Hugh Gloster, *Negro Voices in American Fiction* (1948; rpt. Russell and Russell, 1965), p. 17.

26Paule Marshall, "The Negro Woman in Literature," *Freedomways*, 6 (1966), 22.

27Herbert Aptheker, "Afro-American Superiority: A Neglected Theme in the Literature," in *Black Life and Culture in the United States*, ed. R. L. Goldstein (New York: Thomas Y. Crowell, 1971), pp. 165-79.

28Brawley, pp. 201-02.

29Aptheker, "Afro-American Superiority . . . ," pp. 167, 174.

Family and Early Life: 1882-1919

Jessie "Redmona" Fauset was born on 27 April 1882 in Camden County, Snow Hill Center Township, New Jersey, to Redmon Fauset, age forty-five, and Annie Seamon Fauset, age thirty-seven, their seventh child.[1] The two oldest children were born in Carlisle, Pennsylvania—Ira Redmond on 8 October 1870 and Carolina Susan Mabel on 30 September 1871. The two children nearest in age to Jessie Redmona were born in New Brunswick, New Jersey—Anna Bella on 30 January 1878 and Beatrice Birdie on 26 March 1879. Francis R. Fauset was born in Morristown, New Jersey on 10 January 1873, and Mary Helen Fauset was born in Fredericksville, New Jersey 13 January 1875. Beatrice Birdie lived until approximately 1900, and Mary Helen, later Helen Fauset Lanning, lived until 1936. The other children evidently all died before 1900.

Following the death of his first wife, Redmon Fauset married Bella Huff, a widow with three children—Emma Huff, Mae Huff, and Earl Huff—who became Jessie Fauset's step-sisters and step brother. To this marriage were born Redmond Fauset in 1896, Arthur Huff Fauset in 1899, and Marian Fauset, Jessie Fauset's half-brothers and half-sister.[2] Of these children, Arthur Huff and Marian Fauset are still living. Earl Huff, who was close to Jessie Fauset in her late years, in whose home in Philadelphia she died, and to whom she willed most of her possessions in 1961, died in 1962. Redmon Fauset, the father, died 1 January 1903 (AHF to CS, undated January, 1976), and Bella Huff Fauset died in 1923.

That Jessie Fauset was born in 1882, rather than 1886, as her death certificate from the Department of Health, Vital Statistics, Commonwealth of Pennsylvania, and many other printed sources indicate, or in 1891, as her application in 1928 for the Harmon Foundation Award states, is of some significance in a new look at

her writing career. She was forty-two years old when her first novel
was published, and when, one must add, the publishing world and
the reading public were first ready for the kind of book she could
write. She was fifty-one when her fourth and last novel was published, seventy-seven when she moved back to Philadelphia after the
death of her husband, Herbert Harris, in 1958, and seventy-nine
when she died, having spent at least the last year of her life in senil-
ity. She herself was secretive about her exact age, usually shaving
several years off the accurate total. Recognition now of the age she
had attained when her novels were published helps explain some of
the characteristics of her publication history.

    That Jessie Fauset was born in Camden County, New Jersey,
near Philadelphia but not in it, as most sources give her birthplace,
and that her many older brothers and sisters were born in various
places, were due to her father's occupation as an African Methodist
Episcopal (A. M. E.) minister, subject to assignment by the presiding Bishop (AHF to CS, 10 January 1976). The A. M. E. church,
significant in Philadelphia and surrounding area as the first of the
denominational Black-controlled churches, founded by Richard
Allen and his followers in the late eighteenth century after segregation crept into the church, had reached a membership of about
600,000 by 1908, with seventeen Bishops and with headquarters in
Philadelphia. By 1890 it was one of five denominational church organizations entirely under Black supervision in Pennsylvania.[3]
The importance of the Negro church in the social, political, economic, and intellectual, as well as religious, life of Black America has
been frequently documented. In Jessie Fauset's early world, her
father's position as an A. M. E. minister put her and her family "a
step up the cultural ladder." Leaders in the A. M. E. church were
among the city's "cultural leaders" (AHF to CS, 10 January 1976).

    Together with her father's positon as an A. M. E. minister,
Jessie Fauset's ancestry in Philadelphia is often cited as proof of her
secure and influential early social position. Robert Bone, for example, claims that "undoubtedly, the most important formative influence on Miss Fauset's work was her family background. An
authentic old Philadelphian (known as 'O. P. 's' in the colored society of that day), she was never able to transcend the narrow limits

of this sheltered world."[4] Arthur Davis in *From the Dark Tower* makes essentially the same statement of her early social position and its influence on Fauset's novels (p. 90). Roseann Pope Bell calls Fauset "the darling of the Negro elite," whose "social position" more than talent gave her a "talented tenth" position. "She was born in Philadelphia to an old, established family."[5]

In fact family records of the Fausets (spelled Faucett) listed in the Bible in Arthur Huff Fauset's possession do go back into the 1700s. An "Arthur Faucett" died in the 1820s at age 79, for example. That this Bible record, however, can be translated into Jessie Fauset having been the "daughter of a prosperous and literary, black Philadelphia family"[6] is not clearly verifiable. Documentation on her early life and family background in fact points to modification of these summary estimates toward something quite different than their terms connote.

The misleading terms frequently used to describe Fauset's early life are "prosperous" or "comfortable," implying some wealth, and "middle-class," implying sometimes an economic status and sometimes an attitudinal one. It is reasonable, therefore, to look at evidence of the family's economic situation and at the family attitudes in approaching a more complete and fair estimate of Jessie Fauset's early life. In both the areas of economics and attitudes, Arthur Huff Fauset's memory must be relied upon heavily in the absence, for the most part, of printed or written records.

Arthur Huff Fauset, born in 1899, Jessie Fauset's half-brother, says that "during the period of my earliest recollection, which will be a year or two before my father's death, we were quite poor." Although "it could be that in the 90's and 80's he knew more sufficient days," "apparently our father had no other means of income than the paltry dollars to be squeezed out of the money passed in the church collection plate and provided in the voluntary pledges made by the lowly parishioners." A. H. Fauset was told that his and Jessie Fauset's father once owned property "which he lost because he had little time to attend to business," but in his own memory, "our family was poor, one might say, dreadfully poor" (AHF to CS, 10 January 1976, 26 January 1976, and undated January 1976). Given the large number of children to support, and the probable expense of illness and death among the oldest children, some poverty seems not at all unlikely in Jessie Fauset's first twenty years.

A. H. Fauset says that the term "middle-class" when applied to his and Jessie Fauset's family is misleading. Middleclass "should not refer to the economic situation but to the type of life." One must add that even applied to type of life or attitudes the term "middle-class" is somewhat misleading in its present negative connotations, for Fauset goes on to describe a family which "read newspapers and books," "discussed politics and religion" and "fought against the binding racial biases that made life in the City of Brotherly Love often a burden. It is in these respects that the family was middle class: working; aspiring; discussing; getting their children educated to the extent that biases would permit."

Redmon Fauset, A. M. E. minister, appears to have himself felt much more strongly about the value of learning, of education, of fighting for a principle, than he felt about the value of money. Again according to Arthur Huff Fauset, his son, Redmon Fauset was "very insistent in those things he believed; for years he was remembered for this insistence; on the other hand he paid a price for his strong beliefs—that is, he often made enemies in high places, both white and black; and for this he often had to be satisfied to occupy low places in the generally accepted hierarchy" (AHF to CS, undated January 1976). A H. Fauset recalls his mother, Bella Huff Fauset, telling him of a small instance of what she called her husband's "stubbornness," but which could as well be called courage or principled action given the setting and time in which it occurred. Stepping on a streetcar in Kentucky, and finding no empty seat, he asked a white woman to remove her dog from a seat. Upon her refusal to do so, he removed the dog himself—and nearly got lynched. Evidently outspoken, intelligent, intellectual, self-educated, controversial, and a strong influence on Jessie Fauset by her own evaluation, the real Reverend Redmon Fauset is not the kind of man who comes to mind when one reads of an old established Philadelphia family, or of a comfortable middle class life. While Jessie Fauset could be called a member of a Negro cultured class or intelligentsia in her early life, it is not accurate to call her middle class or prosperous or socially established.

The Philadelphia, Pennsylvania Public School System in 1881 abolished Black public schools as such, giving Black children the right to attend any public school for which they were eligible without regard for their color. But the tendency remained toward separate schools, or social separation in the schools, with whites in the following twenty years becoming more and more reluctant to go to school with Blacks, and with "few friendships" across race lines.[7] Jessie Fauset appears to be one Philadelphia student who benefitted not socially, but educationally, from the 1881 policy.

Her obituary in the New York *Times* in 1961 states that as a public school student in Philadelphia she was the only Negro in her class. There are no school records to show definitely that this was the case prior to her high shcool years, but she herself in an interview in 1929 described the interracial experience of her last school years in Philadelphia. "To this day, it hurts to think of my childhood. My father was a Methodist minister, and his passion was education, so I was raised to be a teacher. I happened to be the only colored girl in my classes at high school, and I'll never forget the agony I endured on entrance day when the white girls with whom I had played and studied through the graded schools, refused to acknowledge my greeting."[8] The racial snub felt on entrance day to high school was evidently long felt by Fauset, appearing in her rather frequent references to hating the uncertainty of dining out under ever-potential segregation, and in her use of similar experiences for characters in her books.

But despite the agony of rejection, stemming, it appears, from a rather intense shyness in unknown social situations, Jessie Fauset achieved a "most enviable mark" at the Philadelphia High School for Girls ("the high school for more scholarly disposed students"). "At a time in our history," her half brother writes, "when blacks scarcely were permitted to participate in educational programs, the school, by way of honoring her, invited her father to offer the graduation invocation" (AHF to CS, 10 January 1976).

The logical next educational step for an honor graduate of Philadelphia High School for Girls, intending to become a teacher, was college. Precedent in Pennsylvania for a Black woman in college was, however, in 1900 invisible. Colleges in Pennsylvania, Richard R.

Wright says in 1902, "evidently have had but small influence upon the Pennsylvania Negroes." According to Arthur Huff Fauset's recollection "there was an effort on the part of faculty and friends to get [Jessie Fauset] a scholarship to Bryn Mawr College, but that school was unable to see its way clear to accept a black student" (AHF to CS, 10 January 1976). Fauset herself, however, wrote in a 1913 letter to J. E. Spingarn, that she had "matriculated at Bryn Mawr 'amid rumors of prejudice,' but that there was no difficulty,"[9] and Wright states in 1912 that "no Negro women have ever applied for admission at Bryn Mawr." A letter to a Miss Mary Mason from M. Carey Thomas of Bryn Mawr in 1903, however, suggests that the institution went to some trouble and expense to avoid accepting a Black student.

> Mr. Kendrick writes me that the $60 for Miss Jessie Fawcett's [sic] tuition fee at Cornell University for which I made myself responsible is now due. You may remember that you were kind enough to say that you would make yourself responsible for $30 of the $60. If convenient will you kindly mail me your cheque for this amount. Miss Fawcett is I believe doing well at Cornell and finds there no prejudice against her on acount of her color. I feel that through your kindness and Mrs Kendrick Bryn Mawr has been relieved of a very great anxiety. I do not at all know how our students would have acted, but I am very sure that a number of Southern girls would have been withdrawn from the College.[10]

The first Black woman to graduate from Bryn Mawr did so in 1931. There are no early policies on race in written form in the archives of the college (Letter to author from Gertrude Reed, Reference Librarian and Archivist, Bryn Mawr, 11 August 1976).

With cautions that his information on these early years is secondhand, though often from Jessie Fauset herself, Arthur Huff Fauset goes on to describe the circumstances leading to his half-sister's college career in the state of New York. "Then the publisher (editor?) of the Philadelphia Press, important newspaper, led an effort to have her continue her work in college, and as a result she was awarded a scholarship to Cornell University" (AHF to CS, 10 January 1976). The *Montclair (New Jersey) Times* in its 1961 obituary of Jessie Fauset states that she was "the first Negro woman to attend [Cornell] University, where she lived with a professor's family. The year after she entered two other Negro girls became students and lived in the college dormitory." It is not possible to document from college records Fauset's being the very first Negro woman at Cornell, but she was certainly one of the first, and one of the few, up to 1915. In 1905 she wrote that she had lived "for the past four years as the only colored girl in a college community of over 3,000 students,"[11] differing thereby from the much later *Montclair Times* report of two Black girls admitted and living in dorms in 1902. In April (p. 29) and May (p. 6) of 1911 the NAACP's *The Crisis* carries an ongoing report of a conflict at Cornell fully a decade later, in which white coeds protest by petition the admission of two Black girls into Sage College and Sage Cottage (269 women petition not to admit Negro girls; 36 women object to this discrimination), indicating that race prejudice among coeds was strong even at this date. The numbers of Blacks—male and female—was exceedingly small at Cornell between 1901 and 1905 when Fauset was there, yet there appears to have been a unity and closeness among the Black men, through their founding of Alpha Phi Alpha fraternity, from which Fauset would presumably have received little beneficial group racial support, being female.

Fauset's Cornell curriculum was a challenging one academically from her first year on, solid in languages. The "Vital Statistics Card" in the university archives indicates that four years of Latin, two of Greek, four of German, two of French, four of English, form the basis for separate courses in Bibliography, Psychology, Logic, Ethics (two years), Archaeology, Political Science. In 1903, in the midst of her Junior year, Fauset describes her work as "chiefly classical," though including, "of course," a good deal of work in English as well as American History, German, French, Psychology. "Of course I am by no means prepared to teach this last." She describes her preference at the time, saying "I would rather teach Latin and rudimentary English—I mean actual English grammar—than anything else."[12]

After this demanding course of study, Jessie "Redmona" Fauset was graduated from Cornell with a Bachelor of Arts degree, and was elected to Phi Beta Kappa by the Cornell Chapter at its meeting of 8 May 1905. Although her "Deceased Alumni Folder" at Cornell does not document her being the first Black in the Chapter, since sex, race, and religion of individuals elected are not recorded, there is a note on her alumni address card by George Lincoln Burr (Professor of History and Secretary to Cornell's first president, Andrew D. White), saying: "Colored student—only one elected to Phi Beta Kappa up to 1921!" Arthur Huff Fauset's children's book *For Freedom*, published in 1927, states that she was the first Black female to be Phi Beta Kappa (p. 189).

But whether or not Jessie Fauset was first Black or first female Black Phi Beta Kappa at Cornell or nationwide is not as important as recognizing the unusual achievement this election represents, given numbers of Black Phi Beta Kappas up to 1936, and, indeed, numbers of Black and women college graduates during the early years of this century. Between 1874 and 1936, 155 Blacks were elected to Phi Beta Kappa, but 78% of these, or 121, were elected after 1914.[13] In December 1911, in his "Opinion" column in *The Crisis*, W. E. B. DuBois reports on an Atlanta University Negro Conference investigation on the college Negro which found only 5,000 Black college graduates in the whole United States at that date (p. 62). In 1889-90, "a little more than 2,500 women had taken a bachelor of arts degree"; in 1900, 5,237 women had graduated from accredited institutions of higher education.[14] Mary White Ovington writes in 1911 that she had yet to find a colored woman university graduate from the state of New York, though she had found teachers who had attended teacher-training normal schools. There were, to be sure, occasional successes, but the colored woman meets "severer race prejudice than the colored man,"[15] says Ovington, in education as in employment.

Fauset's strong and rare academic achievement at Cornell between 1901 and 1905 is unquestionable, but it is also of interest to know of some of her other activities at this time in her life. Her first communications with DuBois date from 1903, while she is at Cornell, and appear to have been occasioned by her contacts with a Cornell professor—Walter Willcox, Head of the Department of Sociology and Dean of Arts and Sciences. Willcox was clearly sympathetic to Black students and to Black history and sociology.

Another Black student at Cornell at the time later recalls that "we took pride in the fact that Professor Walter Willcox . . . quoted Dr. DuBois in his lectures."[16] It is Willcox who, in May 1903, writes to DuBois for assistance in obtaining a summer teaching position for Fauset, "one of the very few Negro students then at the university," and Willcox and DuBois become and remain friends, despite a sharp exchange in 1904 on the subject of economics and the Negro.[17]

Evidently the request for assistance in May 1903 was too late for a summer teaching position in that year, but on 26 December 1903, Fauset writes DuBois from Ithaca, thanking him for his previous letter, and asking whether there might be "some means whereby I could teach school this coming summer of 1904." She would like to have some teaching experience before graduation, she goes on to say, and would have, "my professors tell me," no difficulty getting any requisite recommendations. She would like, if possible, to work in the South: "I know only one class of my people well and I want to become acquainted with the rest."[18]

With DuBois' help or upon his suggestions, Fauset does spend five weeks in 1904 teaching at Fisk University in Nashville, Tennessee. On 16 February 1905 she writes him enthusiastically of the experience, which involved teaching "English branches—English grammar, American Literature and the Interpretation of three or four of the longer standard poems—notably Hiawatha and The Vision of Sir Launfal." "No work will ever have about it again for me the glamor which this summer's work wore," she writes Dr. DuBois. "It was my first attempt at being useful you see—that is a wonderful feeling is it not?" Though her compensation was only board and keep, she prizes the experience." Oh, I was so happy—and I owe it to you in large part you know, for it was you who told me to whom I should apply."[19]

What has been shown here of Fauset's career at Cornell reveals two characteristics which are persistently evident in her life and work after 1905. She was a very hard worker, determined to achieve excellence in whatever she undertook. Accustomed to being in a racial and sexual minority, she determined to be outstanding by other criteria as well. She writes, "Living as I have nearly all my life

in a distinctly white neighborhood, and for the past four years as the
only colored girl in a college community of over 3,000 students, I
have *had* to let people know that we too possess some of the best,
or else allow my own personality to be submerged."[20] Secondly,
she was tolerant of differences from her accustomed life style and
habits. In fact, her desire to go South to teach among people different from her usual group, and her enthusiasm for the experience and
for "being useful" suggest that she sought differences as well as
tolerated them. These characteristics, needless to say, are quite
different than the ease of attained position and the limitations of
view usually touted as resulting from a comfortable, socially secure,
and select early life.

Jessie Fauset's second American degree, the Master of Arts,
was awarded by the University of Pennsylvania in 1919, following
Summer School courses taken by Fauset at the Philadelphia institution in 1910 and 1912 and a year's work in 1918-1919 (Letter to
author from Hamilton Elliott, University Archives, University of
Pennsylvania, 19 February 1976). Sadie T. M. Alexander, who
graduated from the University of Pennsylvania at the same time
("The Horizon: Education," *The Crisis* [August 1919], p. 203)
remembers that Fauset came to study in the Social Sciences on the
advice of Dr. DuBois, and was enrolled with Ms. Alexander in economics classes at the beginning of the year. But Fauset, working for
a "Distinguished Student" designation, and rusty as a student from
having been out of college for years, was discouraged with the results
of her first Economics quiz, and transferred to the French Department. Although her expectation of academic excellence led her to
change courses of study at the University of Pennsylvania, Fauset
evidently kept social contact with those outside her academic area—
Ms. Alexander reports that she and Fauset frequently visited as long
as Fauset remained in Philadelphia.[21]

From a year after her graduation from Cornell in 1905, up
until her appointment as Literary Editor for *The Crisis* in 1919,
Jessie Fauset accomplished a rather long full-time teaching tenure
of fourteen years at M   reet High School (after 1916 called Dunbar
High School), in the P blic School System of the District of Columbia (5 October 1906 to 30 June 1919).[22] One might conclude from

this occupational prelude to the bulk of her literary career that probably the best years of her creative life were exhausted in teaching, yet given the attitudes toward Black women professionals when she began teaching, the employment and economic discrimination against Black teachers in white schools, and the paucity at the time of Black high schools, just the fact that she had such a job becomes an unusual achievement. The job was also a financial necessity, for according to Arthur Fauset, she was not only supporting herself, but helping to educate her sister, Helen Fauset (Lanning) during these years in Washington.

Attitudes toward Black women working as professionals in 1905 were conservative. One of the few articles dealing with Black women directly in D. W. Culp's 1902 *Twentieth Century Negro Literature*, or a *Cyclopedia of Thought on the Vital Topics Relating to the American Negro by One Hundred of America's Greatest Negroes*, by Mrs. R. D. Sprague, is "What Role Is the Educated Negro Woman to Play in the Uplifting of Her Race?" Following the perhaps necessary, and certainly understandable reaction to the decimation of the Black family in slave times, Mrs. Sprague concludes that "the educated Negro woman will find that her greatest field for effective work is in the home."[23] While not every Black or every Black woman at the time would of course agree with Mrs. Sprague, it is clear that the attitudinal climate supported her view for women, but in an exaggerated way for Black women, and that Jessie Fauset was breaking habits of expectation not only in pursuing a college degree but in attaining financial and personal independence in the professional working world.

Patterns of discrimination had also to be broken through. In 1908 Ray Stannard Baker, in a chapter of *Following the Color Line* called "The Negro's Struggle for Survival in Northern Cities," reports of responses in the South and in the North to his question directed to Negroes: "What is your chief cause of complaint?" Southern complaints centered around Jim Crow segregation and political impotence; in the North, however, the "first answer invariably referred to working conditions." Menial work was available, but there was no opportunity for other more skilled trades or professions. Figures in the 1890 census, the first United States census to distinguish laborers by race, show that of 975,530 Black women gainfully employed at that time, 38.74% were in agriculture; 30.83% were "servants"; 15.59% were laundresses; and 2.76% were in manufacturing and mechanical employment.[24]

W. E. B. DuBois in his *The Philadelphia Negro* of 1899 uses to illustrate his statement that colored women in Philadelphia have great difficulty finding suitable work, a couple of instances of honor graduates of Philadelphia High School for Girls (as mentioned before, the academically elite high school in Philadelphia) who were unable to find work after graduation (pp. 335-36). In the entire teaching profession, DuBois counted forty Negroes in the city, all except one teaching Negro children exclusively, and none receiving pay as high as their white counterparts (p. 113).

Jessie Fauset tried to obtain a teaching position in Philadelphia after her graduation from Cornell and failed.[25] Much later she said in an interview: "When I graduated from training school, I found the high schools barred to me because of my color. Philadelphia, birthplace of Independence and City of Brotherly Love—I have never quite been able to reconcile theory with fact."[26] Richard R. Wright, though he names no names, is quite obviously referring to Fauset in his 1912 *The Negro in Pennsylvania: A Study in Economic History* when he states that Negroes are discriminated against by being totally shut out of some lines of work, and goes on to use high school teaching as an example. "A Negro girl wins high honors in our High School, wins a scholarship to Cornell University, graduates with honors and returns to her native city, but finds the doors of our High School shut. This is the 'Negro Problem.' " In another clear reference to Fauset, he contrasts the immigrant to the Negro in America. If the immigrant succeeds, Wright says, success means citizenship. But "if a Negro girl graduates with honors in our High School, wins thereby a scholarship to a leading university, and graduates there with honor, she cannot come back to her native city and teach in her Alma Mater, as white girls who stood below her have done. She must be content to teach in the graded school or go South to teach" (pp. 186, 199).

The alternative to the options Wright lists—teaching in a Black high school—was not easy either in 1905, for there were very few Black high schools at all, and only a handful having the quality and offerings that Fauset's Cornell language training suited her for. A report of the United States Commissioner of Education counted in 1908-09 a total of 112 Negro high schools in the United States, but with only a total of 383 teachers, so many of these schools were exceedingly small and/or understaffed. Seven of a thousand high school-age Black students were enrolled in schools, compared to 100 out of 1,000 whites. Maryland, with 250,000 Negroes, had one Black high school, in Baltimore.[27]

According to a *Negro History Bulletin* note in 1938, Fauset "began teaching in the Douglass High School of Baltimore and transferred later to the Dunbar High School in Washington, D. C." Evidently she did complete the year 1905-06, after her failure to get a job in Philadelphia, at the Baltimore school—her deceased alumni record at Cornell lists her 1905 address as 611 West Hoffman Street in Baltimore. The school she soon moved to, the M Street High School in Washington, D. C. was erected in 1890 at a cost of $107,000, and had in 1911 thirty-three teachers and 726 students,[28] after its humbler origins in the basement of a Presbyterian church, and its several moves from site to site in Washington.[29] When the new Dunbar High School, first occupied 2 October 1916, replaced the M Street High School, the institution had forty-eight teachers and 1,149 pupils, and became the elite Black high school in the country—a photo in *The Crisis* in March 1917 is in fact captioned "The Greatest Negro High School in the World" (p. 221). The claim was understandable after a list of Dunbar's large gyms, banking department, domestic science department and facilities, labs, library, cadets' armory, rifle range, emergency room, greenhouse and roof garden, stadium.[30]

According to testimony of former students at M Street High School, Jessie Fauset was an impressive person as well as teacher of French and Latin there. Ret. Colonel David A. Lane, at M Street from 1910 to 1913, and not a student in Fauset's classes or home-room, yet writes that "now, more than sixty years later, I recall that Miss Jessie Fauset was the first person, as far as I knew, whom I heard use the word *ubiquitous* in ordinary conversation, and on that occasion I hurried to the dictionary to find its meaning" (Letter to author, 29 March 1976). Elsie B. Smith, at M. Street from 1909 to 1913, calls Fauset a "brilliant person, widely read, and interested in literature. She also loved music and always enjoyed the Friday afternoon student music assemblies at M Street." In her teaching, Mrs. Smith goes on, "she was a good teacher for good students" (Letter to author, 7 March 1976).

But joys of teaching and inspiring students were not enough to challenge Fauset or give her happiness during the many years in Washington, D. C. According to half-brother Arthur Huff Fauset, she hated the city itself, with its racial biases, and longed to get into the "frothing New York stream" of growing Black population and cultural activity. Mary Church Terrell's "What it Means to Be Colored in the Capital of the United States," printed in *The Independent* 24 January 1907, tells of the difficulty of getting a bed, a meal, a ride in the nation's capital, as well as of the salary and promotion discrimination practiced in Washington, D. C. Public Schools, and gives a glimpse of what Jessie Fauset must have also found in Washington. Fauset's growing involvement with W. E. B. DuBois, with the NAACP, and with *The Crisis*, which eventually brought her to New York, was the outlet for her non-teaching life in these years.

In looking previously at some of Fauset's correspondence with DuBois between 1903 and 1905 concerning his assistance with obtaining for her a summer teaching job at Fisk University, another side of the letters was not explored—that side showing her deep admiration for his scholarly and creative work, for his ideas, and for his courage in expressing those ideas. When DuBois included his chapter "Of Mr. Booker T. Washington and Others" in *The Souls of Black Folk* in 1903, sharply criticizing Washington's compromising and the losses of franchisement, educational support, and civil liberties that the compromising had meant, he was, as at least one critic has said, "the voice crying in the wilderness" against a man who was at his highest peak of mass support. DuBois' few supporters at the time were either "too young to be influential" or from his close circle of white friends.[31] The beginning of the demise of Booker T. Washington and the beginning of the rise of W. E. B. DuBois from about 1905 until Washington's death in 1915, marks a radical change in Black leadership, which can, in post-Civil War American history, be seen in three stages, as E. Franklin Frazier points out in a 1928 *Current History* article. Following slavery, ministers, politicians, and civil rights activists dominated—Douglass stands out as the prime example. The second period is dominated by Washington with his principles of industrial education, economic advance, social segregation, and non-militant cooperation. The third kind of leader, beginning most notably with DuBois, is distinguished by the best of European and American educational and scientific training; by creativity and absence of servile imitation of whites; and by an international viewpoint.[32]

Jessie Fauset's father, Reverend Redmon Fauset, died 1 January 1903, and in 1903 she begins writing DuBois of her admiration for his work. It is interesting that Fauset, whose admiration for her father is so evident in her early life, makes thereby a transition such as Frazier describes from the Black minister-leader to the scholar-leader as influence on her own life. The transition appears to be there, but it is also clear that Fauset's father and W. E. B. DuBois were in many ways similar, so that there was also a continuity in influence on her life, or at least in backdrop to it. E. Franklin Frazier describes what he sees as DuBois' impetus toward the intellectual life:

> The relatively small number of truly educated Negroes were, like DuBois, isolated and lonely men. They were what sociologists have designated 'marginal men.' . . . They were not accepted by the whites while the ignorance, poverty, and primitiveness of the Negro world repelled them. . . . The marginal position of DuBois and other Negro intellectuals probably provided a stimulus to an intellectual outlook on life.[33]

From what is known of Reverend Redmon Fauset, this summary would seem to be a fair, if partial, assessment of his character, as it is of the character of DuBois.

Jessie Fauset empathizes with the struggle of the "marginal man," herself a "marginal woman." On 26 December 1903 she writes to DuBois about his newly published *The Souls of Black Folk*. She first says thank you, "as though it had been a personal favor," and goes on: "I am glad, glad you wrote it—we have needed someone to voice the intricacies of the blind maze of thought and action along which the modern, educated colored man or woman struggles. It hurt you to write that book, didn't it? The man of fine sensiblities has to suffer exquisitely, just simply because his feeling is so fine."[34]

In 1905 she writes DuBois about another published work of his, a short, oft-reprinted, framed and hung prose piece called "Credo." In "Credo," each generally stated item of belief is follow-ed up by a more specific application of the belief to Black life in America. "I believe in God" is followed by "especially do I believe in the Negro Race"; I believe in "liberty for all men" is followed by liberty to ride the railroads.[35] Fauset expresses gratitude for DuBois' achievements and courage: "I am so proud, you know, to claim you on our side. . . . It has been with much pleasure that I have pointed to you as an example of the heights to which it is possible for some of us to climb." She also adds her own exploration of the racial maze, especially of the struggle to achieve what is good, but to not totally or blindly follow the white definition of the "good." After reading "Credo" in the *Outlook* or the *Independent*, she writes,

> how glad I was to realise that that was your belief, and to ask you if you did not believe it to be worthwhile to teach our colored men and women *race* pride, *self*-pride, self-sufficiency (the right kind) and the necessity of living our lives, as nearly as possible, *absolutely*, instead of comparing them always with white standards. Don't you believe that we should lead them to understand that the reason we adopt such and such criteria which are also adopted by the Anglo-Saxon, is because these criteria are the *best*, and not essentially because they are white? This kind of distinction would in the end breed self-dependence and self-respect, and subjective respect means always sooner or later an outcome of objective respect.[36]

These early letters to DuBois, expressing admiration but not awe, gently lecturing as well as praising, show some of the tone of the long Fauset-DuBois relationship: mutual admiration and support, mutual learning and teaching. In 1918, on the occasion of DuBois' 50th birthday Fauset's letter to him thanks him for the fifteen years of positive influence he has been in her life to that point. "Dear won-derful man," she writes; "for your sake I am willing to rebuild my old creed."[37]

The formation of the National Organization for the Advancement of Colored People in May 1910 marks an important date for Black history, for Black literature, for Black-white relations, for women in America. The paucity of Black intellectuals and educated Blacks early in the twentieth century, the discrimination practiced against them, their isolation from one another, reduced substantially "the capacities of that group for redressing the racial balance."[38] The NAACP, besides pulling together some of these isolated Blacks, added to the slowly growing number of this small group hundreds of concerned, liberal or radical whites, whose access to institutions, to means of communication, and often, to the ears of America, was much broader and greater. For example, the first chair of the organization was Moorfield Storey, Boston civil rights attorney. Wilson Record in a 1956 *Phylon* article, "Negro intellectual Leadership in the NAACP, 1910-1940," points out two other characteristics about the early NAACP sometimes forgotten in concentration on its interracial nature: the organization was made up primarily of the young, with a majority of members under forty, and with many in their twenties; and there was included "a relatively large number of women," mostly white. Record adds that the relatively large number of white women in the organization was not surprising, for feminist and anti-slavery groups were of course linked early, and neither had fully achieved its goals (p. 380).

DuBois, who was invited from Atlanta to become the original and long-time "Director for Publicity and Research" of the NAACP, had himself previously made explicit the link he saw between Black rights and women's rights. Charles Kellogg's thorough *NAACP: A History of the National Association for the Advancement of Colored People*, Volume I, describes, for example, an early DuBois *Horizon* article in which he stated that "the Negro problem was not and could not be kept distinct from other reform movements—women's rights, consumer's leagues, prison reform, social settlements, universal peace." "From the very beginning," Kellogg says, the NAACP "aligned itself with other oppressed minority groups, a policy which has continued down to the present" (pp. 25, 41).

One can understand Jessie Fauset's early attraction to the NAACP—its intellectual leadership, its anti-segregation principles, its emphasis on Black problems without ignoring women's problems of discrimination would presumably have had great appeal for her. Her name does not appear among the early lists of prominent organizers and supporters, but 1912 and 1913 letters from Fauset to Joel Spingarn, who was elected Chair of the New York Branch when it was first formed in January 1911, and who became Chair of the Board of Directors of the NAACP in January 1914, reveal her early behind-the-scenes involvement with conflicts and cases dealt with by the young organization.

In 1912 she writes Spingarn in response to a conflict which was always bothersome within the NAACP. Interracial hassles were ever-present in the organization, if not in its public pronouncements and activities, then in its internal day-to-day workings. The source was sometimes lack of leadership and organizational experience among the Black members, sometimes condescending assumption of superior ability and right to lead among white members, and sometimes over-bearing DuBois. Fauset in the letter to Spingarn is evidently responding to reluctance of Blacks to go as far and as fast in protesting discrimination as the white leadership is anxious to go. She "felt that the average colored man was 'too near the traditions of slavery not to esteem nominal freedom and fleshpots above their real value' " and she urged Spingarn to " 'prod us, prick us, goad us on by unpleasant truths to ease off this terrible outer self of sloth and acceptance. . . . Some of us need to be told that we should be men. . . . Teach us, hammer into us that expediency is not all, that life is more than meat. And don't give us up. . . . For we are worth it.' "39

In the Fall of 1913, an incident of discrimination against a Black woman, Carrie Lee, of New Bedford, Massachusetts, by Smith College, involved Fauset in NAACP case work. Carrie Lee had applied to and had been accepted at Smith, but when she arrived on campus she was denied a room in the dormitories or in college-approved boarding houses. She was told she could live in servant's quarters, with entrance by the back door. According to Kellogg, Fauset and Mary Nerney "worked behind the scenes" to resolve the issue, while Spingarn visited the college to discuss the incident, and Moorfield Storey "protested vigorously" to the President of Smith College. Fauset letters to Spingarn of 9 October 1913, 18 October 1913, and 24 October 1913 deal with the matter. The typical pattern in cases like this is followed by Smith authorities, Fauset reports. The school claims that it is not biased against Miss Lee, a Massachusetts native, but that it must make concession to the discriminating tastes of its Southern students.[40] The same kind of squeamish reasoning by authorities is used later by Fauset in *Plum Bun*, when Black Miss Powell is denied a place on a boat sailing for France after she has won an art scholarship there because the grantors of the scholarships fear offending Southern winners.

Although time and effort by several people—Fauset, Nerney, Spingarn, Storey—went into finding a room for Carrie Lee it is interesting that in the official minutes of the NAACP Board of Directors meeting of 6 November 1913, another person seems to take all the credit. "Miss [Mary White] Ovington reported the successful result of her work in regard to the case of Miss Carrie Lee of New Bedford who was barred from the Campus at Smith because of her color" Library of Congress, Manuscript Division, NAACP Board Minutes). Ovington was a "young white radical social worker" who reported on the Second Annual Meeting of the Niagra Movement, forerunner of the NAACP, for the *New York Post* in 1906.[41] Subsequently she became founder of the NAACP, a member of its first Board of Directors, and Chair of the organization. Ovington was evidently not especially fond of Jessie Fauset, nor was Fauset evidently very fond of her. A later, 1920's exchange between the two reveals a cool formality (uncharacteristic of either of them), despite their long-time and close professional relationship in the NAACP and in work on *The Crisis*. Nor does Ovington mention Fauset in her history of the NAACP, *The Walls Came Tumbling Down*, or include her in her 1927 *Portraits in Color*. One can only speculate as to the cause of such coolness, but racial difference and suspicion, envy of one another's obvious intelligence and prominence, and competition in relation to the intellectual and professional regard of W. E. B. DuBois would seem to be possible sources of the friction.

The absence of closeness between these two women may be

part of the reason that Fauset did not become even more closely tied to NAACP work prior to her *Crisis* Literary Editorship. Retiring secretary Mary Childs Nerney "who believed that Negroes should be given positions of leadership in the [NAACP] proposed Jessie Fauset and several others" as Secretary in 1916. "A white man, however, Royal Freeman Nash, became the new secretary and remained in the post until he left for war duty in 1917."[42] It was not until 1920, when James Weldon Johnson was elected, that a Black was chosen for the important position of Executive Secretary. White domination in the organization's leadership up to 1920 was certainly not assuaged by the kind of personal distrust which seems to have characterized the relationship between Jessie Fauset and Mary White Ovington.

During the same year that Fauset was involved only in the background of NAACP work she became more and more closely and visibly involved with the official NAACP publication *The Crisis*. Involvement with *The Crisis* meant close involvement with DuBois. He continuously battled to make and keep *The Crisis* editorially independent as his own operation.[43] The first number of *The Crisis* appeared in November 1910, with the object of setting forth "those facts and arguments which show the danger of race prejudice, particularly as manifested today toward colored people." The name of the magazine, it was reported, was to signify a critical time for brotherhood in the United States. Intending to be a newspaper, a review of opinion and of literature, an outlet for short articles and editorials, *The Crisis* promised to fall prey to no clique, party, or personal rancour.

At its inception in 1910, *The Crisis* filled a virtual vacuum in reliable printed serial materials by and about American Blacks. Of Black newspapers, the *New York Age* had become "the defender of [Booker T.] Washington's philosophy of racial adjustment in the South," and Monroe Trotter's *Guardian* in Boston had from 1901 attempted to represent views in opposition to Washington. The leading Negro magazine of the first decade of the century, *The Voice of the Negro*, from Atlanta, was closed down and its editor, Max Barber, forced to flee for his life in the "Atlanta Massacre" of September 1906.[44] *Harper's New Monthly Magazine, Scribner's*

(Century), North American Review, Forum, and other white magazines and papers, judging from Rayford Logan's summaries and
examples in *The Betrayal of the Negro, From Rutherford Hayes to
Woodrow Wilson* (originally *The Negro in American Life and
Thought: The Nadir, 1877-1901*), were in their reportage on Black
issues filled with derisive terms, caricatures, ludicrous titles, virtually
every derogatory stereotype designed to perpetuate the plantation
tradition and to support the South. (See also J. Stanley Lemons,
"Black Stereotypes as Reflected in Popular Culture, 1880-1920"
in the Spring, 1977 issue of *American Literature*.) Against such
opinion and images, *The Crisis* appeared as a source of information
and of radical opinion on the issue of race in America.

DuBois' decision to make *The Crisis* a newspaper-magazine
was a good one in 1910. Audience expectation demanded information from a newspaper, culture from a magazine, and DuBois saw
the lack of either kind of communication outlet for Black topics
and materials at the time. He also saw the need for both approaches
to the "Negro Problem"—accurate knowledge and cultural exploration and revision. His conflicts with the NAACP Board of Directors arose partly because of the intense appeal *The Crisis* was designed to have for the Black reader. Charles Johnson wrote in the
January 1928 issue of *The Journal of Negro History* in "The Rise of
the Negro magazine," that "the more direct the appeal to Negroes,
the less the support from that necessary outside group of subscribers
and contributors." Somehow, for twenty-four years, DuBois managed to develop Black reader support and maintain with difficulty
the "outside" support of the white founders of the NAACP. That he
chose Jessie Fauset to assist in this task, and that she did such a
superb job herself in the rather untenable situation is a credit to her
cultural sensitivity, her personal relationships with Blacks and
whites, as well as her efficiency and journalistic skill.

One of the "newspaper" issues the early *Crisis*, as the early
NAACP, became involved in was women's rights, particularly the
right to vote. The handling of the issue over the first five years of the
publication illustrates a couple of characteristics of DuBois' editorship: his own opinion is always strongly expressed, through editorials
and selections; but allowance is made for dissenting views. Beginning

with the second number of *The Crisis*, Mrs. John E. Milholland wrote a series of articles called "Talks About Women," in which she discussed changes taking place in the status of women in business, industry, and the professions. "She urged colored women to expand their efforts and interests from their own circle and race and to join the larger movement—the struggle for women's rights and more particularly for the ballot."[45] The September 1912 issue—the "Woman's Suffrage Number"—includes an editorial by DuBois, "Votes for Women," in which he gives three reasons for his support of women's suffrage. First, it is a human question, and human rights are involved. Second, women's political rights necessarily open anew the question of Black voting rights. Third, votes for women means votes for Black women. Again in August 1915, *The Crisis* presents a "Votes for Women" issue. A regular monthly feature in *The Crisis* called "Men of the Month" in this issue is entirely by women. The following November, DuBois gives space to an opposing view—that of Kelly Miller. In an article called "The Risks of Woman Suffrage" (pp. 37-38), Miller opines that women's domestic role and man's worldly role are both ordained by God. "I am wholly unable to see wherein the experiment of woman suffrage promises any genuine advantage to social well-being," he concludes.

One must turn from the newspaper side of the early *Crisis* to its magazine or cultural side to see DuBois' developing literary leadership, Fauset's early involvement, and DuBois' praise for her involvement. The vacuum described heretofore in accurate printed material on the Black in 1910 of course included lack of work of well-known or widely-disseminated Black authors as well. Three papers on "The Negro as Writer," in D. W. Culp's 1902 *Twentieth Century Negro Literature* . . . can refer only to Paul Lawrence Dunbar, Charles Chesnutt, Francis E. W. Harper, and A. A. Whitman among known Black writers. By 1910 Dunbar was dead (1906), Chesnutt was silent, Harper was eighty-five years old and within a year of her death, and Whitman was dead (1902). Developing interest in Black materials by white writers, as well as encouragement for Black writers, was boosted by existence of *The Crisis*. Robert Hart, in "Black-White Literary Relations in the Harlem Renaissance" (*American Literature*, January 1973), says that in fact "the story of black-white literary relationships could be said to begin with the founding of the NAACP in 1910 and the emergence of DuBois as leader" (p. 612).

In the Spring of 1912 DuBois "met with a group of writers in an effort to interest them in the Negro as a source of literary material and to present the truth regarding the race, rather than fictionalized accounts of a sentimental or sensational character."[46] In August of the same year, *The Crisis* announces a short story competition, describes the kind of literary material it has received, and the kind it is looking for. Stories which had been sent to *The Crisis* at that date were of three kinds: the didactic, "hurt artistically by the always present desire to instruct the reader," a "common fault among writers in America"; the "old time 'darky' stories, too stereotypical; and the non-story or character sketch." Rather than these kinds of material, the announcement goes on, "we want pictures of the real colored America" (p. 189).[47]

Arthur Davis points out accurately that DuBois "anticipated the [Harlem] Renaissance long before 1925. As early as 1915 in the April issue of *The Crisis* he stated what would be two of the most significant themes of the Movement." DuBois said in 1915, that "In art and literature we should try to loose the tremendous emotional wealth of the Negro and the dramatic strength of his problems through writing . . . and other forms of art. We should resurrect forgotten ancient Negro art and history, and we should set the black man before the world as both a creative artist and a strong subject for artistic treatments."[48]

The Crisis attempted to stimulate literary endeavor, and also called emphatic attention to it when it occurred. In June 1917, a regular digest column, "The Looking Glass," quotes extensively from reviews of Ridgely Torrence's three plays—*The Rider of Dreams, Granny Maumee,* and *Simon the Cyrenian*—produced by Mrs. Emile Hapgood at the Garden Theatre, Madison Square Garden, with an all-Black cast. Torrence himself says that he wanted to exploit the capacities of the Negro as actor, and "also the extraordinary, dramatic richness of his daily life" (pp. 80-81). The September 1917 issue includes Torrence among the "Men of the Month"

—crediting him with the existence of a Negro theatre. "No white man has written of colored people more sympathetically than Ridgely Torrence, . . . opening up to them a new field of art, and none ever approached the people of another race in a more generous spirit." (p. 256). The event which Robert Hart ("Black-White Literary Relations in the Harlem Renaissance") calls "a starred date in the calendar of American Negro drama" for the "first serious plays on black life" (p. 613), and the event's originator, Ridgely Torrence, are noted well by *The Crisis*.

The content and nature of Jessie Fauset's book reviews, stories, and poems published in *The Crisis* from 1912 to 1919 will be looked at in discussion of her journalistic work and her fiction, but it is important to point out here that there is evidence in these early years of *The Crisis* that W. E. B. DuBois, in his growing literary leadership, found her work to be excellent, of the kind he wished to encourage and publish in the publication. In November 1912, the "Publisher's Page" announces for the December "Christmas Number" "a novelette, the strongest piece of fiction we have published, by Jessie Fauset" (p. 41). The same section of the December issue states that in "The Crisis for 1913 . . . we shall make a specialty of fiction and expect short stories from Charles W. Chesnutt and Miss Fauset" (p. 146). (Actually, no Fauset stories appear in 1913, and even her "What to Read" column disappears for most of the year, but DuBois' regard is evident in his anticipation. It is rather evident too that the literary quality of the magazine drops in 1913.) Again in 1917, DuBois prepares the way for the first half of a Fauset story in the April Easter Number with a note on the Contents page in March. The April issue, he says, will include "one of the strongest stories which we have ever published." The Contents page of the April issue, in turn, contains the following note: "The May *Crisis* will contain the conclusion of Jessie Fauset's striking novelette." Later, on the Contents page of November 1917, DuBois announces a collaboration between Jessie Fauset and Laura Wheeler the artist, in the Christmas *Crisis*. That DuBois thought highly of Fauset and her work in these years is clear from these references, especially in view of the fact that other writers are not singled out in this way.

Jessie Fauset's life from 1882 to 1919 reveals many things

about her character which gave impetus to her more creative and influential period after 1919. She was devoted to her family, especially to her father, and after his death, to her sister Helen. She was hardworking. She was very intelligent and thoroughly educated in traditional liberal arts. She was at an early date associating with W. E. B. DuBois not as a subordinate, but as an accepted equal. She was active in the most radical interracial organization of the time, but worked in the background, not always getting credit for her activity. Finally, and contrary to printed work on Fauset, least important, she was from a Philadelphia-area family whose name goes back to the 18th century in an old family Bible.

Notes

[1]The middle name "Redmona" is recorded in the Fauset family Bible in the possession of Arthur Huff Fauset, and is also the name on Jessie Fauset's Cornell University records from 1901-1905. Evidently Fauset later chose, however, to use the name "Redmon" instead. Thus, when she became Literary Editor of *The Crisis* in 1919 the full name recorded is "Jessie Redmon Fauset." Variations in family use of the father's first name occur among the children. Arthur Huff Fauset says that the younger children tended to use "Redmon," the older children "Redmond." An alternate spelling of "Fauset" also occurs in early records. In the family Bible mentioned above, early members are listed as "Faucett."

[2]Letter to author from Arthur Huff Fausett, 10 January 1976. Subsequent references to letters to the author from A. H. Fauset in this chapter will be indicated in the text as follows: "AHF to CS, 10 January 1976."

[3]Richard R. Wright, Jr., *The Negro in Pennsylvania: A Study in Economic History* (1912; rpt. New York: Arno Press, 1969), p. 112.

[4]Robert Bone, *The Negro Novel in America*, rev. ed. (New Haven, Connecticut: Yale University Press, 1966), p. 102.

[5]Roseann Pope Bell, "*The Crisis* and *Opportunity* Magazines: Reflections of a Black Culture, 1920-1930," Diss. Emory University 1974, p. 208.

[6]Lee R. Edwards and Arlyn Diamond, eds., *American Voices, American Women* (New York: Avon, 1973), p. 383.

[7]Wright, pp. 126, 169.

[8]Florence Smith Vincent, "There are 20,000 Persons 'Passing' Says Noted Author," *The Pittsburgh Courier*, 11 May 1929, section 2, p. 1.

[9]Charles Kellogg, *NAACP: A History of the National Association for the Advancement of Colored People, I: 1909-1920* (Baltimore: Johns Hopkins Press, 1967), 195.

[10]Bryn Mawr College Archives, M. Carey Thomas Office Files, letterbooks 1897-1950.

[11]Herbert Aptheker, ed., *The Correspondence of W. E. B. DuBois, I: Selections, 1877-1934* (Amherst: University of Massachusetts Press, 1973), p. 95.

[12]Aptheker, ed., p. 66. Letter from Fauset to DuBois, Ithaca, 26 December 1903.

[13]Benjamin Mays, *The Negro's God as Reflected in His Literature* (1938; rpt. New York: Atheneum, 1969), p. 8.

[14]Eleanor Flexner, *Century of Struggle: The Woman's Rights Movement in the United States* (1959; rpt. New York: Atheneum, 1973), pp. 179, 232.

[15]Mary White Ovington, *Half A Man: The Status of the Negro in New York* (New York: Longmans, Green and Company, 1911), pp. 158, 162.

[16]Henry Arthur Callis, "The Legacy of W. E. B. DuBois," *Freedomways* (Winter 1965), p. 18.

[17]Aptheker, ed., pp. 65, 74.

[18]*Ibid.*, p. 66.

[19]*Ibid.*, p. 94.

[20]*Ibid.*, p. 95.

[21]Letter to author from Sadie T. M. Alexander, 30 January 1976.

[22]Letter to author from Vincent E. Reed, Acting Superintendent of Schools, Washington, D. C., 16 March 1976, and enclosed Employment Verification Form.

[23]Mrs. R. D. Sprague, "What Role Is the Educated Negro Woman to Play in the Uplifting of Her Race?" *Twentieth Century Negro Literature, or A Cyclopedia of Thought on the Vital Topics Relating to the American Negro by One Hundred of America's Greatest Negroes*, ed. D. W. Culp (1902; rpt. New York: Arno Press, 1969), p. 170.

[24]Jean Collier Brown, "The Negro Woman Worker: 1860-1890," in *Black Women in White America*, ed. Gerda Lerner (New York: Random, 1973), p. 252.

[25]A letter to Archibald Grimke of 11 April 1905, outlines her plan to teach in "the lower schools of Philadelphia for the next three or four years" in order to complete a graduate degree at the University of Pennsylvania (Archibald Grimke Papers, Moorland-Springarn Research Center, Howard University, Washington, D. C.).

[26]Vincent.

[27]Mason A. Hawkins, "Colored High Schools," *The Crisis*, 2 (June 1911), 73-74.

[28]*Ibid.*, p. 75.

[29]J. C. Wright, "The New Dunbar High School, Washington, D. C.," *The Crisis*, 13 (March 1917), 220.

[30]*Ibid.*, 222.

[31]Horace Mann Bond, "Negro Leadership Since Washington," *South Atlantic Quarterly*, 24 (April 1925), 118.

[32]E. Franklin Frazier, "The American Negro's New Leaders," *Current History*, 28 (1928), 56-57.

[33]E. Franklin Frazier, *The Negro in the United States*, rev. ed. (New York: Macmillan, 1971), p. 556.

[34]Aptheker, ed., p. 56.

[35]W. E. B. DuBois, *Darkwater* (1920; rpt. New York: Schocken Books, 1969), p. 3.

[36]Aptheker, ed., p. 95.

[37]Jessie Fauset to W. E. B. DuBois, 25 February 1918, W. E. B. DuBois Papers, University of Massachusetts Library. Amherst, Massachusetts.

[38]Wilson Record, "Negro Intellectual Leadership in the NAACP, 1910-1940," *Phylon* (Second Quarter 1956), p. 375.

[39]Kellogg, p. 126.

[40]Letters to Joel Spingarn from Jessie Fauset, 9 October 1913, 18 October 1913, 24 October 1913. Moorland-Spingarn Research Center, Howard University, Washington, D. C.

[41]Herbert Aptheker, *A Documentary History of The Negro People of . The United States, The Reconstruction Era to 1910* (New York: The Citadel Press, 1951), p. 898.

[42]Kellogg, p. 112. Based on Letter from Nerney to Spingarn, 6 January 1916; Board Minutes, 14 February 1916, 13 March 1916, 8 May 1916. The author examined the Board Minutes at the Library of Congress and the Nerney letter from the Moorland-Spingarn Research Center, Howard University, Washington, D. C.

[43]For a healthy discussion of DuBois' controversies with the NAACP Board of Directors and with Oswald Garrison Villard over control of *The Crisis*, see Elliott Rudwick, *W. E. B. DuBois: Propagandist of the Negro Protest, Studies in American Negro Life*, ed. August Meier (New York: Atheneum, 1969), pp. 165ff.

[44]Frazier, *The Negro in the United States*, p. 504; Aptheker, *A Documentary History . . .*, p. 862.

[45]Kellogg, p. 53.

[46]*Ibid.*, pp. 139-40. Kellogg's reference is based on a form letter of April 1912 in the DuBois papers and NAACP Board Minutes, 4 May 1912. The Author also examined these minutes at the Library of Congress.

[47]It is not clear that this listing is by DuBois. It could, indeed, be by Fauset, since she was at this date already doing book reviews and stories for *The Crisis*, and some division seems to have already been made by the publication between "newspaper" editorial duties, and magazine cultural coverage. The writing style of the announcement sounds more like Fauset's than like DuBois'.

[48]Arthur Davis, *From the Dark Tower: Afro-American Writers 1900-1960* (Washington, D. C.: Howard University Press, 1974), p. 18.

Life From 1919 to 1961

Jessie Redmon Fauset resigned from her teaching position at Dunbar High School in Washington, D. C. in 1919 and completed her M. A. degree at the University of Pennsylvania in Philadelphia in June of that year. She had evidently taken a leave of absence from her teaching duties the year prior to her formal resignation, for she was working intensively with *The Crisis* in 1918 to 1919 as well as completing work on her degree. In a June 1918 contract letter to her, DuBois stated the terms of the *Crisis* position from July 1918 to July 1919. For $50 per month, Fauset would, from Philadelphia, do designated writer duties, including a study of Colored Building and Loan Associations in Philadelphia, and the writing of the *Crisis* "Looking Glass" column. In July of 1919, DuBois wrote, her salary would be increased to $100 per month, and she would be expected to be in residence in New York.[1] Fauset's full assumption of the Literary Editorship of *The Crisis* came in October in 1919, when she had moved permanently to New York. By December her sister Helen had also moved from Philadelphia to New York City to live with her.[2]

Two of Fauset's half-brothers and one step-brother were physically and socially close to the two sisters in New York. Arthur Huff Fauset "spent a number of years in New York City, . . . and became intimately involved" with his sisters. Brother Redmond Fauset and his wife moved to New York City and came to know Jessie Fauset and Helen Fauset Lanning very well, and their step-brother Earl Huff helped them with real estate matters, according to Arthur Huff Fauset.[3]

From this family contact and support, Jessie Fauset moved

rapidly into European and New York activity on behalf of her race, her sex, and her art. The times were trying, if intriguing, in all three areas of her concern. Boll weevils, labor depression, floods, Jim Crow facilities in the South had resulted in a million Blacks migrating to the urban North by 1918. Educational support for Blacks in the South had been dwindling from 1900 on, when $2 was spent on a Black child, $3 on a white. By 1930, $7 was spent for a white child while $2 was spent for a Black. In Philadelphia in 1919, Fauset interviewed an illiterate Black Southern immigrant, asking him if Northern race friction provoked by wartime migration was enough to make him willing to return South. He answered: " 'If I can't get along here, I mean to keep on goin', but no matter what happens, I'll never go back.' "[4]

Most of the 50,000 Black soldiers who had served in the United States Armed Forces in World War I had been subject to German and American propaganda[5] but had tasted freedom in France. They returned to the twenty-five major riots and the lynchings of the "Red Summer" of 1919. The Ku Klux Klan saw a resurge of membership, claiming 100,000 in its ranks when D. W. Griffith's *Birth of A Nation* appeared on the screen in 1915. Over seventy Blacks were lynched in 1919 alone, ten of them soldiers, some still in uniform. Fourteen were burned publicly, eleven while still alive.[6]

With the war abroad over, W.E. B. DuBois voiced the new militancy of the American Negro returning to battle at home. America "is yet a shameful land," he wrote in his "Returning Soldiers" editorial in *The Crisis* of May 1919. "It lynches. . . . It disfranchises its own citizens. . . . It encourages ignorance. . . . It steals from us. . . . It insults us. . . . We return. We return from fighting. We return fighting. Make way for Democracy! We saved it in France; . . . we will save it in the United States of America or know the reason why."

In the area of sex equality, "Negro women have contributed few outstanding militants," wrote Elise McDougald in 1925. "Their feminist efforts are directed chiefly toward the realization of the equality of the races, the sex struggle assuming a subordinate place." This despite the fact that "true sex equality has not been approximated. The ratio of opportunity in the sexual, social, economic and political spheres is about that which exists between white men and women, . . . even in New York City." But recognition of oppression by sexism as well as racism nevertheless existed in the Black woman in the 1920's. "She is conscious that what is left of chivalry is not directed toward her. She realizes that the ideals of beauty, built up in the fine arts, exclude her almost entirely. . . . Nor does the drama catch her finest spirit. She is most often used to provoke the mirthless laugh of ridicule; or to portray feminine viciousness or vulgarity not peculiar to Negroes."[7] From Wichita, Kansas an unknown Black woman, Mrs. T. W. Fine, expressed strong feminist commonality with other women in a portion of a symposium, "The Greatest Needs of Negro Womanhood," published in the *Messenger* in September 1927. At the NAACP Mary White Ovington expressed the need for more Black women on the Board if their support was to be expected, and Ella Rush Murray presented the Board with a protest over sexism in Griffith's film "One Exciting Night." The female lead's "dances and interviews," she said, "ought not to appear in any movie, (race or no race)."[8]

The post-war period saw a great surge of Black creativity in all the arts, much of it coming out of the communal stimulus of the Black metropolis, Harlem. Jessie Fauset was there. She was on the program as an usher and patron of a 17 October 1921 midnight benefit performance of the smash Black musical, *Shuffle Along*. She worked as well on the preliminary arrangements for the event, held at the Lafayette Theater in Harlem.[9] She collaborated in 1919 with the day's best known Black composer, Henry Thacker Burleigh, writing the words for "Fragments of a Song," sheet music published by Ricordi in New York. She worked with Laura Wheeling Waring, prize-winning painter, on *Crisis* illustrations for poetry and translations, and had her portrait done by Waring.[10] She enlisted support for a voice recital of Alex Auder Galewood at the International House.[11] She published an essay on drama, "The Gift of Laughter," in the anthology edited by Alain Locke in 1925 which gave name and impetus to Black American art in the 1920's (*The New Negro* [1925; rpt. New York: *Atheneum*, 1968]). In the field of literature she corresponded with and partied with and encouraged and competed for publishers against many prominent Black and white writers of the 1920s. She also knew first hand from *The Crisis* the problems created for literary art by the censorship of government and fear and sensitivity of readers which typified the times.

During the years Fauset taught in Washington, D. C. and wrote reviews, essays, stories and poetry for *The Crisis*, editor W. E. B. DuBois was "anxious to add her to his staff," according to her half-brother. In September 1918 DuBois announced in an editorial that the November issue would see *Crisis* enlarged to sixty-four pages, with additional illustrations, a new children's section, an enlarged "Horizon" column. In addition, he wrote, "a literary editor will be added to the present staff, insuring a prompt reading of manuscripts and a larger editorial correspondence." Unfortunately, in November of that year *The Crisis* looked the same. DuBois reported that the National War Industries Board had notified publishers that only 90% of their paper could be used the next year. Circulation was maintained and the enlargement was postponed.

At the November 1918 NAACP Board Meeting, DuBois reported on the necessity of his early departure to France to collect material on the Negro in the Great War. By the time of the December Board meeting, DuBois had sailed, but his report to the Board assured them that he had "left *The Crisis* thoroughly arranged for," with Fauset, Augustus Dill, and "Miss Allison" in charge, Ovington in supervisory position.[12] Charles Kellogg makes the more specific report that "DuBois left his new literary editor, Jessie Fauset, in charge of *The Crisis*, under Miss Ovington's 'general oversight.' "[13] On the same day that DuBois sailed for France on the official press ship, *The Crisis* moved to new roomier offices on the sixth floor of 70 Fifth Avenue, as reported in the January 1919 issue. Moving to New York for most of DuBois' four-month absence, Fauset supervised and/or planned the January 1919-June 1919 issues of *Crisis*.

It is evident from her report to DuBois on his return in April that Fauset wrote the February *Crisis* editorials on Africa and the report on the Pan-African movement in that issue.[14] Though additional editorials by her are not clearly indicated in that report, several others are also likely hers. When DuBois returned, in the May issue, the heading changed back from "Editorial" to "Opinion of

W. E. B. DuBois," and he made a modification to an editorial "written during the Editor's absence" (June 1919). Editorials written by members of the NAACP Board were usually signed. One of the January editorials, "Old Desires," which is likely by Fauset, bears an interesting resemblance to DuBois' later "Returning Soldiers," not in style but in content. A second editorial in the same issue rationally discusses the distinctions between segregation and separation. "Not every builder of racial cooperation and solidarity is a 'Jim Crow' advocate, a hater of white folk. Not every Negro who fights prejudice and segregation is ashamed of his race" (p. 112). Interestingly, Fauset's report to DuBois indicates that she wished to include his "Returning Soldiers" in the April issue, but omitted it on the "insistence" of Mary White Ovington.

The formal announcement of Fauset's position as Literary Editor came in the November, 1919 issue of *The Crisis*, where she is also designated as one of the "Men of the Month" (p. 341). Fauset's choices as Literary Editor from 1919 to 1926 and her own journalistic work published in *The Crisis* during the period will be dealt with in Chapter IV, as will her work with the children's magazine, the *Brownies' Book*, twenty-four issues of which were published from January 1920 to December 1921. Here, however, it is of importance to mention the extent to which Jessie Fauset took over or contributed to various tasks at *The Crisis*. When one looks through office correspondence for the years 1919 to 1926, it is to discover that many duties were handled by Fauset. She corresponded with subscribers, with the NAACP Board, with authors. She handled contest judging details. She managed the office when DuBois made his frequent and extended lecture tours and trips to Europe and Africa.[15]

A most interesting glimpse of Fauset's handling of day-to-day *Crisis* business as well as of her relationship to Mary White Ovington, Acting Chair and then Chair of the NAACP Board from 1917 to 1932, is gained through letters between the two women in November 1923. Ovington wrote Fauset early in the month that

> I understand that in the next *Crisis* there will be an editorial on the Houston soldiers, and that Dr. DuBois did not have time to write a new one but that you are using old material. That would be unfortunate, so I

am asking you to have this editorial written from this office and signed
by whoever writes it. Criticism has come to me, when Dr. DuBois has
been away for a long period, on the use of material taken from the 'stor-
age house.' Perhaps for that reason, it would be well to have one signed
editorial each month while he is away, that will meet the immediate
issue.

Fauset reacted strongly to the stated and implied criticism of her and
DuBois' handling of *The Crisis* operation. She replied immediately to
"My dear Miss Ovington." People who had criticized were "seriously
misinformed," "like yourself," on the Houston editorial issue, she
wrote.

> In the four years which I have been in this office Dr. DuBois has never
> gone away on a long absence and left a mass of material to be used
> indiscriminately; his editorials always come to the office fresh, for he
> writes them while away and sends them on, so that allowing for the loss
> of time in the mail they are quite up to date. Dr. DuBois sailed the 24th
> of October; his editorials were written the 20th, 21st, and 23rd. We went
> to press as usual the afternoon of the 24th. Not much chance for cold
> storage there. I am expecting to receive fresh material from Dr. DuBois
> every month. In case of remarkable happenings in this country, I agree
> that it would be a fine thing to have a signed editorial from some capable
> writer and I shall be glad to ask for it.

Ovington's first letter was quickly followed by a note from her
asking Fauset to be on a committee planning a week on race relations at the Community Church of New York. Fauset, she wrote,
could represent *The Crisis* and also "help . . . materially along the
cultural side." Fauset refused the appointment. "I am already on
more committees than I have any business to be on. . . . My plans
for February and March are a little hazy." In contrast to Fauset's
frequent hand-written notes to others on *Crisis* letterhead, this note
to Ovington is typed by a secretary.[16]

It is probably a mistake to assume that the coolness between
these two women was a simple two-sided hostility. Surely the long
controversies DuBois had had with members of the NAACP Board
is a part of the story. Ovington had attempted peace-making between
DuBois and Oswald Garrison Villard when the latter was Chair of

the Board, and had presented a strong defense of DuBois in 1915.[17] As Chair herself, however, she evidently came close to asking for his resignation at least once. In a letter to Joel Spingarn in 1921 she complained that "I have worked with Dr. DuBois and I know that he is a slippery customer, ready to take advantage of any false step the other side may make." He relies on "power . . . he has over white people. His career has been made by whites. . . . Were the matter in hand to go before the colored members of the Board, men and women, the decision would be less lenient." She says that the others must support her in "saying something drastic to Dr. DuBois, something that shows that we shall not accept his estimate of himself after this" or "I'll demand resignation."[18] There is no reason to question and much evidence to support Jessie Fauset's full loyalty to DuBois at this time, difficult man though he was. If Ovington's and Fauset's relationship lacked friendliness, it may have had some of its source in Fauset's ever-closer connection with DuBois and Ovington's difficulties with him.

Fauset undoubtedly had extensive power and influence in the day-to-day running of *The Crisis* from November 1918 to April of 1926, excluding her months in Europe in 1921 and 1924-25. For this work and for her near full responsibility for the *Brownies' Book* she has not customarily been given credit by historians and critics of the 1920's, including DuBois. She has, however, been mentioned and sometimes praised as having encouraged the young Black writers of the 1920's. George Schuyler has recalled that "Jessie Fauset with her writings in *The Crisis*, short stories and so on, tended to stimulate Negroes' interest in writing, whether one agreed with the theme of her novels or not."[19] Robert Bone does not find Fauset's novels of interest, but he does mention her and Charles S. Johnson of *Opportunity* as having done "yeoman's work for the Negro Renaissance. They encouraged new talent, opened their pages to young writers, and offered cash prizes for outstanding literary achievement."[20] Chapter IV of this study gives evidence of the truth of Schuyler's and Bone's summary assessment. The listing of materials and authors published in *The Crisis* during Fauset's literary editorship does not reveal, however, the extent of Fauset's discovery and encouragement of Black writers in the 1920's, especially Jean Toomer, Countee Cullen, Langston Hughes, and Claude McKay. Autobiographies by Hughes and McKay, and Fauset correspondence show her deep personal support and concern as well as her professional regard and backing.

Fauset wrote Arthur B. Spingarn in January of 1923 about a Jean Toomer poem which she enclosed. Her evaluation of Toomer's work has since been confirmed by other critics. Here was true art, she believed. Toomer would made a "contribution to literature distinctly negroid and without propaganda. It will have in it an element of universality too, in that it shows the individual's reaction to his own tradition."[21] Fauset's earlier, 1922, letters to Toomer himself in Washington, D. C. indicate the same enthusiasm. A 17 February letter responds with pleasure and praise to poetry, a play, and a short African folk tale Toomer had sent to *The Crisis*. Fauset is curious as to the sources of Toomer's technique, and advises him not to sacrifice clarity to it. When she rereads his work, she says, she wants to do everything within her power to assist him in developing his creative abilities. Read the classics, travel, she recommends, and come to New York and visit.[22]

In May of 1923 she wrote Countee Cullen congratulating him on a speech of his she had heard, and asking for a copy of it for possible printing in *The Crisis*. By this time five Cullen poems had appeared in the magazine. The speech was printed in the August issue. Fauset's correspondence with Cullen was long-lived and warm. In August 1923 she expressed her pleasure at his having met "Miss DuBois"—W. E. B. DuBois' daughter Yolande, whom Cullen eventually married in a gigantic Harlem wedding and then later divorced. Fauset asked for Cullen's prayers for acceptance of her first book by the firm of Boni and Liveright. "My friends have been very kind to me in this matter." In October 1925 she wrote him about her contribution to the anthology of Black poetry he was editing, offering to collaborate if he would like, "in work, not in name." In November of the same years she congratulated him on his winning of the John Reed Memorial Prize, expressed her joy at his being at Harvard, and philosophized on her own activities. "We work and dance and gossip and struggle. And many things are in vain. Well a lot of life is vain too." Finally, she praised his own book of poetry, *Color*. "Your book is so lovely! A few Sundays ago it was raining and bitter—there were folks at our house and we made a fire and sat and read—you!" In 1926 Fauset sent Cullen two of her poems, "Noblesse Oblige," and "Le Vie C'est la Vie"—"I knew it to be a favorite of yours." Both were for his anthology, *Caroling Dusk*. After Cullen's death in 1946, Fauset's devotion continued to his widow, Ida. "Remember, you can never weary me talking of Countee," Fauset wrote in one of many letters. Jessie Fauset's relationship with Countee Cullen was characterized by long devotion to one another's work and personal well-being.[23]

Langston Hughes as author was actually "discovered" by Jessie Fauset. In her March 1926 *Crisis* review of Hughes' *The Weary Blues* she recalled how she first "appreciated" Hughes' work in "a charming fragile conceit" in a piece he had sent to the *Brownies' Book*. "Then one day came 'The Negro speaks of Rivers.' I took the beautiful dignified creation to Dr. DuBois and said: 'What colored person is there, do you suppose, in the United States who writes like that and is yet unknown to us?' And I wrote and found him to be a Cleveland high school graduate who had just gone to live in Mexico."

In his autobiography, *The Big Sea*, Hughes describes the sensations of a young unknown discovered and encouraged by someone as prominent as an editor of *The Crisis*

> I had seen the *Crisis* editors but once or twice during my previous winter at Columbia. And then I had had no intention of seeing them—but when I changed the subscription of my magazine from Toluca [Mexico] to Hartley Hall, the editorial department learned of it and tracked me down. Jessie Fauset, the managing editor, invited me to luncheon at the Civic Club. I was panic-stricken. I pictured the entire staff of the *Crisis* as very learned Negroes and very rich, in nose glasses and big cars. I had a tremendous admiration for Dr. W. E. B. DuBois, whose *Souls of Black Folk* had stirred my youth, but I was flabbergasted at the thought of meeting him. What would I say? What should I do? How could I act—not to appear as dumb as I felt myself to be? So I didn't go near the *Crisis* until Jessie Fauset sent for me. Then I asked if I might bring my mother, for I knew she would do the talking.

Hughes' social discomfort was evidently greatly assuaged by Fauset's kindness. "I found Jessie Fauset charming—a gracious, tan-brown lady, a little plump, with a fine smile and gentle eyes. I was thrilled when she told me that readers of the *Crisis* had written in to say they liked my poems. I was interested, too, to hear that she was also writing poems and planning a novel. From that moment on I was deceived in writers, because I thought they would all be good-looking and gracious like Miss Fauset —especially those whose books I liked or whose poems were beautiful."[24] Fauset helped Hughes not only by publishing his early work, but by encouraging his contacts with other writers and artists and by introducing him to many of them.

Claude McKay describes Fauset as similarly gracious and kind while at the same time he gently criticizes what he sees as her propriety and social life style.

> Jessie Fauset was assistant editor of *The Crisis* when I mét her. She very generously assisted at the Harlem evening of one of our *Liberator* prayer meetings and was the one fine feature of a bad show. She was prim, pretty and well-dressed, and talked fluently and intelligently. All the radicals liked her, although in her social viewpoint she was away over on the other side of the fence. She belonged to that closed decorous circle of Negro society, which consists of persons who live proudly like the better class of conventional whites, except that they do so on much less money.

Engaging in some double-edged criticism, McKay goes on to say that "Miss Fauset is prim and dainty as a primrose, and her novels are quite as fastidious and precious. Primroses are pretty. I remember the primroses where I live in Morocco, that lovely melancholy land of autumn and summer and mysterious veiled brown women. When the primroses spread themselves across the barren hillsides before the sudden summer blazed over the hot land, I often thought of Jessie Fauset and her novels."[25]

Two letters of Fauset to a friend and fellow teacher, Harold Jackman, give evidence of her continuing concern for the welfare of Cullen, Hughes, and McKay. From Paris in 1924 she wrote "please see that Langston gets this letter which I'm sending in your care. . . . Isn't it marvelous about Countee! I'm so glad. Have seen McKay.

He's finishing a novel." In 1942 she worte "It's nice that Langston is in New York, isn't it? Oh by the way did you receive a card at Christmas for Countee which I asked you to readress? [sic]"26 With these three Black writers Fauset's role went beyond professional editing to long-standing friendship. The three had widely different writing styles, used different kinds of materials, and had differing political and social sympathies and contacts. Yet Fauset communicated meaningfully with them all while maintaining her own views on literary and social issues.

Some of Fauset's contact with white writers of the 1920's was through her position at *The Crisis*. DuBois inspired and probably wrote the questions which were asked of Black and white authors and publishers in 1925-26, to result in a series of articles called "The Negro in Art: How Shall He Be Portrayed, A Symposium." Fauset, however, did the corresponding. In late 1925 she posed questions to Sinclair Lewis, who had by then published *Main Street* (1920), *Babbitt* (1922), and *Arrowsmith* (1925). Lewis replied to the questions with considerable searching thought. "After reading your letter it suddenly occurred to me that just possibly *all* of the astounding and extraordinarily interesting flare of negro fiction which is now appearing may be entirely off on the wrong foot. All of you, or very nearly all of you, are primarily absorbed in the economic and social problems of the colored race. Complicated though these problems are in detail, yet inevitably they fall into a few general themes; so that there is the greatest danger that all of your novels will be fundamentally alike." Finding himself unable to answer the questions about Negro literature to his own satisfaction, Lewis proposed a conference—though "ordinarily I hate committees, conferences and organizations like the very devil." Some of the questions to be dealt with by twenty or so people would be: "Should American Negroes write as Americans or Negroes?" "Should they follow the pattern of Jewish authors who are quite as likely to write about Nordics as about fellow Jews; or that of Zangwill, who is of importance only when he is writing about Jews?" Should there be a Negro publishing house so that the Negro authors can tell all of the ordinary publishing houses to go to the devil?" "Should there be a club—a comfortable small hotel in Paris to which the American Negroes can go and be more than welcome?"27

Sherwood Anderson replied to Fauset's letter with less interest and concern. "My dear Jesse [sic] Fauset," "Naturally I think it a great mistake for negroes [sic] to become too sensitive.... Why not quit thinking of negro art? . . .As to negroes always being painted at their worst I think it isn't true.... I do not believe the negroes have much more to complain of than the whites in this matter of their treatment in the arts."[28] In publishing Anderson's answer in *The Crisis* of May 1926, the editors capitalized his nouns "negro" and "negroes," in accord with their long battle to make such capitalization common usage. (As far back as *The Crisis* of February 1916 (p. 184), DuBois had editorialized that not capitalizing "Negro" was "a direct, and in these days a more and more conscious insult to at least 150,000,000 human beings.")

W. E. B. DuBois was certainly the dominating figure of *The Crisis* during Jessie Fauset's most intense work there. But some of his dominance was negative, a hindrance rather than impetus to the major force that *The Crisis* was for a few years in the area of Black American literature. "Throughout his career DuBois found it almost impossible to work closely with his fellowmen, black or white," writes Kellogg in his history of the NAACP.[29] James Weldon Johnson, close worker with the editor for years, found that DuBois was within his own circle "the most jovial and fun-loving of men." In battle he was "a stern, bitter, relentless fighter. Outside his own circle he found it hard to unbend," and that quality, Johnson found, limited DuBois' leadership role.[30] Jessie Fauset's evaluation of the man was much like Johnson's, though she tried harder to justify DuBois' irascibility. In what is in balance a highly praising article in *The World Tomorrow* in 1929, she published her evaluation anonymously. If DuBois was found to be haughty, arrogant, just rather than merciful, that might be good, she said. Though "he can and often does irritate," "a man as just, as logical and as often correct as he, is bound to abrade and sting before he heals." As with Johnson, she found DuBois a different person in his own group—a person who would "dance a Highland fling, or eat plebianly hot dogs at Coney Island, or with quip and jest keep the party going."

Though she praised *The Crisis*, Fauset carefully avoided giving DuBois personal credit for discovering the major Black writers of the 1920's. There was "no question but that *The Crisis* has been the greatest single contributing factor in the growth of significant Negro writers. First of all through this magazine DuBois made the Negro theme acceptable, natural and usual. Its pages nurtured assurance and discrimination on the part of the aspiring but timorous colored neophyte. A survey of the numbers of *The Crisis* for the last ten years would show preparation for the present-day output of Langston Hughes, Walter White, Countee Cullen, Franklin Frazier, Jessie Fauset, Georgia Douglas Johnson, Rudolph Fisher, Arthur Fauset, Maria Bonner, Alain Locke and many, many others."31 The establishment of *The Crisis* as a unique and powerful voice for Black people from 1910 on was DuBois' doing. The credit for the magazine's important role in Black American literature must go primarily to Jessie Fauset. It was she who "nurtured assurance and discrimination on the part of the aspiring but timorous colored neophyte." Fauset was never one to praise, glorify, or even describe her own powerful role in the Harlem Renaissance. In this 1929 article she came as close to indicating that role as she ever did, in saying not that it was W. E. B. DuBois, but that it was *The Crisis* that for ten years nurtured and encouraged the young Black writers. Now it is time to weigh all the evidence of office correspondence, autobiography, personal letters, and *The Crisis* pages, and to say that it was Jessie Redmon Fauset who for ten years discovered, nurtured, encouraged, and published the writers who gave new birth to Black American literature.

It is not clear exactly why Fauset left *The Crisis* in 1926. In January she wrote to Arthur Spingarn that she was seeking a new position as of February 28. She requested that Spingarn not inform other NAACP Board members, but said that DuBois was aware of her decision. As for her job possibilities, she had taken the French exam for teaching Junior High School, but indicated that "I prefer not to teach." She asked Spingarn to do whatever he could to assist her in finding work as a publisher's reader, as a social secretary for a private family, "preferably a woman," or with a New York foundation. Her skills, she reported, were typing magazine make-up, speaking and writing French. In a rare note of defeat on her principles, she indicated that if the question of color came up in a job as a publisher's reader, she could work at home. Fauset was perhaps tired of the demands of a job which involved so much contact with strong and independent personalities, and which left her little time or energy for her own novel writing. She concluded her letter to Spingarn by saying, that she was "at sea," and would appreciate any advice or help he might give.[32]

While there appears to have been no major falling out with DuBois as the reason for Fauset's departure from *The Crisis*, since she did continue to do some research for him, and continued her support in testimonial dinners, in articles, in nominating him for the Harmon Prize in 1928, there nevertheless is a cooling of their relationship evident in correspondence following her departure. In contrast to the newsy, chatty "Bulletins of Office News for Miss Fauset" which he sent her during her 1924-25 European stay, and to the cablegrams and telegrams of good wishes on her return, letters between the two in March and April of 1926 are formal and testy. In late March, DuBois writes her with repayment of a $588.85 loan: $590 plus $8.85 interest at 6% for three months, minus $10 paid her on 28 October 1925 by his check number 3277. Also in late March, Fauset writes DuBois a formal invitation to speak at a symposium planned by Mrs. Charles E. Knoblauch, "relating to certain aspects of the race question." In April, DuBois fails to fill out a form on his life's activities which Fauset needs to complete a *Who's Who* entry on him. Instead, he refers her to the first chapter of *Darkwater*. Fauset finally turns the task of his biographical entry over to another writer. "I have never been able to get from you any statement whatever about the questionnaire although other very busy men have been able to fill it out in their own cases."[33]

Fauset did finally turn to teaching in the New York Public School system after leaving her *Crisis* position. From 1927 to 1944 she taught French at DeWitt Clinton High School.[34] Teaching was not an unusual occupation for a Black writer after the 1920's, nor was the New York Public School System an unpleasant place for a Black woman to teach.[35] In 1939 Fauset wrote Harold Jackman, "well how do you like being back on the job? . . . Me I'm glad to be working in these hard times."[36] After leaving her New York City teaching job, Fauset took one other brief appointment as Visiting Professor of English at Hampton Institute in Virginia, from 12

September 1949 to 31 January 1950. She found the campus beauti-ful—"so much natural loveliness"—and "the work comparable with that of the northern schools and very strenuous," but was lonesome for home and husband. "Confidentially," she wrote Ida Cullen, there were "not enough men" there.[37]

During the decades Fauset maintained her positions at *The Crisis* and in the teaching field, she travelled and lectured as well, disseminating her beliefs about the value of the young Black writers, about Black women's role in American culture, about the need for models and inspiration for Black youth. At least twice she travelled to Tuskegee Institute and Talladega College in Alabama to lecture and dedicate buildings. The student paper at Tuskegee in 1923 reported that "in a very charming manner Miss Fauset recounted the struggles and achievements of the lesser known of the race. She also addressed an enthusiastic class of summer teachers on 'Negro Poet-ry.' "[38] In New York at the Schomburg Library and the Internation-al House she judged and read children's poems in programs organized by the James Weldon Johnson Literary Guild ("For Youth," *The Crisis*, June, September 1932). After her move from New York City to Montclair, New Jersey in the early 1940's with her husband, Herbert Harris, Fauset lectured on Black poets and poetry "before many organizations in [the] area"; was a member of the College Women's Club; and was the organization's main speaker at one annual meeting, according to her obituary in the *Montclair Times*.

In 1921 Fauset travelled to the Second Pan-African Congress in London, Brussels, and Paris as a delegate of Delta Sigma Theta Sorority (*The Crisis*, December 1921). It was her second trip to Paris; she had been there briefly in 1914. Notice of her London speeches on Black women was made by newspapers. *West Africa* reported on 3 September 1921 that "notable speeches were made by Mr. White, Assistant Secretary of the Congress, and of the New York NAACP; and Miss Fausset [sic], a journalist from Philadelphia." The Galsgow *Herald* gave an account which was reprinted in the December 1921 *Crisis*, of Fauset's speech,

> on the subject of the colored women in America, who, she said, had been a great moving force behind all the movements for emancipation.

Colored women had taken up social work in the great cities of America, and were rescuing many girls who came into the cities from other parts, and who, through their ignorance, might otherwise be exploited. Colored women were everywhere branching out into every field of activity in the professions and business. She asked the African delegates to carry a message of friendship and encouragement to African women from the colored women of America.

In Brussels Fauset described and showed pictures of Black graduates and the first women Ph.D.'s (*The Crisis*, November 1921).

Fauset's third trip to Europe and first to Africa was in 1924-25. It was made primarily for study at the Sorbonne and the Alliance Francaise, where she earned a certificate, and for private French lessons. The joys of the trip came from her social life and travels, however. She found Paris in winter a different experience than Paris in the summer tourist season. "Grey sky, grey walls, grey mists, these are our portion all day and every day. . . . The other night I stood a moment on my balcony before I went to bed and there was a grey mist . . . like a grey blanket soft and thick and woolly over everything. I sprang up in the morning to see if it was still there and it was,—palpable and mysterious, with the gold eyes of hooting taxicabs peering through."[39] She lost some of her earlier enthusiasm for the French, finding them "too coldly rationalistic and entirely too chauvinistic."[40]

Even with studying, article writing, and working on a book, Fauset found relief in being "outside the pull of routine duties," she said. It was "the first time since I was seventeen that I have been comparatively free from fetters."[41] Café life in Paris was a treat. "I've met a lot of Americans over here, writers etc. who have been most exceedingly kind. They give teas, not social ones, and they meet in the cafés to drink apertifs (perfectly harmless things) somewhere between the hours of 4:30 and 6:00, and to discuss,—well the world at large. And believe me I sit with them whenever I'm invited. I never see such life as this in America and it is worth,—oh so much!" She danced in the cabarets in Montmartre, went to Christmas Eve Mass at Notre Dame, dined Christmas Day with "a very fine and exclusive French family."[42] From January on she travelled—Carcassone, Marseille, Algiers, Nice, Villefranche, Genoa,

Rome, Florence, Venice and Vienna.[43]

Articles published by Fauset based on her European and African travel experiences reveal a sensitivity to lives of the poor and of women, and a curiosity about ways of life other than her own. Both the 1924-25 trip and a later 1934 trip to Paris, Gibraltar, Naples, Rome, Seville, Morocco resulted in articles of historical and personal character.[44] Her Pan-African Congress experience and her African travel made her sensitive to the international relevance of American race issues and the American need for more knowledge of African history and culture. She wrote in 1922 that Americans get the impression that Blacks "are last in the scale of all races, that even other dark peoples will have none of us. I shall never forget how astonished I was to see in London . . . the very real willingness of Hindu leaders to cast in their lot with ours." Africans were misrepresented, with not enough known of "indigenous African art, culture, morals." "We are told of the horrors of polygamy without a word of the accompanying fact that prostitution in Africa was comparatively unknown—until the whites introduced it."[45]

Fauset published four novels between 1924 and 1933, fitting the writing in between duties at *The Crisis*, teaching, lecturing and travelling. She said in the 1930's that she had learned from DuBois' precept and example that "a writer becomes a writer by dint of doing a little every day rather than by waiting for the correct mood or for uninterrupted leisure."[46] Fauset knew Black literature, American literature, European and West Indian literature well when she began her own novels. She saw clearly the kind of pressures a Black writer was under from the negative images of Blacks in American literature, from reluctant white publishers, from self-conscious Black readers, from overly-critical or overly-lenient white readers. "We are constantly being confronted with a choice between expediency and an intellectual dishonesty intangible, indefinable and yet sometimes I think the greatest danger of all," she wrote in 1922. "If persisted in, it is bound to touch the very core of our racial naturalness. And that is the tendency of the white world to judge us always at our worst and our own realization of that fact. The result is a stilted art and a lack of frank expression on our part."[47] One senses an attempt at balance in her own novels. She depicts racial discrimination, but that is not the point of the works. She is more interested in the psychology of characters caught in social and hereditary pressures than in their social morality. She entertains with strong and deceptively romantic plot lines, with descriptions of food, dress, social events, while using these materials to make her more significant points.

Fauset said that she, Nella Larsen, and Walter White were inspired to write their first novels by the publication of T. S. Stribling's *Birthright* in 1922. Sterling Brown later praised *Birthright* for its making a Negro character central, and for its attempt at showing the effects of environment on character.[48] When one reads the book today it is to recognize what a paucity of fictional representation of Blacks must have led Black readers to praise *Birthright*. At the book's beginning, hero Peter Siner returns from Harvard to "Hooker's Bend," Tennessee. "It was the white blood in his own veins that had sent him struggling up North. . . . It was the white blood in Cissie that kept her struggling to stand up, to speak an unbroken tongue, to gather around her the delicate atmosphere and charm of a gentlewoman. It was the Caucasian in them buried here in Niggertown. It was their part of the tragedy of millions of mixed blood in the South." Part of Peter Siner's recognition at the end of the novel is that "no people can become civilized until the woman has the power of choice among the males. . . . The history of the white race shows the gradual increase of the woman's power of choice. . . . That was why his own race was weak and hopeless and helpless. The males of his people were devoid of any such sentiment or self-repression. They were men of the jungle, creatures of tusk and claw and loin."[49] Fauset read *Birthright* and concluded: "Let us who are better qualified to present [the truth of Negro life] than any white writer, try to do so."[50]

There Is Confusion, Fauset's first novel, was published in the United States by Horace Liveright at the firm of Boni and Liveright. This "young, daring, unconventional" publisher of Dreiser, Pound, Eliot, Doolittle, Mencken, Faulkner, Anderson, Crane also gambled on Jean Toomer's *Cane* and Eric Walrond's *Tropic Death*.[51] On those two Black novels he lost, at least as far as sales were concerned, but *There Is Confusion* did sell. By 1928 it had been out of print for some time and a new edition was brought out (*The Crisis*, July 1925). Liveright ads were generous, with pictures of Fauset, quotes from newspapers, descriptions of the dinner given Fauset at the Civic Club as a send-off for the book.

> A few weeks ago a dinner was given at the Civic Club in New York in honor of Jessie Redmond Fauset, which the intellectual leaders of the metropolis attended. They were celebrating the birthday of a new sort of book about colored people—the birthday of a fine novel about Negroes of the upper classes of New York and Philadelphia—as impressive and vital in their special environment as the upper class whites whom Edith Wharton or Archibald Marshall love to write about. . . . Yes, there's something new under the sun, and it is "There Is Confusion."[52]

Floyd Calvin of the *Pittsburgh Courier* remarked in his "The Digest" column on 19 April 1924 that the Boni and Liveright ads "mark the beginning of a new era in the treatment of colored authors." Before, these authors had been neither encouraged before publication or noticed afterward.

Reviews of the book were generally quite favorable. George Schuyler in *The Messenger* praised both Fauset for her work and the publisher "for being sport enough to publish it" (May 1924). Fred DeArmond in *Opportunity* commended Fauset for scorning the precedent of dialect "and other thought-to-be-indispensable earmarks of race literature."[53] The *New York Times Book Section* review pointed out the book's novelty as being by a college-educated Negro woman. The reviewer also could not refrain from digging out and commenting on Fauset's view on racial intermarriage (13 April 1924, p. 9). A positive review was given in London, where *There Is Confusion* was published by Chapman and Hall. The *Times Literary Supplement* (4 December 1924), found the novel an "able and unusual study" which charmed the English reader by its "apt allusions to circumstances of negro life." The character of Peter Bye was singled out for special praise. The *Literary Digest International Book Review* also found the book to be excellent. Fauset "neither demands nor makes any sentimental concessions. She possesses the critical insight and resolute detachment of the novelist, and her picture of the society which her novel surveys is achieved with an art as impersonal as that of Mrs. Wharton. Her novel is neither propaganda nor apology but art" (June 1924).

Mary White Ovington's review of the book for her "Book Chat" column, sent to Negro newspapers, was somewhat negative. "Is this colored world that Miss Fauset draws quite true?" When colored readers responded that yes, it was quite true, in a later column Ovington asked a new question: "Is there sufficient local color to make the story of the Negro interesting without much reference to his relation to the white race?"[54] The reviewer in the *New Republic* was more negative, finding the novel significant only because it was "the first work of ficiton to come from the pen of a colored woman in these United States."[55]

In 1926 the William E. Harmon Foundation set up gold, silver and bronze medal awards for Negroes who had made notable contributions in various fields. According to materials in the Harmon Foundation files in the Library of Congress Manuscript Divison, Fauset was nominated for the Harmon Award in Literature in 1928 by Mabel Carney, Professor of Education at Teacher's College, Columbia University. (Fauset herself nominated DuBois and his novel, *Dark Princess*, for the prize.[56] Her half-brother, Arthur Huff Fauset, was also nominated.) In their letters of support for Fauset's nomination, Julia Derricotte, National Student Secretary of the Young Women's Christian Association, and Leslie Blanchard described the extent to which Jessie Fauset led discussion groups, interpreted Negro thought, and did platform work for student groups. *There Is Confusion* was in great demand on college campuses, with its greatest appeal being "for groups who have read very little." Recognition of Fauset's work would serve as a stimulus to even greater achievement, Derricotte concluded. Others writing in support of Fauset were Gladys Taylor, New York; Dean James Carter of Talladega College, Alabama; President David Jones of Bennett College in North Carolina; Dr. Henry Smith Leiper of New York; and Reverend Fred L. Brownlee.

There was little agreement among the judges. Out of twenty-two candidates Fauset placed second once, third twice, fourth twice, and fifth once. The judge who placed Fauset second, William Stanley Braithwaite, had read *Plum Bun*, Fauset's second novel; the other judges apparently had considered only her first. Fauset did not receive a Harmon Prize, and appears to have been discouraged by that fact. When Mabel Carney, at the request of the Secretary of the Harmon Foundation, asked to nominate her again in 1929, the Foundation files show that Fauset refused. Presumably she would have had a much greater chance of winning in 1929, with *Plum Bun* available for all the judges' consideration. In fact, no gold and silver medals were awarded in literature in 1929; the bronze medal went to Walter White (*The Crisis*, February 1930).

In 1925 Fauset wrote Carl Van Vechten about a manuscript called "Marker" which she described as her second novel. Liveright had rejected the book and it was currently being read by Viking Press. Fauset requested any help Van Vechten might give, since he had volunteered to help her if he could.[57] "Marker" was evidently the same manuscript as *Plum Bun*, which was published in 1929 by Frederick E. Stokes in the United States and by Elkin, Mathews and Marrot in London, judging from a critique of a manuscript DuBois called "Market" on 10 September 1925 (W. E. B. DuBois Papers, University of Massachusetts, Amherst, Massachusetts). Fauset appears to have retained throughout her publishing career the belief that her work was rejected by publishers because of the kind of people she wrote about—educated, sensitive Blacks who were not "pressed too hard by the Furies of Prejudice, Ignorance, and Economic Injustice."[58] Marion Starkey wrote in her 1932 interview of Fauset that "the first publisher to see the manuscript [of *There Is Confusion*] explained as he rejected it, 'White readers just don't expect Negroes to be like this.' And that fact has been Miss Fauset's difficulty ever since."[59] In this belief about publishing problems Fauset was in agreement with DuBois, in disagreement with Charles Chesnutt, James Weldon Johnson, H. L. Mencken and others, who saw such change in attitudes from 1918 on that race and class were no longer by the late 1920s a hindrance to publishing, they thought.[60]

Reviewers of *Plum Bun* were more positive than negative, though no reviewers caught the subtle exploration of women's roles or of Angela's choices in the novel. The *Saturday Review* praised the comparison of white and Negro races and picked out a moral:

honesty is the best policy (5 April 1929). *Booklist* found the plot interesting "in spite of its somewhat sentimental treatment" (May 1929), and the London *Times Literary Supplement* surprisingly, found some parts weaker than others because of "too great a regard for naturalistic detail" (29 November 1928). *Outlook and Independent* described *Plum Bun* as a moving story by a "well-known negress," "interesting, often disturbing and well-written" (13 March 1929). Alain Locke praised the novel in *Survey* for its quiet pool of material, which was "too often disregarded for the swift muddy waters of the Negro underworld and the hectic rapids and cataracts of Harlem," and for its stylistic improvements over *There Is Confusion*. In *Plum Bun* and Wallace Thurman's *The Blacker the Berry* Locke found that "the inner mechanisms of Negro life are close to the surface after generations of repression."[61] Both the *New Republic* and the *New York Times* wrote essentially positive reviews. The story was melodramatic said the *New Republic*, but was nevertheless effective in its handling of Angela's character, desires, *carpe diem* philosophy, and deceptions (10 April 1929). The *New York Times* found in *Plum Bun* "a simple fidelity to character which has nothing to do with race or creed or color" (3 March 1929). In contrast to these reactions, a very negative, imperceptive, and defensive review was made by Ephraim Berry in the *Chicago Defender*. Berry found Angela Murray "disgusting" in her wanting to be white. "I certainly hope the next book [Fauset] writes will be about Negroes. She can do it" (8 June 1929).

Though the Frederick A. Stokes Company published *Plum Bun* in 1929, they balked a bit at Fauset's third book, *The Chinaberry Tree*. In October 1931 Fauset wrote to Zona Gale, who had favorably commented on *There Is Confusion*. "Do you remember Jessie Fauset?" she began. Readers at Stokes, she went on, "declare plainly that there ain't no such colored people as these" in *The Chinaberry Tree*, "who speak decent English, are self-supporting and have a few ideals." Two other readers said the author must know what she was writing about. "If I could find someone much better known than I, speaking with a more authentic voice," to speak for the book, they would accept it, Fauset continued.

By return telegram, Gale expressed her willingness to write

an introduction. In further letters Fauset sent her warm thanks, her own and the Stokes Company's compliments on the introduction Gale wrote, and an invitation "to a very large tea someone is going to give me" on 3 January 1932. The whole publishing difficulty, plus a rush to get the book out by Christmas, upset Fauset very much. She complained to Gale of "a too insistent attack of nervous exhaustion" which left her "without desire for ambition or effort. . . . I'm all distrait just now and correspondingly dull." With particular poignancy she concluded a November 1931 letter: "It's so much simpler to write about life than to live it."[62]

The Stokes Company used Zona Gale's introduction to *The Chinaberry Tree* prominently, with Gale's name on the cover and reference to her statements in its ads for the novel. Fauset has "opened a door on the life of the Negro of intellectual interests and on a society little known to the whites," ran a large advertisement in February 1932 *The Crisis*. "It is, as Zona Gale points out in her introduction, the life of a great segment of Americans which deserve to be better understood." The ads also used a quote from a Countee Cullen letter to Fauset which said that he had read the novel "with extreme pleasure." Fauset had forwarded Cullen's letter to the Stokes Company, asking him later, "You don't mind, do you? I think they are going to use it in their advertising.[63] Jessie Fauset was very anxious for this her third novel to succeed.

W. E. B. DuBois not unexpectedly praised *The Chinaberry Tree* highly in *The Crisis* (April 1932). One wonders how carefully he read the book, however, for he wrote that it would be criticized as artificial for depicting "prim" Negro society and for excluding promiscuous or prostituted sexuality. The novel actually has more sexuality and a freer moral attitude toward it than DuBois evidently perceived. The *New York Times* in a very favorable review found the book "less picturesque and colorful than most novels of Negro life," but "certainly more illuminating" (10 January 1932). The London *Times* called it "an interesting and pleasant piece of work" (23 June 1932). The *Saturday Review* dealt with the book twice. An unsigned review in Febraury 1932 saw the novel as "weighted down" by the "thesis" that Negroes live like whites and are middle class in growing numbers. The review the following month by M. L.

Becker was more perceptive, finding the novel "less concerned with racial than with social handicaps." In the most discerning review the book received, Gerald Sykes in the *Nation* discovered Fauset's intent in the book's style, faulting her only for seeming to avoid the "specifically Negroid, which none but a Negro could contribute" (27 July 1932).

Fauset's last long publication, *Comedy: American Style*, was also published by Frederick A. Stokes Company, in 1933. The *Nation* found it to be a "well-written problem novel, dealing with that isolated group of people who exist on the border-line of race" (3 January 1934). Alain Locke's January 1934 *Opporunity* review was hesitant and disappointed, finding Fauset's art "slowly maturing"; her style too mid-Victorian, her theme not handled forcefully enough; her characterization too close to type. Fauset exploded in anger at Locke's response to her work, writing him a scathing letter which bears evidence of having been crumpled and then ironed out. "I have always disliked your attitude toward my work," she begins, continuing with comments on the pedantry, stuffiness, and poverty of thought in his works, his inept writing, his prejudice as a critic in favor of whites, his malice and lack of discrimination. She challenges him to point out one page where "mid-Victorian style prevails."[64]

Reviewers perceived, present day readers can sense, and Fauset herself recognized that her novel publishing history did not show a gain in literary strengths from her first two novels to her final one. Her half-brother has said that "I think she had a feeling about her prose writings that she had come at the wrong time, ironically too, since it took all the time up to the time of her *There is Confusion* for the establishment to see anything worthwhile in the writings about Blacks" (Letter to author, 10 January 1976). Fauset was fifty-one years old when *Comedy: American Style* was published. One can only wonder what kind of writing she might have done by 1933 and beyond had her writing abilities been encouraged by publishers and readers when she graduated from Cornell in 1905.

Fauset did not give up the idea of writing and publishing after 1933. A 1946 article about her in *The Delta Journal*, publication of her sorority, Delta Sigma Theta, described her as then working on her fifth novel. Arthur Huff Fauset, in trying to explain why his half-sister did not publish significantly after 1933, has indicated that her health became more and more a hindrance to her writing. "She did not and we did not detect the feebleness that bore down upon her over a number of years. In those days she spoke constantly of writing more. She even got down to Philadelphia, to live with her step-brother, in the city that was the inspiration of practically all her writing. . . but it was too late. The strength simply was not there. The death of her full sister, though it had occurred considerably earlier, I suggest was partially responsible for her decline" (Letter to author, 10 January 1976).

Jessie Fauset's essential work at *The Crisis*, her travelling and lecturing, her teaching, and her writing filled the public portions of her life from 1919 to 1961. There remains to be said something of her more private life—her social activities, her family, her last years and her death. Finally, an attempt will be made to briefly define the essentials of her character and attitudes and her contribution to American literature during her life from 1919 to 1961.

Harlem in the 1920s is understandably remembered for its interracial parties and its active night life. In summarizing Black and white literary relations in the Harlem Renaissance period, Robert Hart mentions that most of the interaction between writers was of paraliterary value.[66] Social contacts and activities, encouragement and awareness were at their best beneficial to Black and white writers alike. Fauset was an important figure in two kinds of social event—the testimonial dinner or benefit and the private at-home cultural soiree. She did love dancing and undoubtedly sometimes took part in the drinking and dancing kind of party given by famous Harlem socialite A'Lelia Walker. She also was not a stranger to cabaret life. It is not for these activities that Fauset is primarily remembered, however.

Fauset successfully planned a surprise party for about one hundred guests on the occasion of Mr. and Mrs. W. E. B. DuBois' silver wedding anniversary in 1921.[67] She was at the farewell party for Claude McKay when he left for Russia in 1922. Held at James

Weldon Johnson's home in Harlem, the party was described by the press and by both McKay and Johnson as the "first of the bohemian-elite inter-racial parties in Harlem."[68] In 1924 Fauset was in charge of the "DuBois Dinner Committee" which met throughout February and March setting up the event in honor of DuBois in April.[69] In 1928 she contributed $50 toward the gift for DuBois' 60th birthday party—the purchase of his ancestral Burghardt family home in Great Barrington, Massachusetts (NAACP Files, Library of Congress). Fauset was present at other rather formal events too—a party for James Weldon Johnson when he resigned the secretaryship of the NAACP in 1931 to assume a position at Fisk University, and the award dinner for Johnson when he received the first DuBois literary prize in 1934.[70]

There were of course testimonial affairs for Fauset herself when her books were published. Arthur Huff Fauset recalls these

> "literary teas," which she and our sister Helen arranged for the purpose of giving a "sendoff" to one of her novels. . . . For one of her novels, she had me come up . . . in order to deliver the critical appraisal of her work. These teas were jovial, placid affairs, attended chiefly by the black literati from the New York metropolitan area. . . . They were jolly affairs, where members of the black middle class, chiefly paid homage to the black writer whom they esteemed not only for her literary competence, but as a friend and social companion; many of these were wives of physicians, lawyers, business men (like her husband); and students whose parents were of the black bourgeoisie, as Frazier would have called them. Very genteel affairs; no wild partying, etc. But enjoyed by every one (Letter to author, January 1976).

Langston Hughes remembers Jessie and Helen Fauset's more private gatherings in some detail.

> At the Seventh Avenue apartment of Jessie Fauset, literary soirees with much poetry but little to drink were the order of the day. . . . A good time was shared by talking literature and reading poetry aloud and perhaps enjoying some conversation in French. White people were seldom present unless they were very distinguished white people, because Jessie Fauset did not feel like opening her home to mere sightseers, or faddists momentarily in love with Negro life. At her house one would usually meet editors and students, writers and social workers, and serious people

who liked books and the British Museum, and had perhaps been to Florence (Italy, not Alabama).[71]

Some of the Harlem celebrities "who often attended" Fauset's and James Weldon Johnson's "cultural soirees," Hughes says, were the Van Vechtens, Clarence Darrows, young Paul Robeson, Aaron Douglass, Rebecca West.[72]

The Great Depression changed Harlem social life and Jessie Fauset's social life too. Whites had in the mid-1920's begun flocking to Harlem, "firmly believing that all Harlemites left their houses at sundown to sing and dance in cabarets, because most of the whites saw nothing but cabarets."[73] By 1927 Wallace Thurman estimated that ninety-five per cent of the cabaret frequenters were white.[74] The submerged bitterness of the Harlem Black surfaced when segregation hit even Harlem's own establishments, and the depression brought recognition that the Black metropolis was not a region of prosperous night clubs at all. In 1930 the *New York Herald Tribune* published a report that ninety per cent of the cabarets in Harlem were owned by whites, ninety-two per cent of the Harlem speakeasies were operated by white racketeers. The fact is that this community of 220,000 Negroes is the poorest, the unhealthiest, the unhappiest and the most crowded single large section of New York City." "The October stock slump produced five times as much unemployment in Harlem."[75]

In 1932 Fania Marinoff, wife of Carl Van Vechten, raised the ire of Floyd Calvin at the *Pittsburgh Courier* by not only dropping out of the social scene of which the Van Vechtens had been leaders, but by repenting the years of "hundreds of parties in apartments, night clubs, honky tonks, speakeasies in Harlem, in the Village. It was very hollow. I never liked it." Let this be a "warning to Negroes who bow and scrape to patronizing whites," wrote Calvin. "Nine times out of ten the whites are looking for something, and when they get it, then they go off and make fun of you."[76] In the same issue of the *Courier*, Floyd Snelson wrote that the Van Vechtens had "hosts of followers" and deserved much credit for helping Negro artists and for "bringing about the close relationships and the amicable mingling of races between Harlem and Greenwich

Village."[77] These conflicting contemporary evaluations of the Harlem party craze are similar to the critical conflicts found in evaluating the literature of the period, from Van Vechten's *Nigger Heaven* to Claude McKay's *Home to Harlem* to Jessie Fauset's *Plum Bun.* The parties and interracial contacts of the 1920s were undoubtedly a benefit to some Black writers, an unfortunate distraction to others. The evaluation of the time as a mixed blessing carries over to literary criticism as well.

Jessie Fauset was an active participant in Harlem and interracial social life, but her life was not dominated by it or defined by it. After the depression, and after her marriage in 1929, she continued to invite guests to cultural gatherings at her home, though in smaller, more intimate numbers. Harold Jackman was asked in 1933 if he could "come in Tuesday evening about nine and spend an hour or two with a couple of friends. . . . They are interested in writing, the theatre and kindred subjects which I know attact you."[78] Through the 1940s and 1950s, after Jessie Fauset and Herbert Harris had moved to Montclair, New Jersey, Ida Cullen was frequently asked over with others for bridge, for weekends of music and talk.[79] Fauset's use of the opportunities provided by wide New York social contacts was limited to her isolated requests for help after offers to help had been made, as with VanVechten and the "Marker" manuscript, and her encouragement of the many young Black writers, as in her bringing Langston Hughes to formal and informal gatherings.

Fauset married Herbert Harris in 1929 when she was forty-seven years old. Arthur Huff Fauset recalls that "in 1928 (I believe) I visited my sisters in New York City. There was a very personable young man whom I did not know, and he was introduced to me: Herbert Harris. I had no idea at the time that he was to be my brother-in-law." Harris was an insurance broker, "a talented man in business, and highly esteemed by my sister. I believe he was a native of the upper New Jersey region. He had been a World War I soldier and consequently was somewhat incapacitated by war injuries" (Letter to author, 10 January 1976). *Plum Bun* had just been published, and the publishers "presented [Fauset] with a handsome, bound copy of the new book as a wedding present."[80] Harris was "filled with ambition, and much interested in his wife's success as a writer, although he himself was not active in that realm. Nevertheless, his life was more the kind of life one might expect from an ambitious war veteran with friends among men who enjoyed life, while his wife's naturally ran along the lines of art and literature" (Letter to author from Arthur Huff Fauset, 10 January 1976).

Jessie Fauset and her husband made their home for some years with Fauset's sister Helen Fauset Lanning on Seventh Avenue in Harlem. The building was a "cooperative apartment" which had been in Mrs. Lanning's possession "for some years."[81] Helen Lanning died in 1936, a deep loss to Jessie Fauset. Fauset wrote Mrs. James Weldon Johnson after Johnson's death in a car accident in 1938 that "I know how close you and Jim were to each other—like my sister and myself—no experience, no triumph was perfect until the other knew about it. Well I've lost her and I say to you sadly I know you will never recover from this blow. All I can do is to hope and pray that you'll be given the courage to bear up under it."[82] In 1939 Fauset began working on a memorial to her sister in the form of a "Helen Lanning Corner" in the library of the New York City school at which Mrs. Lanning had taught—P. S. 68 at 127 West 127th Street. "It is to contain books only about colored people, especially colored children," she wrote Jackman.[83] In 1946 according to the *Delta Journal*, Fauset was expanding the memorial to collections of books by and about Negroes "to be given to ten libraries located in various parts of the country."

In the early 1940's the Harrises moved to 247 Orange Road in Montclair, New Jersey, where they lived until Herbert Harris' death in 1958. In 1946, 1948, and 1949 Fauset described herself as "authoress" and housewife, happily married, "enjoying" her own housework and meal-getting and "occasionally" turning out verse.[84] When she accepted the brief stint as Professor at Hampton Institute during the last months of 1949, she wrote Ida Cullen of her longing to get back home,

> never more to roam.... I mean it!... Herbert spent my second and third day here with me, and then finished up his vacation. But now he writes me he is so miserably lonely, he wants me to come home....

We'll think twice before we have another long separation. . . . Herbert is very, very lonely, even more so than I. . . . I'm at the point in my life now when I try to hang on to every minute, but these next five months can evaporate for all of me. Oh ain't HOME grand! . . . Herbert's birthday is Monday. Please send him a card.[85]

Fauset's late life from the time of leaving New York City up to the death of her husband in 1958 appears to have been happy, though not productive as far as any published writing is concerned. Her last two years in Philadelphia, where she moved after Harris' death, were sad despite the devotion of her step-brother Earl Huff, with whom she lived.[86] The immediate cause of Jessie Redmon Fauset's death on 30 April 1961 was heart failure from hypertensive heart disease, with onset of the underlying advanced arteriosclerosis having occured a year and a half earlier. Fauset was buried in Eden Cemetery, Darby Del, Pennsylvania, on the outskirts of Philadelphia.[87]

Many character traits of Jessie Fauset seen in her life up to 1919 remain significant in her most creative period after that date. Devotion to family continued in the many years lived with Helen Fauset Lanning, in the contacts kept with brothers and their wives, and in Fauset's happy and enduring marriage to Herbert Harris. Her early years reveal her to be very hard-working; her later years simply confirm that impression. In her editing, lecturing, travelling, teaching, partying and writing, the 1920's especially show her to be an amazingly industrious person. Fauset's early work with NAACP was not credited to her—she worked quietly but effectively in the background. After her move to fulltime work at *The Crisis* she did even more work for minimal recognition. W. E. B. DuBois later remembered her only as "a very brilliant colored girl . . . , who was born in Philadelphia and has written some lovely things about Philadelphia Negroes," who once said " 'It's so nice to start out in Paris and not have to think where you're going to get lunch.' "[88] Finally, documentation of Fauset's activities and achievements from 1919 to 1961 confirms anew the conclusion reached about her early life that her having come from an old Philadelphia family is not the significant thing to remember about this Black woman, nor is her family's early history an adequate basis from which to evaluate her writing.

Fauset's life from 1919 to 1961 also discloses something of her characteristic thought on the questions of race, of sex and of art. Her having grown up during an intense period of segregation in schools and in public facilities gave her a self-consciousness about race that younger writers such as Langston Hughes were quite free of and often failed to understand. "I cannot if I will forget the fact of color in almost everything I do or say in the sense in which I forget the shape of my face or the size of my hands and feet" she wrote in 1922. Dealing with shop girls, a theater box office, a school, a restaurant waiter one had always to guess at what to expect, how long to wait, whether to credit negative actions to prejudice or to something else.[89] "The Negro moves in a state of child-like bewilderment at being humiliated unnecessarily and denied civic privileges because of something for which he was not to blame," Fauset said in 1929.[90] The description would seem to accurately describe her own bewilderment, originating when she was a school child in Philadelphia. But if Fauset's self-consciousness about race led her into a placing of individual achievement above "race pride," it also kept her from falling into race chauvinism and dependence on race for identity.

Fauset was intensely aware of the discrimination and problems faced by women of any race, and of the dual discrimination faced by Black women. Her own career was a breaking of many occupational barriers to women and a shattering of the image of what a Black woman's role should be, whether that image was manufactured by white or Black society. Her awareness and analysis of sexism comes out partially in her European speeches and her short stories, more fully in her novels. In consonance with her generally balanced and optiministic attitude toward life, her views of Black women emphasize their strengths as well as their difficulties.

Fauset was devoted to art in all forms, not just to literature. She was curious about and self-educated in African and West Indian art as well as in American and European forms. In literature, she was tolerant of and cognizant of value in styles different than her own. She was frustrated by lack of time and energy to devote to her own novel writing. In the writing she did accomplish she was exploratory rather than dogmatic. She was modest in promoting her work. "She never flaunted any of her capabilities" Arthur Huff Fauset has said. "Sometimes when she came down [to Philadelphia] to speak before an interested gathering, I would ask her to wear her Phi Beta Kappa Key. She felt embarrassed to put it on. She never to my recollection praised her own works" (Letter to author 10 January 1976).

Fauset "disesteemed coarseness of any kind." She was lively, vivacious, liked good talk, but did not like "coarse" language. That personal bias did not, however, lead her to either condescension or snobbishness in relation to others who might have other biases.[91] She even loosened up herself on language propriety to close friends as the years went by, writing to Ida Cullen in 1947, "Now Ida don't be a fat black pig but write me."[92]

Jessie Fauset's contribution to Black American literature includes the definable and the indefinable. It is possible to say from extant evidence that she was central to the role palyed by *The Crisis* in the literature of the 1920s, and that she went beyond mere professional assistance to real personal encouragement to Hughes, Cullen, McKay and others. It is not possible to define, but one can estimate, the inspiration provided by *There Is Confusion* in 1924, when the only other current Black novel in the bookstore was Jean Toomer's *Cane*. One can guess at what influence Fauset's many book reviews and articles must have had on young and yet unknown writers; What encouragement and interest in arts was given young people by her lectures and her readings and her teaching. Finally, it cannot be measured, but it can be surmised as to what extent dinners, parties, small art discussion groups, poetry readings by the fireside contributed to an atmosphere of interest, inspiration, and stimulation for Black and white writers and readers alike during the last forty years of Jessie Redmon Fauset's life.

Notes

[1]W. E. B. DuBois to Jessie Fauset, 12 June 1918. W. E. B. DuBois Papers, University of Massachusetts Library, Amherst, Mass.

[2]Jessie Fauset to Mary Church Terrell, 11 December 1919, Mary Church Terrell Papers, Library of Congress, hereafter LC.

[3]Letter to author from Arthur Huff Fauset, 10 January 1976.

[4]Arna Bontemps and Jack Conroy, *Any Place But Here* (New York: Hill and Wang, 1966), p. 309.

[5]W. E. B. DuBois printed some of the Ameican propaganda in the May 1919 "Documents of the War" issue of *The Crisis*. In "Secret Information Concerning Black Troops" the French were warned that social mixing of the races would lead to American Blacks raping French women. This issue of *The Crisis* was held at the U. S. Post Office in New York City for seven days before mailing was permitted (Tenth Annual Report of the NAACP, January 1920, p. 65). The May 1919 issue of *The Crisis*, which also contained DuBois' editorial "Returning Soldiers," was part of the reason for a U. S. Department of Justice Investigation of the magazine (E. M. Rudwick, *W. E. B. DuBois: Propagandist of the Negro Protest* [New York: Atheneum, 1969], p. 240). James Weldon Johnson writes in *Black Manhattan* that when Justice Department agents came to question DuBois, he replied to the query "Just what is this organization fighting for?": "We are fighting for the enforcement of the Constitution of the United States!" ([New York: Knopf, 1930], p. 247).

[6]John Hope Franklin, *From Slavery to Freedom* (New York: Knopf, 1974), pp. 349, 415, 356-57.

[7]Elise McDougald, "The Double Task: The Struggle of Negro Women for Sex and Race Emancipation," *Survey* (1 March 1925), p. 691, 689.

[8]Mary White Ovington (Chair) to A. Grimke, 9 November 1920; Ella Rush Murray to Executive Board, 13 February 1923; Ovington to Murray, 20 February 1923. Ovington's letter to Murray reports that "Dr. DuBois and Mr.

White saw the moving picture of which you wrote and did not feel the Negro was maligned in it. So there you are. Are they less sensitive to things against women than you or I would be?" Rush replied on 7 March 1923 that "Yes, I think men have skins just like *hippopotami.*" NAACP files, LC.

[9]Printed program, and James Weldon Johnson to Jessie Fauset, 21 October 1921, NAACP files, LC.

[10]The portrait can be seen in Sylvia Dannett, *Profiles of Negro Womanhood* (Yonkers, New York: Educational Heritage, Inc., 1966), p. 227.

[11]Jessie Fauset to Mrs. Arthur B. Spingarn, n.d., Moorland-Spingarn Research Center, Howard University, Washington, D. C., hereafter Moorland-Spingarn.

[12]NAACP files, LC.

[13]Charles Kellogg, *NAACP: A History of the National Association for the Advancement of Colored People, I: 1909-1920* (Baltimore: Johns Hopkins Press, 1967), 278.

[14]"Report of Miss Fauset, Acting Managing Editor of *The Crisis* during the absence of Dr. DuBois on her conduct of magazine from 4 December 1918 to 28 March 1919," 2 April 1919, W. E. B. DuBois Papers, University of Massachusetts Library, Amherst, Mass.

[15]Office memos of 5 February 1920 and 26 January 1921 refer inquiries on illustrations and on possible employment of a cartoonist to Fauset (NAACP files, LC). A Fauset note to Mrs. James Weldon Johnson, 1 June 1921, deals with a contributor's copy due date (James Weldon Johnson Memorial Collection of American Literature,The Beinecke Rare Book and Manuscript Library, Yale University, hereafter Yale). An 8 February 1920 letter from John H. Patton to Fauset makes corrections she requested in an article on the history of operations of the 370th infantry (Countee Cullen Papers, Amistad Research Center, Dillard University, hereafter Amistad). A Fauset note of 11 March 1921 to a potential contributor tells the writer that the article, though already printed in an NAACP Branch Bulletin. "The Crisis does not use reprints as main articles" (NAACP files, LC). Orders from the NAACP board to have a 1924 editorial killed because it endangered a Garland Fund grant are addressed "to Dr. DuBois (or Miss Fauset)" (NAACP files, LC). The extent of DuBois' absence from the office can be assessed through his statements in the NAACP Annual Reports. In 1920, for example, he reports having given twenty-one lectures in eight states and having

written *Darkwater*. In 1923, besides attending the Pan-African Conference, he gave lectures in the East, South, and Midwest. A Fauset letter to Arthur B. Spingarn, 25 October 1923, reports DuBois' sailing for Europe and Africa the day before (Moorland-Spingarn).

[16]Mary White Ovington to Jessie Fauset, 3 November 1923; Jessie Fauset to Mary White Ovington, 5 November 1923; Mary White Ovington to Jessie Fauset, 5 November 1923; Jessie Fauset to Mary White Ovington, 8 November 1923, NAACP files, LC. Fragments of these communications are also in the DuBois Papers, University of Massachusetts, Amherst, Mass.

[17]Rudwick, pp. 166 68, 173-74.

[18]Mary White Ovington to J. E. Spingarn, 24 July 1921, NAACP files, LC.

[19]"The Reminiscences of George Schuyler," p. 119, in the Oral History Collection of Columbia University.

[20]Robert Bone, *The Negro Novel in America*, rev. ed. (New Haven, Connecticut: Yale University Press, 1966), p. 58.

[21]Jessie Fauset to A. B. Spingarn, 20 January 1923, Moorland-Spingarn. Two Toomer poems were published in *The Crisis* in 1922.

[22]Jessie Fauset to Jean Toomer, 17 February 1922, Jean Toomer Collection, Fisk University, Nashville, Tennessee. A 24 February 1922 Fauset letter to Toomer expands upon her recommendations on reading and travelling.

[23]Jessie Fauset to Countee Cullen, 1 May 1923, 20 July 1923, n.d. October 1925, 4 November 1925, n.d. 1926, 25 May 1927, 25 January 1932. Jessie Fauset to Ida Cullen, 11 March 1946, 14 May 1946, 24 September 1949, 26 June 1950, 2 August 1951, 20 June 1953, Amistad.

[24]Langston Hughes, *The Big Sea* (New York: Hill and Wang, 1940), pp. 93, 94.

[25]Claude McKay, *A Long Way From Home* (1937; rpt. New York: Harcourt, Brace and World, 1970), pp. 112-13.

[26]Jessie Fauset to Harold Jackman, 21 December 1924, 19 January 1942, Yale.

[27]Sinclair Lewis to Jessie Fauset, 17 November 1925, in Herbert Aptheker, ed., *The Correspondence of W. E. B. DuBois, I: Selections, 1877-1934* (Amherst: University of Massachusetts Press, 1973), 329-30. The Lewis letter, with Lewis' editing, was published in *The Crisis* in May 1926.

[28]Sherwood Anderson to Jessie Fauset, n.d. 1926. In Aptheker, *Ibid.*, p. 342.

[29]Kellogg, p. 55.

[30]James Weldon Johnson, *Along This Way* (1933; rpt. New York: Viking Press, 1967), pp. 203-04.

[31][Jessie Fauset], "Wings for God's Chillun': The Story of Burghardt DuBois," *The World Tomorrow* (August 1929), pp. 334, 336. A letter from Devere Allen, 25 July 1929, an editor of *The World Tomorrow*, identifies Fauset as the author of this anonymously published article, Aptheker, pp. 405-07.

[32]Jessie Fauset to A. B. Spingarn, 26 January 1926, Moorland-Spingarn.

[33]W. E. B. DuBois to Jessie Fauset, 13 November 1924, 4 December 1924, 6 March 1925, 11 March 1925, 6 April 1925, 29 March 1926, 7 April 1926, 12 April 1926, 14 April 1926; Jessie Fauset to W. E. B. DuBois, 31 March 1926, 7 April 1926, 27 April 1926, W. E. B. DuBois Papers, University of Massachusetts Library, Amherst, Mass.

[34]Theresa Rush and A. Myers, *Black American Writers Past and Present: A Biographical and Bibliographical Dictionary* (Metuchen, New Jersey: The Scarecrow Press, 1975), p. 285. Though many of the biographical facts on Fauset given in this reference work are in error, these teaching dates are confirmed by other sources. Errors on Fauset's teaching persist from volume to volume in *Who's Who in Colored America*.

[35]Sterling Brown, "The Negro Author and His Publisher," *The Negro Quarterly* (Spring 1942), pp. 7-20, lists all the Black writers who made their living in some way other than publishing their work. Dr. William H. Maxwell, as City Superintendent of Greater New York City, set the precedent of not distinguishing teachers by race, leading to "happy conditions" in the teaching profession in New York City. Examinations were the same for Black and white teachers, and all taught in racially mixed schools, W. E. B. DuBois, "Some High

School Teachers of New York City," *The Crisis* (July 1926), p. 137. About three hundred Black women were teaching in the New York City School System in 1925, McDougald, p. 690. In contrast, the Philadelphia School System by 1929 employed 264 Negroes, 250 of them elementary teachers in segregated schools, and no Junior or Senior High teachers, "The Far Horizon," *The Crisis* (March 1929), p. 101, quoting the *Philadelphia Tribune*.

[36]Jessie Fauset to Harold Jackman, 15 September 1939, Yale.

[37]Letter to author from Fritz J. Malual, Curator, Collis P. Huntington Library, Hampton Institute, 27 October 1975; Jessie Fauset to Ida Cullen, 24 September 1949, Amistad.

[38]*The Tuskegee Student* (July 1923); *Tuskegee Messenger* (25 June 1927); *The Tuskegee Institute Bulletin* (June 1927); Jessie Fauset, "In Talladega," *The Crisis* (February 1928), p. 48. Langston Hughes and Milton Meltzer, *A Pictorial History of the Negro in America* (New York: Crown Publishers, 1963), p. 275, has a photo of Langston Hughes, Zora Neale Hurston and Jessie Fauset by the statue of Booker T. Washington at Tuskegee in 1927. In *The Big Sea* Hughes says he met Hurston accidentally while travelling around the South and "we stopped at Tuskegee and made speeches on writing to the summer school students—which was our only contact with formal culture all the way from Mobile to New York," p. 296.

[39]Jessie Fauset to Harold Jackman, 21 December 1924, Yale.

[40]Jessie Fauset to Mr. and Mrs. A. B. Spingarn, 10 February 1925, Moorland-Spingarn.

[41]*Ibid*.

[42]Jessie Fauset to Harold Jackman, 21 December 1924, Yale.

[43]*Ibid*.; Jessie Fauset to Mr. and Mrs. Spingarn, 10 February 1925, Moorland-Spingarn; Jessie Fauset to Mrs. James Weldon Johnson, 19 January 1925, Yale.

[44]Jessie Fauset to Harold Jackman, 13 May 1934, Yale, gives most of Fauset's itinerary for the 1934 trip. "Episodes in Tangier," *The Metropolitan: A Monthly Review* (January 1935), pp. 8-9, describes some of Fauset's experiences in Morocco.

[45]Jessie Fauset, "Some Notes on Color," *The World Tomorrow* (March 1922); reprinted in Herbert Aptheker, ed. *A Documentary History of the Negro People in the United States: 1910-1932* (Secaucus, New Jersey: Citadel Press, 1973), p. 357.

[46]Marion Starkey, "Jessie Fauset," *Southern Workman* (May 1932), p. 218.

[47]Fauset, "Some Notes on Color," p. 357.

[48]Sterling Brown, *The Negro in American Fiction* (1937; rpt. Port Washington, New York: Kennikat Press, 1968), p. 115.

[49]T. S. Stribling, *Birthright* (New York: The Century Company, 1922), pp. 98, 277.

[50]Starkey, pp. 218-19.

[51]Walter Gilmer, *Horace Liveright: Publisher of the Twenties* (New York: David Lewis, 1970), pp. 23, 96.

[52]Text of a Boni and Liveright advertisement, *Pittsburgh Courier*, 19 April 1924. The dinner on 21 March 1924, sponsored by the Writer's Guild, is described in "The Debut of the Younger School of Negro Writers," *Opportunity* (May 1924), 143-44. Alain Locke, James Weldon Johnson, Carl Van Doren, Walter White, DuBois, and Fauset all spoke informally. There were about one hundred and ten guests.

[53]Fred DeArmond, "A Note on the Sociology of Negro Literature," *Opportunity* (December 1925), p. 370.

[54]Mary White Ovington, "Book Chat," 1 April 1924; 11 July 1924, NAACP files, LC.

[55]E. D. W. [Review of *There is Confusion*], *New Republic*, 9 July 1924, p. 192.

[56]Jessie Fauset to A. Spingarn, 8 August 1928, Moorland-Spingarn.

[57]Jessie Fauset to Carl Van Vechten, 21 October 1925, Yale. The letter is quoted in Roseann Pope Bell, "*The Crisis* and *Opportunity* Magazines: Reflections of a Black Culture, 1920-1930," Diss. Emory University, 1974, p. 49.

There is no extant correspondence between Fauset and Liveright in the Liveright papers on either the publication of *There Is Confusion* or on the rejection of "Marker." Letter to author from Neda Westlake, Curator, Rare Book Collection, University of Pennsylvania, 19 January 1976.

[58]Jessie Fauset, "Foreword," *The Chinaberry Tree* (New York: Frederick A. Stokes Company, 1931), p. ix.

[59]Starkey, p. 219.

[60]See Charles Chesnutt, "Post-Bellum, Pre-Harlem," *The Crisis* (June 1931), p. 194, reprinted from *The Colophon*; James Weldon Johnson, "Negro Authors and White Publishers," *The Crisis* (July 1929), pp. 228-29; H. L. Mencken, "Burrs Under the Saddle: The Colored Brother," *Montgomery Advertiser*, 18 July 1927, n. p., in Mary Church Terrell Papers, LC.

[61]Alain Locke, "Both Sides of the Color Line" [Review of *Plum Bun*], *Survey* (June 1929), pp. 325-36.

[62]Jessie Fauset to Zona Gale, 20 October 1931 Portage Public Library, Portage, Wisconsin; Jessie Fauset to Zona Gale, 22 October 1931; 25 November 1931; in the Zona Gale Papers, Archives Division, State Historical Society of Wisconsin, Madison, Wisconsin.

[63]Jessie Fauset to Countee Cullen, 25 January 1932, Amistad.

[64]Jessie Fauset to Alain Locke, 9 January 1933, Moorland-Spingarn.

[65]"The Color Line" [Review of *Comedy: American Style*], *New York Times Book Review*, 19 November 1933, p. 19.

[66]Robert Hart, "Black-White Literary Relations in the Harlem Renaissance," *American Literature* (January 1973), p. 627.

[67]W. E. B. DuBois to Yolande DuBois, 31 December 1921, in Aptheker, ed., *The Correspondence . . .*, p. 255.

[68]McKay, pp. 153-54; Johnson, *Along This Way*, p. 376. The quotation is from McKay.

[69]Jessie Fauset to A. Spingarn, 11 February 1924; 25 February 1924; 3 March 1924; 28 March 1924, Moorland-Spingarn.

70*Pittsburgh Courier*, 23 May 1931, p. 9; *The Crisis* (February 1934), p. 50.

71Hughes, *The Big Sea*, pp. 244, 247.

72Langston Hughes, *Fight for Freedom: The Story of the NAACP* (New York: W. W. Norton, 1962), p. 66.

73Hughes, *The Big Sea*, p. 225.

74Wallace Thurman, "Harlem Facets," *The World Tomorrow* (November 1927), pp. 465-67.

75Beverly Smith, "Population Rises Steadily: Illness Takes Heavy Toll; Unemployment and Low Wages Result From Race Prejudice," *New York Herald Tribune*, 10 February 1930, reprinted in Allan Schoener, ed., *Harlem on My Mind* (New York: Random House, 1968), pp. 125-26.

76Floyd Calvin, "Harlem Society Repudiated," *Pittsburgh Courier*, 23 January 1932, p. 2.

77Floyd Snelson, "Van Vechten's Desert 'Gay Spots' of Harlem; Nite Life to Miss Em'," *Pittsburgh Courier*, 23 January 1932, p. 4.

78Jessie Fauset to Harold Jackman, 3 December 1933, Yale.

79Jessie Fauset to Ida Cullen, 11 March 1946; 14 May 1946; 24 September 1949; 26 June 1950; 2 August 1951; 20 June 1953, Amistad.

80Dannett, p. 229; Starkey, p. 220.

81Starkey, p. 220.

82Jessie Fauset to Mrs. James Weldon Johnson, 29 June 1938, Yale.

83Announcement enclosed in Jessie Fauset to Harold Jackman, 5 October 1939; Jessie Fauset to Harold Jackman, 15 September 1939; 21 September 1939, Yale.

84*Delta Journal*, p. 5; Cornell University Deceased Alumni File, 1948; "Poets," *Ebony* (February 1949), p. 42.

85 Jessie Fauset to Ida Cullen, 24 September 1949, Amistad.

86 Interview with Attorney William Zeitz, Philadelphia, Pennsylvania, 1 April 1976. Arthur Huff Fauset has said that Jessie Fauset was senile in her last years (Interview, 1 April 1976).

87 Death Certificate, Department of Health, Vital Statistics, Commonwealth of Pennsylvania; Fauset's date and place of birth are both stated in error on her death certificate.

88 "Reminiscences of W. E. B. DuBois," p. 123, in The Oral History Collection of Columbia University. This is DuBois' only reference to Fauset in this recollection.

89 Fauset, "Some Notes on Color," p. 355.

90 Florence Smith Vincent, "There are 20,000 Persons 'Passing' Says Noted Author," *Pittsburgh Courier*, 11 May 1929, section 2, p. 1.

91 Interview with Arthur Huff Fauset, 1 April 1976.

92 Jessie Fauset to Ida Cullen, 24 September 1949, Amistad.

Jessie Fauset: Journalist

The Crisis *and the* Brownies' Book

The November, 1919 issue of the NAACP's publication, *The Crisis*, is the first issue to list "Jessie Faucet" as "Literary Editor" after its customary introductory phrase of "conducted by W. E. B. DuBois." The following month's issue corrects the spelling to "Jessie Fauset," and from that time until April of 1926, this Black woman is the continuing literary editor of the magazine that proved to have extensive influence on the work of Black artists in America during the Harlem Renaissance. Several things are of interest in her work as literary editor. Fauset included on *The Crisis* pages numerous works by Black writers who were later to become well-known to American literature. She included many articles dealing with literary movements of the day. She published a large number of women writers, some Black and some white, whose views as revealed in stories, poems, and essays range from conservative to radical on racial and sexual issues. Finally, Fauset's own published writing during the period includes many book reviews, essays, and articles which are of interest for the range of experience and knowledge they reveal about this Black woman as a journalist.

The Crisis is in magazine format, its lynching tallies tucked in with ads for Madam C. J. Walker's Superfine Preparation For the Hair and For the Skin, and S. D. Lyons' East India Hair Grower ads from Oklahoma City, Oklahoma; its poetry juxtaposed to the winning baby pictures of the year from Duluth, Minnesota. Because of this format, it is not readily apparent that the major Black writers of the 1920s and later received their first exposure and first published some of their best work in *The Crisis* while Fauset was literary editor. However, a look at a bibliography of work by these writers published in *The Crisis* shows the importance of the magazine.

Langston Hughes' first published poem, "The Negro Speaks of Rivers," appeared in *The Crisis* for May, 1921. His fifty-some works which appeared in the magazine during Fauset's editorship include sketch and essay as well as some of his most frequently anthologized poems, such as "Dream Variation," "Cross," "Negro Dancers." Countee Cullen was first published in *The Crisis* when he was still a New York High School student. The excellence of Jean Toomer was recognized early by Fauset, evidenced by her letters to him and by his poem from *Cane*, "Song of The Son," receiving a full-page printing in April of 1922, the only poem to be so honored until Langston Hughes "A Song to A Negro Washerwoman" in January of 1925. Late writing of Paul Lawrence Dunbar in the form of letters to a friend, and of Charles Chesnutt in the form of a serialized story printed in 1924 and 1925 indicate the Literary Editor's respect for the best of the earlier Black American authors as well as for the young innovative writers. *The Crisis* during the period of Jessie Fauset's literary editorship was an important publishing outlet for Black writers.

The Crisis articles on art and literature from the 1919-1926 period demonstrate an understandable emphasis put on Drama in reviews and discussions. With Black theatre becoming popular, especially if one includes productions of such works as Eugene O'Neill's "All God's Chillun Got Wings" under that broad heading, and with Black actors, such as Charles Gilpin, becoming very well-known during the period, it is reasonable that *The Crisis* would be dealing with the area of drama, so difficult, however, to represent adequately with published plays on its pages.

Other choices of Fauset in the areas of literary and artistic discussion are also interesting. There are, for example, articles on the nature and structure of short stories and plays evidently designed to educate a wide audience. These explanatory articles also intend to encourage new writers to enter such competitions as the Amy Spingarn awards for Black writers of Poetry, Drama, Essay, and Short Story (winners from various competitions such as the Spingarn are published in *The Crisis* as well). *The Crisis* is in the center of the 1920s controversies over how "the Negro" should be depicted by Black artists—illustrated by the Symposium of reactions by writers, white and Black, to a series of questions posed by DuBois early in 1926, appearing in the magazine at the time of Fauset's moving from the position of Literary Editor to Contributing Editor, in April of 1926. Both the range of opinions and materials discussed and the public-minded attitude of combined education and encouragement, suggest a careful selection of literary and artistic criticism in Fauset's work as editor.

When one picks out and looks closely at the selections written by women which Fauset chose to publish during the seven years she worked closely with *The Crisis*, one begins to see her concern for balance. Some poems, such as Ethyl Lewis' "The Optimist," published in January of 1920, are conventional, cliché-ridden rhymed couplets about suffering being really all right because one will be rewarded later. Other poems, such as Georgia Douglas Johnson's "Attar," of March 1920, are more skillful and original in their statements of an optimistic philosophy. Still others approach a militancy of thought, a subdued threat, such as that in Carrie W. Clifford's "An Easter Message," which moves from Spring's message of the "pink-fingered Easter" to "black folk choked within the deadly grasp of racial hate," and ends with an:

> *Assurance* their death-stupor is a mask—
> a sleep, with elements potential, rife,
> Ready to burst full-flowered into life.

In "The Looking Glass," a column which begins in each issue of *The Crisis* with a section on literature, Fauset began the habit soon after assuming the literary editorship of prefacing her remarks or views or lists of books and articles with a poem, sometimes a translation, sometimes by a well-known American or British author, sometimes from some other magazine. One of these reprints, appearing in the column in September of 1921, is taken from a Miriam Allen de Ford poem in *Call Magazine*. Entitled "Tulsa," the poem connects the veterans of the Tulsa riots with other historical fighters for freedom, and contains some rather direct imagery in its "Little black babies, homeless in black streets/against a curtain of flames and sighs." From these few examples, it is clear, perhaps, that varying views as well as varying literary skills are represented in Fauset's choices.

It is important, though, to mention that there do seem to be some excellent writers among these women published by Fauset and DuBois who have not, for some reason, become known to a wider or later audience than the readership of *The Crisis* represented in the 1920s. Anita Scott Coleman's stories are excellent. Her "Etisico," in the March, 1920 issue, could be described as a kind of literary debate on the nature of patriotism. It is effective in its establishing of setting, a Santa Fe Railway Station restroom, and character, including a sick Black Banjo player who gives his earnings to the Red Cross. Leila Amos Pendleton's dialect tales of Sallie Runner, a maid who translates her white mistress's educational conversations into relevance, can be compared favorably to Langston Hughes' later Jesse B. Semple (Simple) tales. When Sallie Runner learns of Socrates' devotion to law and justice she asks: "Don't yo' wisht we had one million of dem Sockertees down here in ameericas sunny Soufland?" More precisely feminist issues are addressed by many of the selections during these years, too. When Sallie Runner learns of Socrates' customary daily activity she says "Hole on, Miss Oddry. . .Jes 'wanta ax yo one question. While ole Sockertees was runnin' round the streets, shootin' off his lip an' makin' peepul cry, who was takin' keer uv his fambly? Sounds mo' an' mo' lak Brudder Runner to me." Ruth R. Pearson's "The 'Barrier' (White Womanhood Speaks)" subtly translates the barriers to Blacks in America into a consideration of the barriers to women. "I can see further than I saw before;/Smoke in the valley—pines against the sky—/And little dreams curled close on every hand."

Jessie Fauset's own work published in *The Crisis* during the years of her literary editorship includes a large number of poems and stories, one a rather lengthy "novelette"; translations from French and West Indian and African writers; many essays, some based on her experiences during the six months of study at the Sorbonne and travel in France and Algeria in 1925-1926; book reviews; articles on topics ranging from Egyptian nationalism to Brazilian emancipation; reports on the Second Pan-African Congress held in Europe in 1921, which she attended as a delegate of Delta Sigma Theta sorority.

What is noticeable in this range of selections is her thorough-going awareness of the American social and literary scene, as well as her cosmopolitan awareness of the relationships of American life to what was being lived and written in other countries. Her own writing undergoes some changes during the period. Change is noticeable particularly in the poetry, which does not exactly become more militant, but which does become a bit more direct and somewhat less conventional from early (1919) to late (1926). Change is noticeable also in the essays, which seem to gain in confidence of expression throughout the period.

Fauset is a very good essayist. Just as with James Baldwin later, the intelligence, the precise language skill, the wide-ranging interests, the intense sensitivity of Jessie Fauset often seem more suited to the essay form than to the fictional. A couple of Fauset essays printed in *The Crisis* in the years before she became Literary Editor of the magazine illustrate early her possibilities in the form. "My House and a Glimpse Therein" from the July 1914 issue delves into her imaginary ideal living space and life style with enough detail to let the reader observe personality and intellect of the author. Fauset reveals herself and her own experiences and strengths and fears much more readily in essay than she does in fiction. "Tracing Shadows," from *The Crisis* of September 1915 reveals early her skill with the travel essay. In relating the experience of being a student in Paris during the outbreak of World War I in August 1914, Fauset shows the awareness of others' differing experiences, the deep interest in various classes and types of people, and the ability to make relevant universal significance out of personal observation that make her essays of the 1920's so incisive.

The first three essays published in *The Crisis* during Fauset's tenure as Literary Editor make use primarily of personal memory and experience. "Nostalgia" (1921) closely and effectively describes nostalgia for "home" of three New York and Philadelphia inhabitants—a Greek flower-vendor, an Italian cobbler, and a Roumanian Jew—in order to make the point that for the American Negro, here or abroad, homesickness is "a nostalgia of body and soul." "In

France he will want the comforts of America; in America, he cries out for the rights of man which he knew in France" (p. 158). "Sunday Afternoon" is more reflective, less attached to making a point. The memory of the enforced quiet and inactivity of her childhood Sundays in a "very conservative, not to say very religious household" (p. 162) becomes an "oasis" for Fauset in adulthood. The "Sunday Afternoon" feeling is a sense of mental clarity, of completeness, of sweet melancholy. "Everything takes on an exquisitely true value which is immediately recognizable without any extra adjustment. It is as though the picture, the view had been focussed just for my special degree of short-sightedness. My heart and my mind are without strain" (p. 163). "—When Christmas Comes" puts less emphasis on conveying an internal state, more on memories of particular childhood Christmas sights, sounds and smells that convey the joy and warmth of the recollected time. The snow "falling softly, thickly, warmly," the "light in every window" "so like a conventional Christmas card," the "warm, soft ginger cookies," the grownups "stodgy" on Christmas Day, "too redolent of the taste of 'the day after the night before,' " are all remembered images that Fauset also makes use of in her Christmas descriptions in *The Chinaberry Tree*. Perhaps the use of personal memories accounts for some of that novel's feeling of nostalgia and time duality. In the essay, the nice detail of the memories makes for an evocative piece of writing appropriate to Christmas publication.

Five essays which deal with Fauset's experiences and observations in France and Algeria in 1925-1926 show her concerns and methods as she contemplates national and geographical class differences. Fauset is very interested in and sensitive to the lives and strengths of the poor. In "Yarrow Revisited" (1925) she contrasts the summer Paris she knew in student days and the Paris of the Second Pan-African Congress with the working October Paris of her current visit. "I am glad to have had those golden memories of former visits. Yet I am glad to be here now in this workaday season. . . . 'The visions of the past/Sustain the heart in feeling/Life as she is—' " (p. 107). On this visit, Fauset reports, she has mapped out a plan: "Two weeks in a cheap pension . . . ; A month in this small, comfortable hotel . . . ; A month in a 'good' French family; A month in a first-class pension" (p. 107). "Yarrow Revisited" describes with both architectural and emotional detail the "dampness" and "dreariness" of the cheap pension.

"This Way to the Flea Market" describes with even more detail and with great sensitivity the extreme poor of all nationalities clinging to the fringes of the fortifications of Paris. Journeying to the Sunday *Marché aux Puces* outside one of the city gates, Fauset and her companion pass a carpentry shop which is "part of a large school for poor children." "Not only is the instruction free," she comments approvingly, "but a luncheon is served gratis to the pupils every day" (p. 161). She uses the sight of the market goods to make an anti-materialistic evaluation: "Life is the important, the supreme end of existence; how can people be encompassed about with all these gee-gaws and yet find time to live?" She recognizes the driving force and the strength of poverty. "The poor of Europe are very poor. . . . Life, the mere business of living, is their supreme occupation, let its trappings be as sordid, as infected, as repellant as may be; so long as the precious jewel of life is contained therein, what matter? It is a hard philosophy, but an inevitable one in a people who have fought so long and so often for the right to survive; and it is a philosophy too, mind you, born of terrific experiences, not a mere dumb, driven acquiescence to the inequalities of life" (p. 162).

While Fauset inevitably directs her attention to the poor in Paris and Algiers, it is to the women that she especially is drawn in sympathy and wonderment. At the flea market "the women merchants are the hardest bargainers, seldom if ever yielding." Fauset speculates as to why this should be so.

> Her attitude, her calmness, her determination even to the point of grimness is characteristic of this class. There is something tremendously hard and stratified in the French character, a granite-like quality which results from this continuous necessity of being at grips with life itself. One always comes back to some evidence of that, the struggle for existence, the struggle with soil and the struggle to keep the soil. And this struggle with its resulting hardness shows nowhere more plainly than in the poor and middle-class French woman. It is an extension of that instinct which makes the small and cornered animal fight so bitterly, converting him finally into a truly formidable opponent. Woman being the weaker creature must harden herself proportionately just that much

more to meet the exigencies of her existence (p. 163).

"Dark Algiers the White," published in two parts in April and May of 1925, revolves around women. Upon arrival in the city at dusk, Fauset observes a young Arabian wife—"mystery shrouded her; her two eyes stared unseeingly before her; she was like an automaton beside her lord; there was no conversation"—and an old Arabian woman—"the triangle of flesh appearing above those faded eyes could scarcely ever have been smooth, so crissed and crossed was it now by a pattern of tiny lines. But old and faded and wrinkled as she was her clothing and her veil lent her mystery and marvel." In the disenchanting revelations of the following day-time, Fauset finds that the "voluminous garments" of the women nevertheless show "the misshapen bodies, broken and distorted by neglect, abuse and much bearing of children" (p. 256). Fauset's two visits to the Kasbah, the Arab quarter, expand upon her observations of women's lives. Escorted by a French woman, she enters an Arab house. "At the first turn of the staircase we come to a curtained door opening on a dark oblong room five feet perhaps by eight. In a moment my eyes, accustomed to the gloom, pick out three figures of women sitting on the floor near a brazier of live coals. Their backs are against the wall, their feet are bare, their hands are in their laps. They sit thus, listless, doing nothing, absolutely nothing; life slips by" (p. 17).

Fauset's methods in the five travel essays published in *The Crisis* in 1925 and 1926 reveal an inventiveness and mastery of effectiveness that is at times lacking in, or inappropriate to, her fiction. Some material is used effectively in both essay and fiction. For example, the description of life in the cheap Paris pension of "Yarrow Revisited" is used for Olivia Cary's demise in the final section of *Comedy: American Style*; Fauset's familiar distress over segregated eating places in New York is reversed in her Paris delight in having tea "at the first tea room which takes my fancy" ("Yarrow Revisited," p. 109). Other kinds of material and means of conveying it are effective in the essay but do not prove advantageous for Fauset's narrative style. "The Enigma of the Sorbonne" makes good use of her ability to amass and arrange historical and sociological facts; the introduction of such factual background in the novels is often intrusive and lecture-like. Literary allusions in the essays, such as the use of Wordsworth in "Yarrow Revisited" and the comparison of an Algerian man to Dr. Aziz of Forster's *Passage to India* in "Dark Algiers the White" are smooth and natural, whereas in the novels use of such references approaches irritating pretension. The essays reveal a quiet humor which is not evident in the novels, perhaps because the novels are being taken too seriously as dealing with the inflammatory topics of race characteristics and race relations in the United States. Writing of the French passion for having everything close at hand in "Yarrow Revisited," Fauset describes the shops along the street leading to her hotel. "One would never have to walk a mile for a camel here either a literal or figurative one. If French people elected to use camels, they would be found, I am quite sure, along Rue de Sèvres tethered a bit too near perhaps to the exposed cheeses and cuts of meat" (p. 108).

Finally, use of concrete detail is more thorough and appealing in the essays than in the novels, and Fauset's sparse figurative imagery highlights an essay effectively whereas a novel having such minimal figurative language seems sometimes thin and insipid. Algiers beckoning travelers from Marseille "was twenty-eight hours away, beyond a sea that smiled and faintly rippled; a sea warmed and gilded by the sun which had forsaken Paris; curtained and lighted at night by stars and constellations which we had never seen; mellowed by a saffron moon climbing from below the surface of the world to the warm, rich velvet of the sky" ("Dark Algiers the White," p. 255). The Kabyles at the flea market outside Paris, thin, swarthy, wearing "dull red fezzes, their hair . . . lank and oily," yet with an impression of pride and aloofness, make Fauset think of "sick eagles." ("This Way to the Flea Market," p. 163). "The Eucalyptus Tree" (1926) concludes with the emerging from the dank, death-filled darkness of Rome's catacombs to the "green and perfect, towering, . . . huge, graceful pyramid" of the wind-swept tree. "The tree, the eucalyptus tree, had caught and preserved the essence of all that the early martyrs had lavished so profusely on the iron pride of Rome. . . . The Christian Church now centres at Rome. The roots of the eucalyptus tree are plunged deep in that cemetery but its branches bear a beneficent sap within their veins" (p. 117).

Fauset's essays reveal a strong and gentle woman with happy childhood memories, an intense intellectual life and wide social contacts, a deep sensitivity to the lives of the poor and the foreign, particularly women. They reveal also a writer with wide reading experience, figurative and imagistic skill with words, and ability to make a point subtly and entertainingly. The personal essay form was particularly suited to Fauset's thought and writing skills. In a relaxed but attentive manner she explores in her essays opinions and experiences that are invariably forgotten in critical consideration of Fauset and her materials.

Though here and there reference is made to her Literary Editorship and journalistic work, it is done with a cliché-filled unspecific summary that makes one wonder if any of her essays were actually read by the critic. Arthur Davis, for example, writes that "the most cursory of glances at the pages of *The Brownies' Book* and *The Crisis* will show that Jessie Fauset was a prolific and versatile contributor to both periodicals during the twenties." Glancing cursorily, Davis lists titles only of some Fauset articles, and concludes that she had a "clear, keen, no-nonsense type of intellect."[1] Jessie Fauset's *Crisis* essays are well worth careful reading, both for their own values, and also as a prelude to fairer consideration of her novels than has previously been made. The essays' revelation of sympathetic curiosity about and understanding of the poor Arab women of Algiers or the lower-class French marketwoman makes it much less likely that the reader will turn to Fauset's novels with the preconceived belief that this author's *raison d'etre* was to promote the pretensions of the Black American middle class.

A brief look at the kinds of books reviewed by Fauset for *The Crisis* also reveals a woman and an author with wide-ranging interests and knowledge. Jean Fagan Yellin comments on *Crisis* book reviews in the very useful *CLA Journal* article of June and July 1971, "An Index of Literary Materials in *The Crisis*, 1910-1934: Articles, Belles Lettres, and Book Reviews." "Reading a list of titles of books reviewed in *The Crisis* 1910-1934, one is struck by the breadth, the scope," Yellin says. "For *The Crisis* discussed not only volumes written in English but also books in German and French, not only fiction, drama, poetry, folklore and journalism, but also biography, criticism, and literary history.... Not only books, but special issues of magazines and even articles of particular concern to black people were also periodically reviewed.[2] Of this listing, Fauset is represented by reviews in all the categories except German books. In fact, it is Fauset's reviews that give the *Crisis* list its breadth.

Neither Fauset's reviewing technique nor the scope of kinds of materials she considers changes from her earliest *Crisis* reviews, which appear in a monthly "What to Read" column in 1912 and part of 1913, to her later reviews while Literary Editor. Her standards of form are invariably high even when she is strongly moved by content. Her negative criticism is kind and polite while nevertheless clearly stated. She attempts to find something to praise even where the sum of a review is negative. A review in July of 1912, for example, of Otis M. Shakelford's autobiography *Seeking the Best,* says that while the book is not great literature, it has an "attractively simple" style and Shakelford a praiseworthy motive for writing. On fiction she repeatedly praises novels that she finds not propagandistic, and is disappointed by those that are too intent on proving something. In February of 1924 in "The New Books," for example, she writes of a Gertrude Sanborn novel: "My feeling is that what the entire black reading world, and to a large extent the white reading world also, is awaiting is something at once more subjective and less 'purposeful',— at least less obviously purposeful than 'Veiled Aristocrats'. The successful 'Negro' novel must limn Negro men and women as they really are with not only their virtues but their faults" (p. 177).

Fauset's review assessments of the works of Black American authors who are now highly regarded do not differ from assessments by well-known critics writing since 1930. She reviewed James Weldon Johnson's *Autobiography of an Ex-Coloured Man* in November 1912 when it was first published anonymously.[3] She calls the book "an epitome of the race situation in the United States told in the form of an autobiography." Accurately, she finds that the incidents, localities, settings of the book suggest "a work of fiction founded on hard fact.... Practically every phase and complexity of the race question is presented at one time or another" (p. 38).

In May of 1922 Fauset highly praises Claude McKay's first

volume of verse, *Harlem Shadows*. "Mr. McKay possesses a deep emotionalism, a perception of what is fundamentally important to mankind everywhere—love of kind, love of home, and love of race. . . . He has dwelt in fiery, impassioned language on the sufferings of his race. Yet there is no touch of propaganda. This is the truest mark of genius" (p. 66). In March 1926, she commends Countee Cullen's verse in *Color* for its subjective interpretation of "the inner workings of the Negro soul and mind" (p. 239). Finally, despite her confession that "I am no great lover of any dialect," in the same 1926 review she extensively praises Langston Hughes' verse in *The Weary Blues*.

> Mr. Hughes is not always the calm philosopher; he has feeling a-plenty and is not ashamed to show it. . . . While I do not think of him as a protagonist of color,—he is too much the citizen of the world for that—, I doubt if any one will ever write more tenderly of the life of Harlem shot through as it is with mirth, abandon and pain. Hughes comprehends this life, has studied it and loved it. . . . Indeed all life is his love and his work is a brilliant, sensitive interpretation of its numerous facets" (p. 239).

Fauset was always greatly interested in biographies, especially of historical Black personages, and especially as corrective models for youth. Her book reviews reflect the interest, as do her articles and her *Brownies' Book* writing, as shall be seen later. In 1912 Fauset reviewed two biographies, one of Black Matthew Henson at the North Pole, the other of an anti-slavery crusader, George Thomas Downing. "What to Read" of July of the same year suggests that readers of Leila Amos Pendleton's *A Narrative of the Negro* put it in the hands of their children, for "there is nothing finer in all history" than stories of brave people of color. In Fauset's February, 1924 review of William Pickens' *Bursting Bonds* she says the book confirms her "old theory" that "the life of an American Negro who has risen from obscurity to distinction forms the most inspiring material for a biography." She hopes that "this book will be read widely by our boys and girls and by the younger group of men and women. It affords an often needed stimulus" (p. 176). In *The Crisis* of March 1922 she deals even more specifically with the way a book like Elizabeth Ross Haynes' *Unsung Heroes* can be used to educate and inspire youth. "It is just the sort of book we need to offset the tendency of American shcools to impress upon children of both races that the only heroes in the world have been white heroes. . . .

The influence of the printed word is so great that these stories gain greater authenticity by the mere placing of them between the covers of a volume, instead of leaving them as we have too long in the form of anecdotes and personal recollections to be handed down from father to son" (p. 209).

Fauset felt strongly that Black biography could inspire the young to greater courage and achievement. However, she also felt strongly that for the youth who wished to write effectively, it was obligatory to become thoroughly familiar with the world's great literature, from whatever nation or race, and to read widely in numerous subject areas. She outlined the necessity for stylistic models and for teaching methods making use of models in a 1923 summary of entries in Alpha Kappa Alpha Sorority Prize Story competition (January 1923).

No matter how much a person desires to write he cannot write unless he has practice, and he cannot practice without models. . . . Do our colored pupils read the great writers and stylists? Are they ever shown the prose of Shaw, Galsworthy, Mrs. Wharton, DuBois or Conrad, or that old master of exquisite phrase and imaginative incident—Walter Pater? . . . Does a teacher tell them this?—'Select a passage which appeals to you, find out why it appeals, and try to write a passage in the same style, but on another subject.' Or 'Makeup a story which is full of the real but unusual.' Or lastly: 'Try to spin a yarn which is obviously unlikely, but none the less fascinating' " (p. 58).

"Some Books for Boys and Girls," written by Fauset for the October 1912 *Crisis*, suggests for the young fairy tales to stimulate the imagination, Lewis Carroll, Eugene Field's *Nonsense Rhymes*, Stevenson's *Child's Garden of Verses*, Hawthorne's *Wonder Book* and *Tanglewood Tales*, *Swiss Family Robinson*, Louisa May Alcott, Tennyson's *Maud*, some Longfellow, Keats, Shelley, Browning. For the older reader, the range of materials Fauset reviews for *The Crisis* indicates what wide areas of knowledge she believes the adult writer must be acquainted with. An economic study, George Edmund Haynes' *The Negro at Work in New York City* is reviewed in September 1912. The April issue of the same year prints her summaries and assessments of three magazine articles, including a reprint of William James on Robert Gould Shaw and a Ray Stannard Baker piece on Hawaiian natives. Fauset's "On the Bookshelf" in May 1921 includes reviews of a contemporary Englishman's account of travels through the seaboard slave states in Stephen Graham's *The Soul of John Brown*, and an "intimate and authentic account of the life of the colored soldier who fought for his country in France" in Addie W. Hunton's and Kathryn M. Johnson's *Two Colored Women with The A. E. F.* The detailed accounts in the latter book were certainly of use to Fauset as she described the World War I experiences of Maggie, Philip, and Peter in her first novel, *There Is Confusion*. Fauset reviews many books on the Negro church, including Carter Woodson's *The History of the Negro Church*. Frederick Detweiler's *The Negro Press in the United States* is reviewed in February 1923, as is Lothrop Stoddard's *The World of Islam*. An unusual short book by John P. Turner, M. D., *Ringworm*, which traces phases, history, manifestations, diagnosis, and remedy for the disease, is reviewed as valuable because "the ringworm . . . works more ravages among Negroes than among whites."

One must turn to books on countries other than the United States, however, to see most clearly Jessie Fauset's encompassing intellect and interest. She regularly reviews books printed in French, commenting not only on the information or form of the book, but also on its potential difficulties for a reader who has studied French as a second language. Paul Reboux's *Romulus Coucou*, for example, reviewed in June 1920, is said to be "written in language simple enough for the most casual student of French." The most extensive example of Fauset's educational treatment of a French book occurs with René Maran's Prix Goncourt-winning 1921 novel, *Batouala*. She first reviews the book in its original French version in March 1922, citing it as "really a great novel. It is artistic, overwhelming in its almost cinema-like sharpness of picturization. And there lies its strength. No propoganda, no preachments, just an actual portrayal of life . . . (pp. 208-09).

In September 1922 a longer review deals with the English translation of the book—" 'Batouala' is Translated." The translation, Fauset says, "barring a few defects" has "achieved a result almost as starkly simple and magnificent as the original." Fauset's recognition of Maran's achievement puts her in touch with a surging 1920's international current. As Harold Isaacs describes it in *The New World of The Negro American*, "the white literati had developed a new interest in primitivism. Picasso taking up African sculpture, Gide writing of the Congo, and a great vogue for African naturalism following the award of the 1921 Prix Goncourt to Batouala, a novel of African tribal life by René Maran, a Martinique-born Negro," were the evidence.[4] Jessie Fauset attempts in her reviews to introduce and educate *Crisis* readers into areas which her training and position have allowed her to delve.

Many other books on Africa and African literature are also selected for reviews by Fauset. The May 1921 *Crisis* includes three such books. *Africa: Slave or Free* by John H. Harris is both an "encyclopedia" and an "indictment" in amassing facts and in arraigning colonial rule, she tells the reader. *The Bantu—Past and Present* by S. M. Molema, "himself a member of the Bantu folk," is less comprehensive but more important in its "dispassionate" tracing of South African history, its "thorough" bibliography, maps, copies of "treaties, articles, and legislative documents." Finally, Natalie Curtis' *Songs and Tales from the Dark Continent*, with its book decorations of African textiles, wood-carvings, and utensils, as well as its songs and legends, fixes "once for all the place of the native African high up in the scale of Art and Literature."

It is interesting that the appeal of African folk materials was evidently much greater for Fauset than was the appeal of Black American folk materials. Heavy use of dialect always bothered Fauset, perhaps because that characteristic alone was enough to relegate a Black to the bottom of any heap in her growing-up years for mocking, scornful humor. Her May 1922 review of Thomas W. Talley's *Negro Folk Rhymes* is extensive and fair in describing what "salient characteristics of the Negro are traceable in these songs"— "his sense of humor, his dryness, his tendency to make fun of himself, and above all his love for the sudden climax." Fauset cannot refrain from expressing her bias on dialect, however. "From the standpoint of beauty," she says, "these songs fail to satisfy, but from the standpoint of sociology they are both valuable and enlightening" (p. 68). February 1923 finds her reviewing *The Black Border. Gullah Stories of the Carolina Coast*, complied by Ambrose E. Gonzales.

"Only the philologist or the sociologist will take the time to wade through this mass of unrecognizable, unpronounceable dialect." Fauset finds Gonzales' Foreword "interesting and informative" but concludes with the hope that "the compiler of the 'Gullah Stories' will soon translate his patience, industry and knowledge of Negro conditions in the 'Black Border' into a form which we can more readily absorb and appreciate" (pp. 164, 165). Here as in Joanna Marshall's "Dance of the Nations" in *There Is Confusion* Fauset finds it necessary for the folk to be translated by the conventionally-trained artist to be artistically meaningful.

As concluding illustration of Fauset's range of interests let it be mentioned first that she looks thoroughly at the indigenous literature of Haiti in an article of September 1920, " 'Pastures New.' " She considers four French books with selections of prose and poetry, a critique of Haitian literature, and the works of one Haitian poet. Through reviewing these works, she traces the background and history of Haitian literature, its prominent themes and influences, and gives, finally, some of her own translations of illustrative examples. Secondly, in March of 1922 she shows her unchauvinistic concern for persecuted minorities in reviewing Elias Heifetz' *The Slaughter of the Jews in the Ukraine in 1919*—"the cruelest and bloodiest butcheries of human beings that the world can ever have known." Jessie Fauset's involvement with the creative arts and with the analytic arts knows no barrier of race, class, or academic discipline.

Fauset's *Crisis* articles reaffirm and extend the impression one has from her essays and book reviews of great openness to new experiences and ideas and places. Some articles are mere competent reportage. "Out of the West" (November 1923), on the Black community of Denver; "The 13th Biennial of the W. A. C. W." (October 1922); and "The 'Y' Conference at Talladega" (September 1923) fall into this category. Other selections show her deepest predilections. Her interest in educating and education is evident here as in the reviews and essays, taking such form as a July 1912 explanation of "The Montessori Method—Its Possibilities" and a February 1928 piece on the atmosphere and curriculum of Talladega College near Birmingham, Alabama. *Crisis* articles by Fauset include a number of biographical sketches of Black people—"Saint-George, Chevalier of France" (May 1921); Robert Brown Elliott, Reconstruction Legislator (" 'Looking Backward,' " January 1922); Bert Williams (May 1922); "Henry Ossawa Tanner" (April 1924); Martin Robinson Delaney (" 'Rank Imposes Obligation,' " November 1926).

The interest in and opinions on Black literature found scattered liberally through her reviews is made more specific in Fauset's portion of the 1926 *Crisis* series "The Negro in Art: How Shall He Be Portrayed: A Symposium." Fauset's answers to the series of questions are printed in June 1926. Though she believes that an author should be under no limitations in portraying Negro character, she does see a tendency for writers to write and publishers to publish only works about the sordid, foolish, and criminal elements among Negroes. To the rather loaded DuBois question "Can publishers be criticized for refusing to handle novels that portray Negroes of education and accomplishment, on the ground that these characters are no different from white folk and therefore not interesting?" Fauset gives a sharp answer. "I should think so. And what is more, it seems to me that white people should be the first to voice this criticism. Aren't they supposed to be interesting?" (Alfred A. Knopf writes in answer to the same question: "This question seems to me to be senseless.")

Fauset's competent observing and reporting as well as her great concern with the international implications of racial identification and with Black Africa are all shown in her lengthy articles on the Second Pan-African Congress. One of the articles—"What Europe Thought of The Pan-African Congress" (December 1921)—quotes and translates widely from British, French, Belgian, Scottish, and American newspapers and magazines, with some commentary-transition. The other article reveals more of Fauset's own reactions to the Congress, which held consecutive meetings in London, Brussels and Paris with a subsequent trip to Geneva to present a Manifesto to the Assembly of the League of Nations. Summarizing both fact and feeling, Fauset contrasts the warm and friendly and open atmosphere of the London Meetings to the rigidity and jealous fear of the Belgian gathering. "We were all one family in London," but in Belgium "the shadow of Colonial dominion governed. Always the careful Belgian eye watched and peered, the Belgian ear listened. For three days we listened to pleasant generalities without a word of criticism of Colonial Governments, wihout a murmur of complaint of Black Africa, without a suggestion that this was an international congress called to define and make intelligible the greatest set of wrongs against human beings that the modern world has known" (p. 14).

Fauset concludes her evaluation of the results of the Congress with a strong statement of need and determination.

> The most important result was our realization that there is an immensity of work ahead of all of us. We have got to learn everything—facts about Africa, the difference between her colonial governments, one foreign language at least (French or Spanish), new points of view, generosity of ideal and of act. All the possibilities of all black men are needed to weld together the black men of the world against the day when black and white meet to do battle.
>
> God grant that when that day comes we shall be so powerful that the enemy will say, 'But behold! these men are our brothers.' ("Impressions of the Second Pan-African Congress," November 1921)

The concept of Black Power as prerequisite to Black equality was not an invention of the 1960's. Seemingly mild and gentle Jessie Fauset gave strong voice to the concept in 1921, tucked away in one of her ignored and forgotten articles for *The Crisis*.

In the May 1926 issue of *The Crisis* W. E. B. DuBois writes in his "Opinion" column that "Miss Fauset," after seven years of "active service" as Literary Editor, would be moving to the "less exacting duties" of Contributing Editor. "The office will miss her monthly cooperation" he adds. From this issue through the February 1927 issue Fauset is listed on the Masthead as Contributing Editor. In March 1927 *The Crisis* changes its format to larger pages, and Fauset's name disappears to be replaced by "Aaron Douglas" as "Art Critic." As it turned out, it was a good time to leave. With an economic crunch already being felt and the advent of the Depression imminent, DuBois was rapidly losing his editorial independence as *The Crisis* lost readers and its financial independence. Between 1929 and 1934, $35,000 of NAACP money went into the expenses of *The Crisis*.[5]

While increasing financial problems of the magazine cannot be said to be the direct result of Jessie Fauset's departure as Literary Editor, there are indications of editorial problems at the magazine which are just that. The Black writers who gained recognition partially through *The Crisis* and who then in turn lent their prestige to the publication become upset with sloppy office work there after 1926. Sterling Brown writes DuBois on 28 March 1927 that he opened the April *Crisis* to find a poem of his there. "I am properly thankful that you thought it worth publishing, but I am in the dark as to how it got into your hands." DuBois replies that he assumed Brown had sent him the manuscript, for how else would he have had it.[6] On 11 February 1928 it is Langston Hughes' turn. He is understandably a bit more impatient with *The Crisis* editor, this being his second letter on the problem. "Some months ago I asked for my old manuscripts in your office, but they couldn't be found. I was hoping they were really lost, but lately some of the poems have been in *The Crisis* and I don't think they are quite good enough to be there so please throw them in your wastebasket if there are any more."[7]

Finally, Claude McKay writes on 18 June 1928, thoroughly disturbed at DuBois' audacity and sloppiness. In the June *Crisis* DuBois had printed his scathing review of McKay's *Home to Harlem*. "For the most part" the book "nauseates me," he wrote, and went on to suggest that McKay had "set out to cater to the prurient demand on the part of white folk." In the same issue, DuBois placed a McKay poem. McKay explodes. "I think I beseeched you over a year ago *not* to publish those poems I sent to the 'Crisis' towards the end of 1925. . . . I particularly resent the publication of my poem in the same number of the 'Crisis' in which, in criticizing my novel, the Editor steps outside the limits of criticism to become personal."[8]

Complaints are made by young unknown contributors too. In the July 1929 issue of *The Crisis* DuBois prints a letter from one such contributor. "A little over a year ago, I submitted a short story to you which you at that time accepted, but so far it has not appeared in print." DuBois, without ever answering the specific complaint, writes a long reply in an editorial called "Negro Journalism." In his reply, DuBois attacks young Black writers who get refused publication by a Negro editor and then get bitter. It is clear from these surfaced examples that DuBois and *The Crisis* were more dependent than anyone knew on Fauset's efficiency and ability to relate smoothly to temperamental artists—and to her temperamental editor. "The office will miss her monthly cooperation" was in May of 1926 a polite commonplace. By 1930 it appears to have become a way of life at *The Crisis* editorial offices.

Predictably, the literary appeal of *The Crisis* weakens after Fauset's departure. Arna Bontemps in 1970 recalls of the 1920s that "the magazines *Crisis* and *Opportunity* . . . became more interesting than before" and "went out of their way to attract the new writers."9 By the late 1920s, after Fauset left *The Crisis*, the magazine returned to its early dominance by DuBois. He makes some attempt to keep literary materials up to Fauset's standards, but without much success. In November of 1932, for example, he writes in the "Contents" that "for a month or so, we have been neglecting poetry, just as America has been neglecting souls. We recant," There are four poems in the issue.

Evaluators of the contribution of the 1920s *Crisis* to the history and development of Black American literature make a common mistake. Those who see the period and the magazine as the single great impetus to re-awakening and re-birth of Black literature give all credit to DuBois as Editor. Those who find the middle class and mulatto-dominated *Crisis* a hindrance to development of truly Black features in the literature look also only at DuBois, though Fauset's name is lumped in, without evidence, as being one and the same in belief and action.10 In truth, from 1919 to 1926, while Jessie Fauset was Literary Editor of *The Crisis*, she was the one who discovered Langston Hughes and Countee Cullen; who got along with radical Claude McKay; who corresponded with the white authors who took part in the symposium "The Negro in Literature: How Should He Be Portrayed"; who ran the office while DuBois made his numerous trips in the United States and abroad; who made the literary selections of widely representative philosophies and kept track of their contributors; who wrote reviews and articles and essays and poetry and novels at the same time.

W. E. B. DuBois has also typically received credit for the

values of another publication of the 1920s which is even more obviously Jessie Fauset's achievement. In *Dusk of Dawn* DuBois wrote of 1920 and 1921 that "I made one effort toward which I look back with infinite satisfaction: an attempt in the *Brownie's* [sic] *Book* to furnish a little magazine for Negro children, in which my efforts were ably seconded by Augustus Dill and Jessie Fauset; It was really a beautiful publication, but it did not pay its way."[11] The children's magazine published its first issue in Janaury 1920, with Fauset writing the dedication, "To children, who with eager look/ Scanned vainly library shelf, and nook,/ For History or Song or Story/ That told of Colored People's glory,—/ We dedicate the *Brownies' Book*." The last issue of the publication appeared in December 1921. In between, in the twenty-four issues of this remarkable publication, Jessie Fauset wrote hundreds of signed and unsigned stories, poems, dialogues, biographies, articles, and did the editing of manuscripts and correspondence with contributors as well.

Elinor Sinnette in an article called "The Brownies' Book," published in *Freedomways* in 1965, is exceptional in crediting Fauset with the prime work on the *Brownies' Book*. Though the periodical was under the direction of the "team" of DuBois, Fauset, and Dill, Sinnette reports, the actual day-to-day labor fell to Fauset. Jessie Fauset was "a lady of distinction from similar background and education as Dr. DuBois." She "found the same attractiveness in her people, black people, as Dr. DuBois. She was moved by their beauty, warmth, understanding, tolerance and fellowship. She believed her people could find themselves through searching in the past. As a teacher . . . she saw daily the need for children and young people to have insight into their past and hope and pride in their future. . . . It was she who gathered stories, poems, biographical material, words of wisdom for the children."[12]

The magazine itself "was a magnificent publication," with nothing since to compare with it, Sinnette believes. In contrast with the earlier famous illustrated magazine for boys and girls, *St. Nicholas*, published by Scribner's from 1873-1943, she finds the *Brownies' Book* better. *St. Nicholas* illustrations included no colored faces; *St. Nicholas* treatment of social issues was immature.[13] The first ad in *The Crisis* for the *Brownies' Book* in September 1919 announced a magazine "Designed for all children, But especially for *ours*," a magazine that "will seek to teach Universal Love and Brotherhood for all little folk." Both aims are lasting ideals of Jessie Fauset's life and both aims are skillfully accomplished in the magazine.

Fauset encourages and includes contributors other than herself in the *Brownies' Book*. Langston Hughes' very first publication was there. "I could not put the bullfights down, so, wanting to write prose, I wrote instead an article about Toluca, and another about the Virgin of Guadalupe, and a little play for children called *The Gold Piece*," he writes in his autobiography. "I sent them to *The Brownie's* [sic] *Book*, a magazine for Negro children just begun in New York by Dr. DuBois and *The Crisis* staff. These pieces of mine were accepted, and encouraging letters came back from Jessie Fauset, who was managing editor there." Because of Fauset's encouragement on the *Brownies' Book* pieces, Hughes sent her "A Negro Speaks of Rivers," which appeared in *The Crisis* in June 1921.[14] Hughes is frequently represented on *Brownies' Book* pages by various kinds of writing. The January 1921 issue uses another poem, "An April Rain Song," and an essay, "In a Mexican City." Other contributors include James Weldon Johnson and Georgia Douglas Johnson (January 1920); Arthur Huff Fauset (March 1920); Nella Larsen Imes (June and July 1920); Helen Fauset Lanning (February 1920); and many children of various ages.

Fauset herself is shown to be adept at writing children's stories. Tales like "Ghosts and Kittens" (February 1921) and "Cordelia Goes on the Warpath" (May 1921) make use of a large happy family of six children whose escapades occur without much adult participation or interference. The stories use dialect here and there, and effectively depend on suspenseful build-up. Fauset's ability to see and write things from a child's point of view is evident in her *Brownies' Book* stories; one wishes she had felt free to innovate with such a viewpoint in the "Oliver's Act" section of *Comedy: American Style*.

There are additional Fauset writing contributions to the children's magazine that are impressive for the glimpse they give of her skills in education. Each issue of the *Brownies' Book* contains a short biographical sketch of a Black person—from Harriet Tubman to Alexander Dumas to Denmark Vesey. Fauset makes use of a regular column she calls "The Grown-Up's Corner" to in one issue comment on the lack of positive Black models for Black children. "Heretofore the education of the Negro child has been too much in terms of white people." Textbooks, pictures, authors, heroes and heroines are all white. In movies, "if a Negro appears on the screen, he is usually a caricature or a clown." The Black child "unconsciously gets the impression that the Negro has little chance to be good, great, heroic, or beautiful." (February 1921) As late as 1932 Fauset was still planning to write biographies aimed at Black children. "No part of Negro literature needs more building up than biography. . . . It is urgent that ambitious Negro youth be able to read of the achievements of their race. . . . There should be a sort of 'Plutarch's Lives' of the Negro race. Someday, perhaps, I shall get around to writing it."[15] Fauset does not ignore the need for female models as well as male Black models. In the April 1920 issue a biography of Sojourner Truth, "A Pioneer Suffragette . . . ," concludes that "her mind was so keen and so broad that she quickly realized that the refusal of the right to vote to women was only another form of slavery. . . . Her interest in this cause is the surest proof that she was a sincere advocate of liberty." As has been seen with *The Crisis* as here, this emphasis on forgotten Black lives as part of world history and American history was very much at the center of Fauset's journalistic work. The *Brownies' Book* was to be for all children, but especially for those needing positive models.

The other of the announced aims of the juvenile publication—"to teach Universal Love and Brotherhood"—is accomplished first of all through wide-ranging selections of materials. Games and songs from other lands, frequent African and West Indian folk tales, American Indian legends, biographies and photographs from around the world, all give the publication an international flavor. Secondly, Fauset uses a very well-done dialogue-column called "The Judge" to teach love and brotherhood even more directly. The Judge introduces himself in the first issue of the *Brownies' Book*, "I am the judge. I am very, very old. I know all things, except a few, and I have been appointed by the King to sit in the Court of Children and tell them the Law and listen to what they have to say. The Law is old and musty and needs sadly to be changed. In time the children will change it, but now it is the Law." The regular "Judge" section uses several children of ages six through seventeen with names that suggest they could be one and the same child at different ages and of differing sex. "Billikins" is the youngest; "Billie" a bit older; "William" older still; and "Wilhelmina" the eldest. In conversation with "the Judge" the children speak with perceptions and problems suitable to their respective ages. The Judge always has something to say, but he doesn't always win the arguments. When he gets pompous, a child will break in to stick a poker in an inkwell or to tell him that his robe is looking frayed. The column teaches, but is always saved from preachiness by the dialogue form and by the children's reported actions.

In one dialogue Billikins has been caught teasing a Chinaman living in the neighborhood. "But I'm an American. I'm better than they are. *I'm* the way *they* ought to be." The Judge looks sadder and sadder, finally saying: "What you are saying is the kind of thing that sets the world by the ears, that makes war, that causes unspeakable cruelties. . . . Think of the world as being a desert island, and all of the people as being just wrecked on it. Hasn't each one of us a right to everything on the island—joy, light, love, 'life, liberty and the pursuit of happiness'?" "That's from the Declaration of Independence," says William. "You know it Billy. You recited it at the school picnic" (May 1921). In another column, when the Judge amazes the children by picking out Africa as the greatest continent, he is asked if that means historians are wrong. "No," says the judge. "There are lots of things to be known, and few to know them. Our duty is therefore not simply to tell what we believe is true, but to remember our ignorance and be sure that we know before we speak" (June 1921). When one child wants to quit school the Judge expounds on the difference between schooling and experience, describing books as a shortcut to what can be learned by experience. "Just the same," Billikins pipes up, "I'd like to learn how to add sums in a candy shop" (April 1921). In the February 1920 column one of the children is upset over having received a whipping. In answering the difficult question "Why should there be pain in the world?" the Judge admits that there is sometimes too much of it.

But, he goes on, "in a world where there was no sacrifice, no need of hard and unpleasant work, it is a question whether we could develop the kind of sound, strong character in human beings that we ought to have. . . . It is the law of the world that we achieve beauty only through suffering. Perhaps that law could be improved; but I do not know."

The *Brownies' Book* is a delightful publication; it expands one's impression from *The Crisis* materials that Jessie Fauset was an efficient editor, a friend to young writers, a creative and interesting person and writer. It is appropriate to let the words of a writer who was discovered, befriended, and encouraged by Fauset sum up the effectiveness of her journalistic work. Langston Hughes writes in *The Big Sea* that there were three midwives of the Harlem Renaissance. "Jessie Fauset at the *Crisis*, Charles Johnson at *Opportunity*, and Alain Locke in Washington, were the three people who midwifed the so-called New Negro literature into being. Kind and critical—but not too critical for the young—they nursed us along until our books were born."[16]

Notes

[1] Arthur P. Davis, *From the Dark Tower: Afro-American Writers, 1900-1960* (Washington, D. C.: Howard University Press, 1974), p. 94.

[2] Jean Fagan Yellin, "An Index of Literary Materials in *The Crisis*, 1910-1934: Articles, Belles-Lettres, and Book Reviews," *CLA Journal*, XIV (1971), 223.

[3] Yellin in the July *CLA* issue mistakenly lists the reviewer of *Autobiography of an Ex-Colored Man* as anonymous. The mistake is easy to make in the 1912 *Crisis*, for during some months Fauset's reviews are only initialled; sometimes her name is given in the Table of Contents and not on the column; sometimes her name is on the column but not in the Table of Contents.

[4]Harold Isaacs, *The New World of the Negro American* (New York: Viking, 1963), pp. 232-33.

[5]Raymond Wolters, *Negroes and the Great Depression: The Problem of Economic Recovery* (Westport, Connecticut: Greenwood Publishing Company, 1970), pp. 272-73.

[6]Herbert Aptheker, ed., *The Correspondence of W. E. B. DuBois, I: Selections, 1877-1934* (Amherst: University of Massachusetts Press, 1973), p. 346.

[7]*Ibid.*, p. 374.

[8]*Ibid.*, pp. 374-75.

[9]Arna Bontemps, "The Black Renaissance of the Twenties," *Black World*, XX (November 1970), 7.

[10]Two examples of this lumping of Fauset into a negative assessment of DuBois occur in William Muraskin, "An Alienated Elite: Short Stories in *The Crisis*, 1910-1950," *Journal of Black Studies*, 1 (1971), 282-305; and in Roseann Pope Bell, "*The Crisis* and *Opportunity* Magazines: Reflections of a Black Culture, 1920-1930," Diss. Emory University 1974. The Muraskin article is weak because it is unfairly selective in its attempt to prove the point that *Crisis* short stories reveal "the mind of the Middle Class." Muraskin ignores all dialect and lower-class stories—those of Sallie Runner, for example. In trying to show that "DuBois, Jesse [sic] Fauset . . . and later editors had policies that reduced the type of stories which were published," Muraskin says: "For example, in the 1920's, DuBois withdrew his support from the Harlem School of Literature when those writers began to glorify the lowest structures of Negro life." In fact Muraskin does not deal with Fuaset's editorship at all, even to distinguish the years during which she was active.

Bell ignores the fact of Fauset as Literary Editor completely in dealing with *Crisis* literary choices, though she does mention her briefly in writing of the *Crisis*-sponsored contests. When she is critical of DuBois, however, she dumps Fauset in with him. "DuBois and Fauset were of the same social strata— they both belonged to an elite black society. Their comments about the nature of Negro literature often contained allusions to 'decent' Negroes as opposed to the 'sordid' elements of the 'folk.' Consequently, many of the participants in *The Crisis* contests wrote vapid, unrealistic dramas about Negro life" (p. 172).

[11]W. E. B. DuBois, *Dusk of Dawn: An Essay Toward an Autobiography*

of a Race Concept (New York: Harcourt, Brace and Company, 1970), pp. 271-72.

[12]Elinor Sinnette, "The Brownies' Book: A Pioneer Publication for Children," *Freedomways* (Winter 1965), p. 137.

[13]*Ibid.*, pp. 142, 134-35.

[14]Langston Hughes, *The Big Sea* (New York: Hill & Wang, 1940), p. 72.

[15]Marion L. Starkey, "Jessie Fauset," *Southern Workman* (May 1932), p. 211.

[16]Hughes, p. 218.

Poetry, Translations, Short Stories

Jessie Fauset said in 1932 that she began writing poetry as a child while her sister "wrote romances all over the laundry paper."[1] "All my life I have wanted to write novels. . . . But usually, in spite of myself, I have scribbled poetry."[2] Fauset's half-brother says "I think she was deeply proud of her poetry, as was I. . . . She seemed to write her poems with an ease and fluidity that came more naturally than her prose" (Letter to author, 10 January 1976). At the same time, perhaps because poetry writing came readily to her, Fauset took "no serious interest in her poems, [and] . . . made no effort to publish a collection of her own."[3] As a result, though Jessie Fauset's poems are scattered through the pages of *The Crisis* and sprinkled in Black American poetry anthologies, they are not in print in large enough numbers to form a basis for evaluating either what she unquestionably achieved as a poet or what she was capable of achieving had time and publishing outlets been more readily available to her. What Fauset's available poems can tell readers is something of her personal delights and pains behind her more public concerns.

There is much pain over lost love in Fauset's poetry, touched with a bit of wry cynicism about life as bringer of pleasure and pain together. "Again It Is September," published in *The Crisis* in 1917, illustrates the combination. "It seems so strange that I who made no vows/ Should sit here desolate this golden weather/ And wistfully remember," the poem begins. The remembering brings back a passionate moment rather unusual on the pages of *The Crisis*— "A sigh of deepest yearning,/ a glowing look and words that knew no bounds,/ A swift response, an instant glad surrender/ to kisses wild and burning." Concluding, the poem returns to "Again it is

September," and the speaker sitting "lone,and spent, and mutely praying/ That I may not remember!" (p. 248.)

"Dilworth Road Revisited" appeared in *The Crisis* in August 1922, after Fauset had made her second trip to France. This poem of lost love is unusual in Fauset's poetry in attaching the loss of the loved one to death in World War I rather than to quirks of fate or passion. "Sad years ago my love and I/ Strolled all its sunny length one day,/ To Dilworth's ivied church,—and then/ Sighing, we turned away./ Ah, Dilworth Road, can you still laugh/ When on another road's expanse,—/ 'The Ladies' Road,' they call it,—lies/ My lover,— dead for France!" One other lost love poem suggests parting by death, although it may refer to death of love or companionship rather than physical death. "Fragment," included in Countee Cullen's anthology, *Caroling Dusk*, uses life and death imagery with quiet effectiveness.

> The breath of life imbued those few dim days!
> Yet all we had was this,—
> A Flashing smile, a touch of hands, and once
> A fleeting kiss.
>
> Blank futile death inheres these years between!
> Still naught have you and I
> But frozen tears, and stifled words, and once
> A sharp caught cry.[4]

More frequently, loss of the loves is not explained so readily, but is simply felt. "Recontre," for example, in its briefness, gives no reason for separation, pain, new meeting, and pain again. The pain simply is. "My heart, which beat so passionless,/ Leaped high last night when I saw you./ Within me surged the grief of years/ And whelmed me with its endless rue./ My heart which slept so still, so spent,/ Awoke last night—to break anew" (*The Crisis*, January 1924, p. 122).

Fauset's best known and lightest poem dealing with this combination of love and pain and irony is "La Vie C'est La Vie." The speaker sits "quiescent" in the park by the man who loves her, idly watching sunbeams and squirrels while his voice breaks "with love and pain." The concluding three stanzas complete the story.

> I know a woman who would give
> Her chance of heaven to take my place;
> To see the love-light in your eyes,
> The love-glow on your face!
>
> And there's a man whose lightest word
> Can set my chilly blood afire;
> Fulfilment of his least behest
> Defines my life's desire.
>
> But he will none of me. Nor I
> Of you. Nor you of her. 'Tis said
> The world is full of jests like these-
> I wish that I were dead.
>
> (*The Crisis* [July 1922], p. 124)

Seasons of the year and the balm and promise of nature are used rather frequently as analogy to hope after love has gone. "Here's April!" and "Rain Fugue," both in *The Crisis* in 1924 (April, August), convey the comparison. The first uses the "dark," "mean," "dank," "raw," "drear" winter of yesterday compared with the "verdant," "gold-tinted," "budding" April of today to remind the speaker of "all the healing places of the Earth,/ Where one lays by his woe, his bitter pain,—/ For peace and mirth." If the blighting seal" of winter can vanish to be replaced by the "faint, shy jargoning of spring birds, then so can the heart be renewed. "Oh foolish heart to fret so with your grief!/ This too shall pass!" "Rain Fugue" describes in its first four stanzas the differing emotional responses the speaker has to Summer, Fall, Winter and Spring rains. The "slanting, driving," passionate rain of summer washes the heart of pain and inspires pride and courage. Autumn's soaking rains blot and blur the past, urging forgetfulness. The hurtling winter rains "but make me hug the hearth/ Laughing, sheltered from your wrath." It is, finally, spring rains that "set me to remembering/ Far-off times and lovers too,/ Gentle joys and heart-break rue/ Memories I'd as lief forget." Th final quatrain of the poem restates the ease of pain found in Summer, Autumn, and Winter rains, and concludes that even the "hurt" brought by the "whispering, wistful showers of Spring" is loved.

The Fauset poems that do include the loved one present and returning love nevertheless reflect some disillusionment through inevitable conflicts. "Words! Words!" compares the language of a lovers' quarrel with "the things we used to say," like " 'Love, we shall always love, come what may.' "[5] "Touché" presents the man remembering an early blond love each time he puts his hand to his lover's dark hair. She discerns his thought and responds: "Nay, no excuses; 'tis little I care./ I knew a lad in my own girlhood's past,—/ Blue eyes he had and such waving gold hair!"[6] "Enigma" presents the kind of lover one cannot get along with or get along without; the poem effectively repeats the line, "There is no peace with you,/ Nor any rest," with slight variations, and the wish "If only you were you and yet not you!"[7]

Fauset's later love poems are expressed in a more detached, objective way than her early ones, with tighter control and command of feeling. In "Noblesse Oblige" an ironic distance is achieved by setting up a scene contrasting "Lolotte, who attires my hair" in her dramatic outbursts of pain, to the speaker, whose pride prevents her from revealing hurt. The rhyme and rhythm of the verse suit the overly-dramatic, but happier Lolotte, while the speaker suffers without cathartic outlet.

> What a silly thing is pride!
> Lolotte bares her heart.
> . . .
>
> What I hide with my soul's life
> Lolotte tells with tear and cry.
> Blurs her pain with sob and sigh.
> Happy Lolotte, she![8]

"Stars in Alabama," in *The Crisis* in January 1928, contrasts in three stanzas the passionate heat of noon cotton-fields with the pure holiness of the Alabama night. "In Alabama/ Stars hang so low,/ So low they purge the soul/ With their infinity" the poem begins. At noon "A Negro lad and lass/ cling hand in hand,/ And Passion, hot-eyed, hot-lipped,/ Lurks unseen." But in the evening, "When the skies lean down,/ He's but a wistful boy/ A saintly maiden she." The first lines are again repeated as evening returns. Fauset has moved through this poem from personal feeling to a quietly effective comment on passion and its context.

A Fauset poem included in Langston Hughes' and Arna Bontemps' collection of Negro poetry seems to sum up Fauset's love poetry. "Dead Fires" concludes that despite love's pain, loss, conflict, suppression, passion is better than lifelessness.

> If this is peace, this dead and leaden thing,
>   Then better far the hateful fret, the sting.
>
> Better the wound forever seeking balm
>   Than this gray calm!
>
> Is this pain's surcease? Better far the ache,
>   The long-drawn dreary day, the night's white wake,
> Better the choking sigh, the sobbing breath
>
> Than passion's death![9]

On topics other than love, Fauset's poetry shows a sensitive touch in conveying a thought. "Christmas Eve in France"[10] does not rage in order to ask the unanswerable questions about the meaning of war and death. The childlike question posed to "little Christ": "Why must this horror be?" gains its power from its innocence and directness. "Return" tells of religious struggle—of denial and belief—in few words and one sustained image (*The Crisis*, January 1919). "Oriflamme" uses a quotation from Sojourner Truth and then a brief poetic restatement in order to jar and move the reader into recognizing both the pain of slavery and the enduring strength and faith that continue to sustain after slavery's end. I think I see her sitting bowed and black,/ Stricken and seared with slavery's mortal scars/ Reft of her children, lonely, anguished, yet/ Still looking at the stars" (*The Crisis*, January 1920). " 'Courage!' He Said," one of Fauset's longest poems, uses a quotation from Ulysses to his men "debarking in The Lotus Land," and a narrative of this experience to make its point. " 'To be courageous is to face despair.' " Though the concluding stanza is rather intrusive and moralistic, it is interesting in reflecting Fauset's own quiet fortitude and modesty.

> For he who is courageous
> Seeks no meed. Naught flashing nor white
> Blazons the fortitude
> With which he bears his burden,
> Signalling him to the world
> For all men's seeing.
> His heart is calmly conscious of its might.
> The fact of courage,—a sufficient guerdon—
> Like beauty is its own excuse for being
> (*The Crisis*, November 1929).

The ease with which Fauset evidently wrote poetry and the simplicity of her style suited her particularly for the children's poems she wrote for the *Brownies' Book*. There are many of Fauset's game poems and light-hearted poems in the magazine's twenty-four issues. "Spring Songs, Verses" in the May 1920 issue (pp. 146-47) includes a whole group of poems on kites, tops, hoops, jumping ropes, roller skates. "That Story of George Washington" " (February 1920) points out a facetious moral of the cherry tree legend (p. 64). "After School. A Poem" tells of a boy who rebels at school until the last bell rings, and then begins to work. "But just let that old teacher go—/ There's nothing Bill and me don't know" ([January 1920], p. 30). More serious Fauset poems are also included in the *Brownies' Book*. The December 1920 issue includes a particularly lovely poem called "Crescent Moon," as well as "Christmas Eve," both with religious connotations.[11] The Easter issue of April 1920 uses a two-page hand-printed and illustrated copy of "The Easter Idyl," again a religious poem (pp. 112-13).

Jessie Fauset's poetry is not difficult in either the feelings and thoughts conveyed or in the forms used to convey them. Much of the stilted "poetic language" and most of the classical allusions of an early poem like "Rondeau" (*The Crisis* [April 1912], p. 252) disappear in later poems, which are more naturally spoken. Fauset maintains a great love for words, however, seeming to delight not just in finding the right word, but in finding the unusual and unexpected word. Arthur Davis has written a fair summary of Fauset's verse as far as its impact on Black literature is concerned. "Typical lyrics of love and nature, [they] were light and sophisticated, and neither good enough to become an impressive part of the canon of New poetry or bad enough to be overlooked entirely."[12]

Fauset appears to have used her poetry writing for delight and pleasure rather than for promoting art—Black art or her own art. Race is not discussed in most of her poems; they are interesting to a student of Fauset, however, in suggesting that she knew well the joys and pains of passion and of love, and that she attained about these portions of life an "ironic disillusionment," as Sterling Brown called it.[13]

Given the very personal nature of Fauset's poetry and reasons for writing poetry, it seems particularly harsh to imply, as Saunders Redding once did, that Fauset wrote her poetry to hide her Negro ancestry. "Jessie Fauset did not write *vers de société* in French and give some of her English language poems French titles merely to exercise her command of the language."[14] In fact Fauset often slipped naturally into French even in letters. More important, Fauset recognized the importance of French to Black people world wide in a way that seems to have escaped Redding. Fauset's recognition can be seen partially in her translations. "She has made skillful translations from the French of some of the Negro poets of the French West Indies," wrote James Weldon Johnson accurately in *The Book of American Negro Poetry* in 1931.[15]

Writing about the translating of Haitian poetry in 1920, Fauset showed awareness of the selection and process which goes into adequate rendering of poetry from one langauge to another. Poetry, she wrote, was the "perfect blending of idea and form" and for that reason "there are a few poems which bear resetting into another tongue—but not many. Fewer if any endure the translation from one language to another of essentially different stock. French poetry does not lend itself easily to our harsher, less flexible mould. So it is almost impossible to bring over to the reader in English, the verse of Haiti and have him perceive its charm. It *is* there, however, ranking with the charm of the poetry of France."

The Fauset translation included in the Langston Hughes and Arna Bontemps anthology, *The Poetry of the Negro: 1746-1949*, as well as in Johnson's *The Book of American Negro Poetry* is

"Oblivion: From the French of Massillon Coicou (Haiti)." The poem
is quite like the kind Fauset herself wrote after 1920, though its
detached intellectual disillusionment is more exaggerated than in
Fauset's verse. "I hope when I am dead that I shall lie/ In some de-
serted grave. . . / There I should lie annihilate and my dead heart
would bless/ oblivion—the shroud and envelope of happiness."

In "Pastures New" in *The Crisis* in September 1920, Fauset
chose to translate another kind of verse by Coicou and other Haitian
poets. "One is struck by the patriotic motif," she wrote in her review of Haitian poetry. "A country whose struggle for freedom has
been so persistent and so beset must reflect that condition in the
hearts of her sons. . . . Massillon Coicou bids all children 'Love with
all your hearts, your Fatherland,/ . . . / Preserve for her a worship
grave and pure.' Pierre Faubert, born in the troublesome days following the fall of [Toussaint] L'Ouverture, sings:

> 'Brothers, we've cast beneath our feet
> The infamous yoke that bowed us so;
> Yellow or black—what mattered our skins
> When we sought revenge on our common foe?
> God who is just gave strength to our arms,
> Yellow or black we breasted the flood;
> Crying "What matters? We've built for our race
> A common land bathed in common blood!" ' (pp. 225, 226)

Speaking as well to the issue of influence on Black Haitian poetry
from France and the classics, and the issue of universality in poetry,
Fauset says

> But why not? Both France and the classics are the property of the world.
> In *Le Secret d'Etre Heureux* of Jules Solime Milscent, son of a white
> father and a black mother, one finds a familiar note. It is the *Carpe
> Diem* of Horace, the *Freut Euch des Lebens* of Nägeli and the "Gather
> ye rosebuds while ye may" of Robert Herrick. Milscent sings:
>> "Take this lesson to your hearts,
>> Lovers young and maidens fair:
>> Hug your fond illusions fast,
>> Do not seek the truth to bare.
>> Do not seek to penetrate

Why's and wherefore's of life's pleasure
Ignorance is often bliss:
Knowledge may destroy joy's treasure!"
Thus the Haitian poet singing over a century ago shows that life with its
ideals, its problems, and its solaces, flows on always the same, though
lived under different skies and in varied climes (p. 226).

When one looks at Jessie Fauset's stories published in *The Crisis* between 1912 and 1923, one concludes as with her poetry that there is not enough material to make an evaluation of this Black writer as an artist of the genre. There is, however, value in reading the stories for the insight they give into some of the themes and forms Fauset developed more fully in her four novels. By comparing the shorter to the longer fictional works, one can see something of Fauset's composition and revision techniques.

Two early stories, "Emmy," in *The Crisis* in December 1912 and January 1913, and to a lesser extent "There Was One Time" in the same periodical in April and May 1917, show Fauset's interest in certain themes later developed in her novels. Emmy Carrel in the first story is a dark-skinned Black girl and then woman satisfied with her race, her color, her family. She is loved by Archie Ferrers, Black but light enough to pass for white. Ferrers obtains a position with the president of a Philadelphia engineering firm who assumes the young man is white. Ferrers advances rapidly to the point of being pegged and trained for the top job. Mr. Fields, the president, accidentally discovers Ferrers' engagement to dark Emmy. Ferrer, unable finally to bear Field's insults to Emmy, announces that he too is Black, and he promptly loses his job. Emmy, who has renounced Archie while he hides his race, returns to him when his honesty makes him poor and jobless. Together, they receive the happy word that Archie is to return to Mr. Field's firm, receive the man's apologies, and once again take over his former job.

"Emmy" shows Fauset's early interest in the ironies of American discrimination based not only on skin color but on invisible "Black blood." The story explores childhood sources for attitudes toward racial identification, just as Fauset's *There Is Confusion*, *Plum Bun*, and *Comedy: American Style* do. Racial identification, sometimes but not always attached to skin color, creates conflicts not only between Black and white, but between Black and Black. Fauset's primary interest in racial and interracial conflicts, however, is not in the externals of teachers' prejudice, employment difficulties, broken engagements, though she depicts all these trials both in "Emmy" and in the novels. Rather, Fauset is interested in what characters do with their heritage and their experiences. In "Emmy" the conflict centers around Archie's honor. Will he gain his position by acquiescing to deception? Will he allow the woman he loves to be insulted in her absence? Will he live by the philosophy that "the end justifies the means?" A wealthy but liberal young white man who gives Archie his first occupational chance voices the essential conflict. " 'So it's all a gamble with you, isn't it? By George! How exciting your life must be—now white and now black—standing between ambition and honor, what?' " (p. 84.) "Emmy" uses a girl/woman as central character, as do all Fauset's stories and novels, but in this early narrative, the psychology of the man rather than the woman is explored. Emmy remains static in her racial acceptance, her honesty, her satisfaction with herself and her role. In *Plum Bun* and *Comedy: American Style* Fauset makes both the static and developing characters women—Virginia and Angela in the former novel; Olivia and Phoebe in the latter.

James Weldon Johnson's novel *The Autobiography of An Ex-Colored Man* was first published the same year as was "Emmy," and was sensitively reviewed by Fauset for *The Crisis*. It is of significance that Fauset was at the same time as Johnson exploring not just the externals of racial discrimination but the psychology of race by using Black characters who could pass for white, and who were thereby intimate with two worlds in America. Fauset added another element to her exploration, not exploited as much by Johnson, that being the barrier race and color present to romance in America. With "Emmy" Fauset entertains a wide and somewhat unsophisticated readership with a plot line of romantic conflicts but a happy ending, while she simultaneously begins looking at the deeper relevance of both race and romance. Essentially the same method in a refined form is used to good effect in *There Is Confusion* and *Plum Bun*.

"There Was One Time," subtitled "A Story of Spring," in

The Crisis in April and May 1917, is a less serious story than is "Emmy," designed essentially to pleasantly entertain. The story does show Fauset's interest in the form of the romance, however, in its combination of a French tale of a little shepherdess and a Prince and the parallel tale of Anna, a high school French teacher, and Dick, a potential race leader. Fauset's use of romance for formal structure is deliberate and explicit here; in *Plum Bun*, as shall be seen, such use is more subtle and more meaningful.

The two early stories introduce some thematic and formal concerns which Fauset develops more fully in her novels. Two stories published in *The Crisis* in the 1920's are even more directly related to two of Fauset's novels. "The Sleeper Wakes" from the August, September, and October issues of 1920 is an early working out of the race and sex issues of *Plum Bun*. "Double Trouble," from the August and September issues in 1923 is an early version of the barely-avoided incest of *The Chinaberry Tree*.

Amy of "The Sleeper Wakes" is of unknown racial origin. As a baby she lived with a wealthy white woman, but was brought at a young age to the home of Black Mr. and Mrs. Boldin, where she was raised as a foster sister to their son Cornelius. Very beautiful, teenage Amy has no problem finding a job as a waitress after she runs away from the Boldins and goes to New York. Through a woman met while waiting tables, Amy comes to know a rich white man, Stuart Wynne, who eventually convinces her to marry him, though she does not love him. Living with Wynne in Southern spendor, Amy grows to love him despite her extreme dislike of his treatment of their Black servants. Amy senses in his attitude toward Blacks a sort of white world in microcosm—a combination of "hate and yet desire" (p. 272). One day Wynne's valet, who reminds Amy of Cornelius Boldin, strikes Wynne for insulting his sister. With Wynne ready to lynch the valet, Amy interferes to claim first that the young man is her brother, then to admit that she herself is Black.

Amy's awakening occurs in the third and last section of the story. She is amazed that Wynne divorces her despite all the protestations of love he had made before she claimed Negro ancestry. She lives unthinkingly on his money after the divorce until he shocks her by returning not with a new marriage proposal, as she expected, but with a proposal of another sort. Recognizing that she had in effect sold herself in her marriage and in her financial dependence, she goes to work and eventually pays Wynne back. Accomplishing this, she has "a feeling that at last her training, her senses were liberated from some hateful clinging thralldom" (p. 272). At her point of freedom from Wynne she writes the Boldins about her desire to return to them and her home with them. At the end of the story she is packing her bags while thinking of Cornelius and his parents.

"The Sleeper Wakes" shares with other Fauset stories some weaknesses of trying to crowd too much into a short narrative and of covering too lengthy a time span; and some strengths of dialogue and psychological probing. The parallels with *Plum Bun* are clear beneath surface details. A girl from a poor but close Black family goes white and is attracted to marrying a rich white man. Eventually recognizing the hollowness of wealth and whiteness as ideals, the girl develops and acts on sounder moral principles. At that point the girl returns to her former poor but secure Black home. Beyond this skeletal plot of both the story and the novel, the details differ. The changes Fauset makes from the 1920 story to the 1929 novel are of interest.

Amy in "The Sleeper Wakes" does not know if she is Black or white. When she recognizes in white people a coldness and cruelty toward the unfortunate which is foreign to her and to the Blacks she has grown up with, she concludes that she is Black. In *Plum Bun* Fauset is not so foolish as to extend the suggestion that kindness and cruelty can be biologically inherited. By making Angela Murray clearly Black but light enough to pass for white, Fauset explores cultural and environmental differences, and Angela's psychological motivation, not biological differences and determinism. Amy's racial judgement appears in *Plum Bun* only in the form of sister Virginia's brief speculation that Angela gets her cruelty from her "white blood." Nor does Fauset depict in *Plum Bun* as she does in "The Sleeper Wakes" all bad white characters and all good Black characters. *Plum Bun* is thus more realistic, less propagandistic than is "The Sleeper Wakes."

In the short story Amy marries rich, white Stuart Wynne. In

Plum Bun Fauset has rich, white, spoiled Roger Fielding more real-
istically pressure Angela into an affair. By letting Angela become
Roger's mistress while retaining her financial independence, by caus-
ing her to break off the affair because of Roger's treatment of women, and by having Angela later refuse Roger's offer of marriage,
Fauset makes a much more radical statement in *Plum Bun* about sex
roles and sexuality than she does in "The Sleeper Wakes." Amy
wakes; Angela actually leaves the bed.

"Home" in "The Sleeper Wakes" is literal—it is a return to the
three Boldins. In *Plum Bun* Fauset has Angela return not to the
Philadelphia house she left, for her parents are dead and the house
has been sold. Rather, "Home" becomes a kind of racial loyalty
and honesty, a development of one's own moral standards, and a
discovery of others who can be one's true friends because their moral
standards are similar. Again, Fauset is more realistic, less simplistic,
in the novel.

A final difference between the early 1920's short story and the
late 1920's novel shows Fauset's conscious development of a formal
structure to contain her thought. The story simply moves from Amy
as a young girl to Amy packing her bags for returning home. Though
there are numbered divisions, they appear to be only for convenience
in serial publication. *Plum Bun*, on the other hand, as will be seen in
Chapter VI, uses nursery rhyme, fairy tale, and controlled imagery
to create a formal adjunct to themes developed.

When one looks at another 1920's Fauset story, "Double
Trouble," in comparison to her 1931 novel *The Chinaberry Tree*, it
is to make much the same observation. The novel more carefully develops character and situation, but its primary development as compared to the short story is in its conceptual frame in the form of settings dominated by the chinaberry tree. "Double Trouble" has the
same central characters as does the novel: Aunt Sal; her illegitimate
daughter Laurentine; her niece Angelique (Melissa in the novel);
Angelique's boyfriends Asshur and Malory. Of these characters, only
Angelique is developed to any extent in the short story. The novel's
depiction of the ideal love affair of Aunt Sal and Laurentine's father,
and of Laurentine's own struggles with longing to be respectable and

ordinary, are not present in the story. Nor does the story develop the contrasting ideals of "respectability" maintained by the community and by the characters of Asshur and Dr. Denleigh.

For any appeal it might have, the story depends almost entirely upon the sensationalist connotations of Malory's and Angelique's growing involvement with one another. The community and Laurentine whisper and gossip and try to keep the two young people apart, for they are unknowningly half-brother and sister. There is some attempt to get at Angelique's feelings as an outsider in town who is judged and ostracized and assumed an easy mark by the boys, all for something of which she is unaware. This psychological exploration is minute, however, when it is compared with the way in which community and individual morality are defined and contrasted in *The Chinaberry Tree*.

The framework of the tree itself, what it means to each of the women, what it stands for as a remembrance of the interracial love of Aunt Sal and the Colonel, is essential for drawing together the characters and thoughts of the novel. The tree is not present in "Double Trouble," nor are external settings of any kind in particular evidence. Although the small kernel of unwitting near-incest remains from short story to novel, in the novel Fauset has made significant thematic impact beginning with that event, primarily through more carefully using scene and material surroundings for structuring.

In discussing Jessie Fauset's short stories, it is only fair to look at a story which does not impress one as being essentially a trial run in theme or form for a later novel. A story idea later developed into a novel is perhaps always likely to look weaker and thinner by comparison with the later and longer work. "Mary Elizabeth," from *The Crisis* of December 1919, is unusual in Fauset's ficiton in that it is told in first person, and in that it uses dialect extensively. It also limits its time frame drastically as compared to other Fauset stories, which often cover years.

Mary Elizabeth, Black servant to a Black couple, Sally and Roger Pierson, is late for work one morning because she has been out looking for her senile and wandering husband. Sally, who has been forced to fix breakfast, tells the story of the day. "The coffee boiled, or stewed or scorched, or did whatever the particular thing is that coffee shouldn't do" (p. 51). Roger is enraged about the botched breakfast, and flings out of the house. "Mary Elizabeth came in about eleven o'clock. She is a small, weazened woman, very dark, somewhat wrinkled, and a model of self-possession. I wish I could make you see her, or that I could reproduce her accent, not that it is especially colored,—Roger's and mine are much more so— but her pronunciation, her way of drawing out her vowels, is so distinctively Mary Elizabethan!" (p. 51.)

Sally follows Mary Elizabeth around, listening to her talk, until she mentions her father's many marriages. "That shocked me out of my headache." Mary Elizabeth tells the story of the slave marriage of her father and mother—" 'they jumped over a broomstick and they wus jes as happy! But not long after I came erlong, they sold papa down South, and mamma never see him no mo' fer years and years. Thought he was dead, So she married again' " (p. 53). Twenty-six years later he returned; Mary Elizabeth tells the story with all its surprise and drama. " 'My sister Minnie and me, we jes' stood and gawped at 'em. There they wus, holding on to each other like two pitiful childrum, en he tuk her hands and kissed 'em.' "

At the end of her day, Sally says "I watched from the window til she was out of sight. It had been such a long time since I thought about slavery. I was born in Pennsylvania, and neither my parents nor grandparents had been slaves, otherwise I might have had the same tale to tell as Mary Elizabeth, or worse yet, Roger and I might have lived in those black days and loved and lost each other futilely, damnably, met again like Cassius and Maggie" (p. 55). Roger comes home; the pair make up. Sally's narrative concludes, "So thus, and not otherwise, Mary Elizabeth healed the breach" (p. 56).

Jessie Fauset's published poetry, translations, and short stories are not her primary accomplishment in the history of Black literature. That accomplishment is shown in her journalism, including essays, and in her novels. What the shorter compositions do show, however, is a woman attuned to universal experiences of love and joy, loss and pain, a woman sensitive to both the universal and the unique in the writings of Black poets throughout the world. Her stories are a working out of many themes and patterns which are developed and perfected in the novels. Her literary development in fiction was not as impressive as it might have been had her opprotunities been different and had they occurred earlier in her adult life. Nevertheless, comparison of the short stories to the later novels demonstrates conscious artistic development on her part. In both theme and form, the novels are an advance over the stories.

Notes

[1] Marion L. Starkey, "Jessie Fauset," *Southern Workman* (May 1932), p. 218.

[2] "Jessie Fauset," *Caroling Dusk*, ed. Countee Cullen (New York: Harper and Brothers, 1927), p. 65.

[3] Starkey, p. 218.

[4] Jessie Fauset, "Fragment," *Caroling Dusk*, pp. 70-71. The life/death imagery was added to what was evidently an earlier version of the poem in "Fragments," set to music by Burleigh in 1919.

[5] Jessie Fauset, "Words! Words!" *Caroling Dusk*, pp. 65-66.

[6] Jessie Fauset, "Touche," *Ibid.*, pp. 66-67.

[7] Jessie Fauset, "Enigma," *The Poetry of the Negro: 1746-1949*, ed. Langston Hughes and Arna Bontemps (Garden City, New York: Doubleday, 1949), p. 65.

[8] Jessie Fauset, "Noblesse Oblige," *Caroling Dusk*, pp. 67-68.

[9] Jessie Fauset, "Dead Fires," *The Poetry of the Negro*, p. 66.

[10] Jessie Fauset, "Christmas Eve in France," *The Independent* (22

December 1917), p. 552. Reprinted in "The Looking Glass: Literature," *The Crisis* (February 1918).

11Jessie Fauset, "Two Christmas Songs. Verses," *Brownies' Book* (December 1920), p. 384. A manuscript of "Crescent Moon" is at the Beinecke Rare Book and Manuscript Library, Yale University.

12Arthur P. Davis, *From the Dark Tower: Afro-American Writers, 1900-1960* (Washington, D. C.: Howard University Press, 1974), pp. 93-94.

13Sterling Brown, *The Negro in Poetry and Drama* (1937; rpt. New York: Atheneum, 1969), p. 67.

14Saunders Redding, "Problems of the Negro Writer," *Massachusetts Review* (Autumn-Winter, 1964-65). Reprinted in Jules Chametzky and Sidney Kaplan, eds., *Black and White in American Culture: An Anthology from the Massachusetts Review* (University of Massachusetts Press, 1969), p. 262.

15James Weldon Johnson, *The Book of American Negro Poetry*, rev. ed. (New York: Harcourt Brace, 1931), p. 205.

Content and Form in Fauset's Novels:

There Is Confusion *and* Plum Bun

There Is Confusion, 1924, and *Plum Bun*, 1929, form a rather convenient pair for studying content and form in Jessie Fauset's longer fiction, for the first novel, while in many ways weak in execution, is nevertheless thorough in revealing Fauset's fictional themes and concerns and the second is more consciously formed and styled while not departing significantly from the first in theme. Previous studies of *There Is Confusion* have over-emphasized and sometimes misread the "theme" of middle-class Black social depiction, and have assumed emphasis on protest against racial discrimination, to the exclusion of other important explorations in the book: the influence of history, of heredity, of environment and the possibility of free will; life as a corrective for obsessions; the reconsideration of religious tradition; folk material as basic to Black art; the limiting roles of women and departures from the roles. Previous studies of *Plum Bun* have for the most part emphasized its picture of "passing," a topic liable to sensational inferences in Black and white readers alike, while ignoring the novel's formal and stylistic strengths: the use of setting to reveal character, change, growth; the plot closely woven with psychological exploration of change in the character of Angela; the imagery emphasizing chance and gamesmanship; the formal use of the fairy tale and nursery rhyme for structuring what is essentially romance. Emphasizing here the range of ideas in *There Is Confusion* and the careful form of *Plum Bun* will hopefully aid in moving toward a full and fair critical assessment of Fauset's novels.

One need not go far to discover weaknesses in execution in *There Is Confusion*. The work includes a rather large number of important characters. Joanna Marshall is shown from about age five to several years after her rather late marriage to Peter Bye and the birth of their son. Less central to the book, but significant in representative ways are other members of the Marshall family—Sylvia, Joanna's sister, whose domestic proclivities contrast to Joanna's artistic ambition; Phillip, her brother, whose interracial organization and newspaper are clearly modelled on the NAACP and *The Crisis*; Joel, the father, whose basic beliefs and actions mold and inspire the children's lives. Outside the Marshall family, Peter Bye, from age twelve to his marriage to Joanna, is shown rather fully in his physical and psychological development, and Maggie Ellersley and her first husband, Henderson Neal, are given a great deal of space as representative of different heritage and different environmental experience than either the Marshalls or Peter Bye. The sheer number of primary characters has been labelled confusing by some readers, among them Zona Gale, whose review of the novel prompted a reply from Jessie Fauset agreeing that fewer characters might be a better idea, but justifying her inclusion of persons for their representative impact. "I feel myself that I could do a much better piece of work with the introduction of fewer characters, though on the other hand, when I was writing the book I was not trying consciously to introduce a great many people. I think I was simply trying to show on how many strata the life [sic] of colored people in Joanna's class impinge."[1]

The social range and number of characters alone is not necessarily a weakness in the novel, but there is a failure to develop these characters enough as full people, tied to failure to bring physical detail and description of setting fully into focus, and a failure to use original figurative language for its brightening and revelatory capabilities. By moving back into the early adult life of Joel Marshall and even further back into several generations of the Black and white Bye families, Fauset does succeed in delineating the various effects of heredity and environment on her characters, but in the present time of the novel, the characters are not shown in full enough physical or mental or emotional detail to make them live. Inexplicably, the detail which stands out in the book in contrast to generally prevailing abstract summary is devoted to people's clothing. When young Joanna first catches young Peter Bye's attention in an otherwise all-white classroom, she is wearing "a very fine soft sage-green middy

suit with a wide buff tie."2 When Joanna first hears with horror of
the growing affection between Maggie Ellersley and Joanna's brother
Phillip, information which causes her to write Maggie the letter
which nearly destroys two lives and does, indirectly, destroy Henderson Neal, she is "a little prim in her pale yellow dress and soft
floppy hat of tan chiffon" (p. 77). When Maggie, in shock from Joanna's letter, runs off with Henderson Neal to Atlantic City, he buys
her "a blue silk dress, a white satin skirt, two or three smart, deli-
cately tinted blouses, a wonderful wrap, light but warm, tan and
white shoes and stockings" (p. 114).

This halting approach toward preciseness in external description is only infrequently used to reveal the intenal workings of
Fauset's characters in *There Is Confusion*. When Maggie, married
several months to Henderson Neal, first finds out that his mysterious wealth comes from dishonest gambling, "outside a steady
soaking rain had begun to fall in the gray somberness of the November afternoon. The gas-heater cast a ruddy oblong of light on the
white ceiling. Maggie. . . crossed the room and threw her slight figure
on the couch, huddling close against the wall. She shivered a little in
the luxurious warmth" (p. 122). And when Joanna mails Peter the
cool, demanding letter which temporarily alienates him from her and
turns him to the less demanding, newly-divorced Maggie, Joanna
"got up and walked bare-footed across the room to the desk, shiver-
ing a little as the chilly January morning air struck at her, bellowing
her thin nightdress. She thought she would read it again, but the
envelope was sealed. It slipped out of her hand and she ran back to
bed again, cuddling luxuriously" (p. 165). But frequently, any external description of physical appearance, of setting, and of activity
in the book sits apart from any revelation of thought or emotion,
and even more frequently, the world of sight, sound, touch, smell,
feel, disappears altogether into an amorphous summation. Maggie
and Henderson Neal ride into the country prior to her receipt of Joanna's letter and her rebound acquiescence to Neal's desires. Only
once does the world appear in their trip, when "he turned and swore
fluently at a motorist who passed him too closely." The remainder
of the scene is conveyed in generalities: "She thought with the
ignorant pride of a young girl that it would be very easy for her to

manage him. Shortly after that they turned around and came home"
(p. 84).

Occasional figurative image stands out in the book for its
rarity and often for its triteness. Sylvia as a child, flitting around
dressing both her and Joanna's dolls, "was like a firefly in comparison with Joanna's steady beaconlike flood of light" (p. 17). In their
dance, "Sylvia was as light as thistle-down on her feet, but Joanna
was like the spirit of dancing" (p. 18). When Peter and Joanna first
discover mutual attraction and passion for one another, "something
leaped, something fluttered within their hearts, like a fettered, struggling wing. And it was beautifully, it was magically, first love!"
(p. 102) The young beautiful Maggie Ellersley, living in honest and
virtuous, but dangerous, poverty in the New York Tenderloin district, "blooms." "She was like a yellow calla lily in the deep cream
of her skin, the slim straightness of her body" (p. 57). Henderson
Neal, one of her mother's roomers, of course notices. ' "You're like
a little yellow flower, growin' in that house' " (p. 83).

There are some instances in the book where a rather trite or
excessively sentimental image is made to work by the quick intrusion of an antithetical viewpoint. One such noticeable device occurs
when the reconciliation to his past, his present, and his future are
depicted for Peter Bye in a symbolic tableau in the World War I
mud of France. Meriwether Bye, Peter's first white friend and also
his relative, dies wearing Peter's coat, lying in Peter's wounded arms.
"When the stretcher-bearers found them, Meriwether was lying across
Peter's knees, his face turned childwise toward Peter's breast. The
colored man's head had dropped low over the fair one and his black
curly hair fell forward stright and stringly, caked in the blood which
lay in a well above Meriwether's heart.   'Cripes!' said one of the
rescue men, 'I've seen many a sight in this war, but none ever gave
me the turn I got seein' that smoke's hair dabblin' in the other fellow's blood' " (p. 253). More frequently, however, the impression
of either too little originality in form or too great a tendency toward
unqualified sentiment prevails in *There Is Confusion*.

Fauset's intent in the book to show historical, hereditary, and
environmental influences on personality and action, and to show life

as a corrective, necessitates a rather lengthy time frame, in itself not necessarily a weakness, as simple number of characters is not a weakness. In novelistic movement forward and backward in time, however, *There Is Confusion* reveals both some confusion and some awkwardness. The confusion occurs primarily in the charting of the early history of the Black Byes and the white Byes, Peter's ancestors. The early pattern of the book is to introduce a character, as first Joanna and then Peter are introduced, and then to work back to a description of parentage. In the case of Joanna, there is little difficulty, for the central influence on her life is her father, Joel, and Joel's character determinants have been experiential more than hereditary. After the introduction of Peter, however, Fauset goes back to his father, Meriwether Bye (Black); to his grandfather, Isaish Bye; to his great-grandfather, Joshua Bye; and to the person who is only at the end of the book revealed to be his great-great-grandfather, Aaron Bye, patriarch of the white Byes as well. Aaron Bye's and Dinah Bye's youngest white son, Meriwether Bye, is the same age as and childhood friend of Isaiah Bye, and is still living as a very old man at the end of the novel. His grandson, (white) Meriwether Bye, has become reconciled with Peter Bye, his Black counterpart, during World War I, dying, as has been seen, in Peter Bye's arms in France. Peter and Joanna have named their baby son Meriwether Bye after this Meriwether Bye (not after Peter's dissolute father, Black Meriwether Bye).

Clearly, some of the confusion inherent in family trees tangled with the rotten fruits of slavery is meant to be present in Fauset's description of the Byes, simply to illustrate one of the impingements on Black life and white life in America. But the point being made thereby is only one of the themes present in the book, and the time and energy spent by a reader unravelling Peter's involved heritage is out of proportion to that point. (The previous simplified description has even left out half of the participants—the wives, mistresses, bearers of the children.) The nature of the involved historical racial mix and interaction bears much resemblance to William Faulkner's customary material, but Fauset did not develop the formal experiment to contain it, the lengthy exposure to large numbers of characters in a long time span, or the clarification that repetition lends.

It is rather obvious that Fauset is struggling with devising smooth time transitions in the book, not yet having discovered, as she does by the time of the writing of *Plum Bun*, that closely described scenes, years apart but juxtaposed, are transition enough. One example will illustrate resulting awkwardness. When Peter and Joanna, after his medical school and war experiences, and her success on the stage, are finally reunited in new understanding of what life and success and they themselves are all about, "he persuaded her to go to Philadelphia, to Bryn Mawr in fact. 'I've got to give these pictures and the locket [of the dead young Dr. Meriwether Bye] to Dr. Meriwether Bye and to Mrs. Lea.' " After about a minute's worth of dialogue, " 'Gosh!' Peter exclaimed inadequately, don't you do funny things when you're kids? Well, here we are at Bryn Mawr' " (pp. 279-280).

There Is Confusion shows some of Fauset's adeptness at dialogue, including an ability, though not a tendency, to write in dialect when called for. Maggie Ellersley at age twelve listens to her mother and mother's cousin "Mis' Sparrow," discuss the ways of white folks the latter works for. Young Mr. Proctor of the family has married "jes' a little teeny slip of ole white gal. No money, no fambly, no nuthin!" Upon hearing that the girl does not love Mr. Proctor, Maggie asks, "What she marry him for then?' " " 'H'm child, wouldn't you do anything to get away f'um hard work, an' ugly cloes an' bills? Some w'ite folks has it most as bad as us poor colored people. On'y thing is they has more opporchunities' " (p. 56).

Here and there in the book, however, one of Fauset's irritating habits pokes out—a need to remind the reader that while her character may be saying something ungrammatical, she herself knows better, and a thoroughgoing assumption that the "right" way to speak is better. Young Maggie says " 'Aw, quit your kiddin!' " and Fauset tells the reader: "Poor Maggie. Her calla-lily charm visibly lessened in those days when she opened her pretty mouth. She disclosed herself then for what she was, a true daughter of the Tenderloin" (p. 58). When a white society woman and patron of the arts, Miss Sharples, comes to Joanna with her long-awaited chance to break into the discriminatory performance world, she tells Joanna of her dancing predecessor in "The Dance of the Nations" that

" 'she's all right as a white American, or as a red one, but when it comes to the colored American, she simply lays down on her job,' " and Fauset tells the reader that "Miss Sharples' eloquence drowned her sense of grammar" (p. 227). Benjamin Brawley once credited this "self conscious air" of Jessie Fauset's works to her having been for "several terms" the only Negro in her school classes.[3] Whether or not this is the source, there is a lessening in self-conscious intrusion of this kind in her following three novels, helping give them greater artistic coherence than *There Is Confusion* displays.

While weaknesses in form are rather obvious in this, Fauset's first novel, there are strengths in content—in ideas and themes— that make the book well worth reading. This assessment does not differ much from that of early white and Black readers of the book. The *New York Times* review of 13 April 1924 judges that "considered exclusively as fiction, the novel is mediocre; fairly well written, loosely constructed," but goes on to a lively discussion of content.[4] George Schuyler, writing in the *Messenger*, found *There Is Confusion*, though "not very engrossing as a work of fiction, . . . of compelling interest as a picture of Northern Negro urban society," with an author skillful, truthful, having a "wealth of understanding" and a "feeling" for the material coming from "intimate knowledge." Schuyler reports that in reading the book he was "never bored," but felt "like a traveller returning to familiar scenes."[5] Close reading of the 1920's best-seller, Carl Van Vechten's *Nigger Heaven*, reminds one that the weaknesses in form in *There Is Confusion* are not unique to Fauset's work, but that the unique material lent by Black life at all social levels outweighs those weaknesses in value.[6]

In overlooking form in the book to deal with content, however, readers have tended to pick out a single characteristic of *There Is Confusion*—its use of middle class characters—and to take that characteristic to be Fauset's point in writing the book. Hugh Gloster, in summarizing Fauset's contribution to American fiction, says that "in her novels, she shows that in the country there are respectable, middle-class colored people whose lives are twisted and distorted because of race prejudice," and that "Fauset's description of the lives and difficulties of Philadelphia's colored elite is one of the major achievements of American Negro fiction."[7] The above-mentioned *New York Times* review points out differences in background in Fauset's characters in *There Is Confusion* and goes on to say that "this note of insistence on distinctions of birth and background among the Negroes themselves is emphasized again and again." For other readers (or possibly, people who have not read the books carefully at all, but only summaries of them), Fauset's *depiction* of middle class characters becomes *pushing* them, promoting them, elevating them above other Black people. Wallace Thurman claims that *There Is Confusion* was "an ill-starred attempt to popularize the pleasing news that there were cultured Negroes, deserving of attention from artists, and of whose existence white folk should be apprised"[8]; Arthur Davis calls Fauset the "most prolific, and in many ways the most representative, of [the] glorifiers of the Negro middle class," whose novels "told white America" that apart from negligible color differences high-class Negroes are like high-class whites"[9]; and Nick Aaron Ford describes the theme of *There Is Confusion* as one which "exalts the artistic tastes, good manners, and normal American conduct of Negroes."[10]

With this basic, though unwarranted, assumption that Fauset's intent is to promote middle class Negroes, it is predictable that critics then go on to castigate both the way she shows the middle class Negro and what the critic believes to be characteristic not of Fauset's work, but of the middle class Negro. Sterling Brown criticizes Fauset for too often showing not typical middle class experience, but the more spectacular "passing" and exceptional Negro artists and cosmopolitans.[11] Arthur Davis, again, calls *There Is Confusion* Fauset's "fullest and most representative novel" because it renders "more of the typical attitudes and shibboleths held by the New Negro middle class of the 1920's than any of her others," assuming thereby that this is her aim. Davis in fact extends this notion of her aim to add that Fauset is trying with her middle class characters to show *all* Negroes. *There Is Confusion*, he says, is "limited" because a reader is not apprised of the presence of thousands of "low-class-vulgar-loud-and- wrong-ghetto-type Negroes" in metropolitan areas across the country. "She is really trying to make a very small group of Negroes represent all Negroes."[12]

Addison Gayle, in *The Way of the New World*, shows the

confusion incumbent on a critic who believes from all that is written of her work that Jessie Fauset's purpose is to promote middle class Negro life, and who would like to believe this since it buttresses his political "Black aesthetic" assumptions, but whose own reading of her novels begins to discover something else in Fauset's themes and concerns. Gayle tells us that Fauset speaks for the bourgeoisie, is more the oracle than Nella Larsen, whose two novels otherwise bear some similarity in theme to Fauset's. She believes, Gayle says, in "the unique ability of affluent Blacks to serve as mentors to whites and missionaries to Blacks." Before Joanna, of *There Is Confusion*, "can become the perfect middle-class model, . . . she must undergo a baptism, must be cleansed of the evils of snobbery and obsession." Gayle then begins to confuse the "major concerns of the class [Fauset] represented" with the content of her books. The concerns are "marriage, security, family, respectability" first, with race pride and interest as "necessary elements." But the "salient quality" of Fauset's work is not any of the above, Gayle finds, and as other careful readers will find, but an "appeal to tolerance on the part of her major characters."

Weakly, Gayle sums up his confusion by blaming Fauset indirectly for books which readers, both middle-class and proletarian, misread. "Had the class for which she spoke divined in her philosophy dedication to work and progress as a suitable norm by which one validated his worth, their position might not have been so contemptible. However, they settled instead for an ethic based upon appearance, upon status attained by skin color and one's distance in things material from the poor." "The black poor came to believe with most of them that the possession of Nordic skin, Nordic manners, and Nordic culture defined one as human beings [sic]. The men and women of *There Is Confusion* and *Plum Bun* became the new models, the new images, for members of the lower class, the Anthonys and Angelas were the paradigms against which they measured their worth." Spurred by attitudes created in part by the literature of James Weldon Johnson, George Schuyler, Nella Larsen and Fauset, Gayle says, "they joined in chasing the white phantom with all too often disastrous results."[13] Gayle's difficulty as a careful reader of Fauset is clear. Wanting to condemn her for the class of herself and her characters, he is forced to recognize that Fauset does by no means indiscriminately praise the Black middle class or redeem or hide all its faults. Lee R. Edwards and Arlyn Diamond, in their introduction to a selection form *Plum Bun* in *American Voices, American Women*, are more accurate than Gayle in stating that Fauset sympathizes with the Black bourgeoisie, but "realizes the potential sterility and destructiveness of their overwhelming concern with whiteness and respectability."[14]

If the promotion of the Black middle class, the displaying to whites the virtues of socially and economically select Blacks, is not Fauset's central concern in *There Is Confusion*, it is necessary to look at the book carefully, without preconceptions, to discover the themes which do emerge. There *is* exploration of the kind of racial discrimination and inheritance a Northern urban Black faces. Beyond this exposure, Fauset looks at a wide range of characters and actions possible given American slave history, racially mixed heredity, and various environments. In quiet, subtle ways, she tiptoes across "acceptable" topics and conclusion to explore alternatives to her society's sometimes limiting norms. Religion in the Black church is looked at not as accepted supernatural truth or embodiment of truth, but as a social institution of varied support to varied characters. Biblical motifs, similarly, are used not for religious but for historical significance. Black folk material as the basis for possible uniqueness in Black artistry is a nicely underplayed but repeated idea present in Joanna's use of a Black children's dance-game as her entree into the theatrical world. The entire book explores the limited alternatives available to women, especially Black women, and also shows women breaking out of these limits without being excessively punished. If it is desirable to select "a" theme in *There Is Confusion* to include all the above thematic ideas, probably the best statement of it would be: Life is a corrective, individually and collectively, experientially and historically.

Ambitious Joanna, longing for and battling for success on the American stage as a singer and dancer, at first sees racial prejudice as "an awful nuisance; in some parts of this country it's more than a nuisance, it's a veritable menace' " (p. 98). Fauset documents both the nuisance-nature and the menace of discrimination with small incidents and references throughout *There Is Confusion*. Having to guess as to one's likely reception in a "public" eating place was always a nuisance to Fauset herself. Her fictional Joanna echoes the aggravation. Standing hungry on the steps of the New York Public Library, she wonders where to eat. "All about her flashed the lights of restaurants, but she was not sure of their recption of colored patrons, and being in a slightly irritable mood, she wanted consciously to spare herself any contact which would be more annoying." She has been shopping, and was invited while trying on a coat to use the mirrors near the rear of the store rather than those toward the front. "The incident was a slight one, possessing possibly no significance, but Joanna had walked out of the store hot and raging, the more so because she was not completely sure whether the slight was intentional or not" (pp. 195-96).

The constant guessing game as to what white reaction will be, the protecting oneself from potentially embarrassing or insulting situations, is thoroughgoing. When Miss Sharples comes to Joanna's home to request her trying out for the part of Black America in "The Dance of the Nations," "the older woman held out her hand. Joanna had neglected to do this, having, like most colored people of her class, carefully schooled herself in the matter of repression where white people were concerned" (p. 225). Very much as W. E. B. DuBois points out in his sociological study, *The Philadelphia Negro*, protection tactics create an at-home society among middle and upper class Negroes. "Like many of the better class of colored people, the Marshalls did not meet with the grosser forms of color prejudice, because they kept away from the places where it might be shown. This was bad from the standpoint of development of civic pride and interest. But it had its good results along another line. The children took most of their pleasures in their house or in those of their friends and devoted their wits and young originality to indoor pastimes" (p. 49).

Some of the discussion and prejudice Joanna and Peter encounter is stronger than nuisance; it moves toward menace to their economic and psychological well-being. Joanna's study with the French dance instructor, Bertully, must be done in a class of Black girls got up by herself, meeting from 7:30 to 10:00 three days a week, because " 'I'm sorry, Mees, but the white Americans like not to study with the brown Americans. Vair seely, but so. I am a poor man, I must follow the weeshes of my clients!' " (pp. 95-96) It is the same pattern of discrimination Fauset dealt with for the NAACP at Smith College in 1913, and that the character Miss Powell faces in *Plum Bun*. Peter, in Medical School at the University of Pennsylvania, is not allowed to work in some white hospitals, marring the quality of his surgical training. Peter also deplores the stupidity of prejudice which warps and destroys what would otherwise be the warmest of human impulses and deeds—the comforting of another's sorrows. When he returns from the war in France with the mementoes of the dead Dr. Meriwether Bye, and goes to visit the woman Bye loved, and who loved him, Mrs. Lee, she greets Peter, "tears streaming down her face," with " 'To think that the Lord would let Meriwether Bye be killed and would let his nigger live!' " While Peter reports Meriwether's words to her, as he later tells Joanna, " 'she leaned back and moaned—moaned, Janna. I wanted to pick her up in my arms and comfort her,' " he goes on, " ' and if I had, do you know what would have happened to me— . . . Well, this is Pennsylvania, so probably I'd have got off with imprisonment, here, but if it had been in Georgia, and I'd have dared to touch her—' " (p. 281).

In short references to minor characters, Fauset shows more of the American menace to Black life and living. Vera Manning is a light-skinned Black woman whose love for a dark-skinned man, Harley Alexander, has been frustrated by her "color-struck" mother. " 'As soon as my mother . . . realized we were in earnest, up she went in the air. None of her children should marry a dark man. It only meant unhappiness. . . . You know the funny thing is she doesn't like white people any better than I do—she just didn't want me to marry a dark man because, she says, in this country a white skin is such an asset' " (pp. 198, 199-200). Harley, insulted by the mother and disappointed that Vera is so easily disuaded from marrying his dark self, decides to remain in France after the war. " 'No more insults for him, no more lynching news' " (p. 272). Vera finds that with her white skin she can, as did her non-ficitonal counterpart, NAACP's Walter White, go into the South and spy on anti-Negro white activity. " 'You remember they mobbed some colored soldiers in Arkansas because they'd worn their uniforms in the street? Well it made me sick, it made me think of—of Harley. So I rushed to a newspaper . . . and I told them: " I'm colored, see, but nobody would guess it; send me down there. See if I can't get a line on those people." . . . Those white bullies, thinking I was one of *them*, told me the most blood-curdling, most fiendish tales. I really got an investigation started' " (p. 270). Vera, when she tells Joanna of her experiences, has fled one Southern town, but is ready to go back for more. Her loss of Harley makes her " 'glad there's the South to go to—I've got to choose between life and death. Even if I should lose my life in Georgia or in one of those other terrible places where they lynch women too, I'll save it, won't I?' " (p. 273).

The young white Dr. Meriwether Bye, who succeeds by his sensitivity to historical and present-day racism in breaking through Peter Bye's hatred of whites, finds the same urge toward extremism on the race question nationally as Vera Manning seeks and finds in the South. To young Dr. Bye's cumulative and incapacitating feeling of guilt and regret for his slave-holding Quaker ancestors and his inheritance of white wealth redolent of Black sweat, Peter says " 'I like to hear you acknowledge your indebtedness, . . . but I don't think you should take on your shoulders the penitence of the whole white nation.' " Meriwether Bye replies: " 'No, I don't think I should either, . . . but that sort of extremeness seems to be inherent in the question of color. Either you concern yourself with it violently as the Southerner does and so let slip by all the other important issues of life; or you are indifferent and callous like the average Northerner and grow hardened to all sorts of atrocities; or you steep yourself in it like the sentimentalist—that's my class—and find yourself paralyzed by the vastness of the problem' " (p. 246). In proof of his sentiment and his principles, Dr. Bye has refused to marry his beloved Mrs. Lea because of her hatred for Negroes.

Two rather long speeches in *There Is Confusion*, the first by a Joanna educated in some of the trials of life, less idealistic and unrealistic than the young ambitious Joanna was, and the second by a minor character, Sylvia's husband Brian, commenting on the creative and hard-working Blacks he has known, provide summaries of the psychological chasms of American discrimination, and the superiority which can come from successful crossing of those chasms. Joanna says:

"Of course I'll marry you, Peter. Dear, don't think I don't understand how hard things have been for you. I was such a stupid, before when we were young. I didn't allow for the difference in our temperaments. Why, nothing in the world is so hard to face as this problem of being colored in America. See what it does to us—sends Vera Manning South and Harley overseas, away from everybody they've ever known, so that they can live in—in a sort of bitter peace; forces you to consider giving up your wonderful gift as a surgeon to drift into any kind of work; drives me, and the critics call me a really great artist, Peter, to consider ordinary vaudeville. Oh, it takes courage to fight against it, Peter, to keep it from choking us, submerging us. But now that we have love, Peter, we have a pattern to guide us out of the confusion" (p. 283).

Brian says:

"Of course, what Joanna doesn't realize is that she's up against the complex of color in Peter's life. It comes to every colored man and every colored woman, too, who has any ambition. Jan will feel it herself one day. Peter's got it worse than most of us because he's got such a terrible 'mad' on white people to start with. But every colored man feels it sooner or later. It gets in the way of his dreams, of his education, of his marriage, of the rearing of his children. The time comes when he thinks, 'I might just as well fall back; there's no use pushing on. A colored man just can't make any headway in this awful country.' Of course, it's a fallacy. And if a fellow sticks it out he finally gets past it, but not before it has worked considerable confusion in his life. To have the ordinary job of living is bad enough, but to add to it all the thousand and one difficulties which follow simply in the train of being colored— well, all I've got to say, Sylvia, is we're some wonderful people to live through it all and keep our sanity" (p.179).

Selecting and repeating these instances of discrimination and prejudice in the book, including tirades against the white world and American society (carefully put, however, into the words of characters who are not Fauset and do not necessarily represent her full view) might suggest that *There Is Confusion* is exclusively a novel of protest. Such is not the case. Fauset does not underestimate the barriers to "life, liberty and the pursuit of happiness" for the 1920's American Black, but neither does she content herself with showing those barriers. Rather, her interest centers on what a character can do with life, with action, given facts of history, of biology, of birth and education. Both Roseann Pope Bell and Kenny Williams have mistakenly written that Fauset characters lack free will. Bell says that Fauset "omitted the surging, vibrant, cosmic possibility of Negroes who were agents in determining their own fate,"[15] and Williams that she "does not allow for the free will nor independent actions of her characters." Her characters, for the most part, says Williams, remain "caught within the maelstrom of American prejudice," and respond by attempts "to join rather than battle their oppressors and oppressions."[16]

Such readings go only half way. Fauset is in fact very careful to show change, learning, "free will" in her characters in *There Is Confusion*, and provides several characters as well whose differing uses of the same heritage and setting support the principle of freedom within limits. Solutions posed to American and Black identity in the lives lived by Fauset's characters are surprisingly unranked. It is particularly in this posing of unranked alternatives that what Addison Gayle calls Fauset's "salient quality" of "appeal to tolerance" comes through in *There Is Confusion*. There is no one "best" way to be Black and to Black American. Such moralizing is foreign to Fauset's interest in individual psychology. There are, however, often "better" ways for each character to deal with his or her life, and the book's plot becomes the story of how each major character makes the discoveries and changes which lead him or her to the best individual perspective. This plot pattern is essentially the same as that of the traditional British *Bildungsroman* where growth of character is depicted in the movement from disordered and confused value distinctions to a revelation of true differences.

One value distinction is not changed as much as it is expanded. "Black American" identification retains both its halves. Early in the book Joanna argues with Brian, her sister Sylvia's husband-to-be, about what he calls her " 'wildcat schemes of getting on the stage. Better stick to your own, Janna,' " the Harvard graduate advises, " 'and build up colored art.' 'Why, I am,' cried Joanna, astonished. 'You don't think I want to forsake—*us*. Not at all. But I want to show *us* to the world. I am colored, of course, but American first. Why shouldn't I speak to all America?' " (p. 76). Later, after Joanna has been "niggered" by manager after manager and after she has as a result lost some of her idealistic belief that simple excellence will be automatically recognized, she sees and makes the relationship between "Black" and "American" more explicit. Called on to dance not only "Black America" in the "Dance of the Nations," but "Indian America" and "White America" as well (with a mask), after the white dancer, Miss Ashby, has resigned (" 'I've really been violating my principles in staying this long,' she told Mr. Hale with meaning" [p. 231]), Joanna is encored, " 'Pull off your mask, America! . . . Let's see your face, America!' " The mask off, "there was a moment's silence, a moment's tenseness. Then Joanna smiled and spoke. 'I hardly need to tell you that there is no one in the audience more American than I am. My great-grandfather fought in the Revolution, my uncle fought in the Civil War and my brother is "over there" now' " (p. 232). Peter adds slave history and the kind of love which prevails over the errors of the loved to his American identification in deciding that he must fight in World War I. " 'America makes me sick, you know, like I used to make you, I guess,' " he tells his Aunt Susan, who has raised him from age twelve. " 'But darn it all, she is my country. My folks helped make her what she is even if they were slaves' " (p. 207).

While Fauset clearly presents the basic principle that "American" should include "Black" for white and Black people alike, she is more various in showing the day-to-day and generation-to-generation lives of her characters. Individual difference in dealing with the same basic heritage is shown in Peter's ancestors. Peter's grandfather, Isaiah, blood grandson of the white patriarch Aaron Bye, legal grandson of a surly white-hating ex-slave, Ceazer, and son of a devoted servant to his master/father, Joshua, early in life discovers limits placed on him by the white world, and rebels not only with dislike, but with "a sturdy independence and an unyielding pride," founding a school, saving money and buying property, becoming an A. M. E. Church leader (pp. 27, 29-30). His son, (Black) Meriwether Bye, however, raised "to be a great man—a doctor, his father . . . said emphatically," develops only the dislike for whites, along with a belief that the white Byes owe him a living. Squandering his inheritance in gambling, he passes only the hatred for whites and "the world owes me a living" on to his son Peter. Contact with white discrimination from within the same family has in each case led to a different result. As Fauset summarizes, his "grandfather's connection with white people resulted in pride, his father's in shiftlessness; in Peter it took the form of a constant and increasing bitterness" (p. 34).

It is partially through his environment that Peter develops into other than an unproductive bitter man. His father dies when he is twelve, and Peter is put in the care of his dead mother's sister, Susan Graves. The huge New Jersey Graves clan, Fauset tells us in an interesting anecdotal aside, is the result of the 18th century, run-away marriage of two white sisters to two of their father's slaves. "Nature and God alike, instead of being disconcerted at this utter contravention of the laws of man, presented each couple with numerous children" (p. 37). Cast out from both the white and Black community, the clan has inter-married happily. Susan Graves, with not enough Graves males to go around, has chosen to remain single rather than give up her family pride. With this strongly positive, though slave, history, Miss Graves is a good influence on Peter, as are the mannerly and ambitious Marshalls, whose house Peter frequents from the time he first sees Joanna in his classroom.

But influence is not all the determining factor for Peter's ultimate achievements; he also makes some choices. His weariness with battling to live up to Joanna's expectations leads him to the less demanding comforts of Maggie Ellersley's traditionally feminine treatment of him. His aims lower, his manners become inconsiderate, his feeling that "the world owes me a living" returns as Maggie urges him to his easy chair and newspaper, cooks for him and waits on him. It is only when he chooses Joanna again that the best of his character is once more made dominant.

Maggie's way of life, representing a different social class, different ambitions, and a freedom from documented heritage, is not, however, pictured as negative because of its negative influence on Peter's susceptible character. The lesson Maggie must learn through living is that respectability in simple societal terms is a hollow ideal. As a young girl, she loves the Marshall family for its respectability; she loves the son, Phillip, who can give her the security of name and position that she is obsessed with. She is repelled by her discovery of Henderson Neal's gambling life for she has unwittingly thrown away her most desired goal in marrying him on the rebound. She latches on to Peter's attentions for his family name, his potential position, though she does not love him.

Though the shock of her near-murder at her divorced husband's hands, and his own suicide, Maggie views her life. She feels responsible for Henderson Neal's death—" 'I did poison his life' " (p. 255); she frees Peter of his unhealthy commitment to her; she begins to do war work, no longer promoting herself, but unselfishly helping others. "She came to understand and to analyze for what it was that quality of hers, that tendency to climb to the position she wanted over the needs and claims of others" (pp. 255-56). Going to France with a small contingent of Black women sent by the YMCA to help nurse Black men at the front, Maggie is rewarded for her new kindness with the assignment of the wounded Phillip Marshall. Phillip's obsession, the opposite of Maggie's, has been his unselfishness, his determination to forget self in order " 'to strike a blow at this great towering monster,' " the " 'awful business of color in America' " (pp. 266-67). Though he has loved and still loves Maggie, he will not marry her now as an invalid attempting to make what is to be an unsuccessful recovery from gassing. " 'Then,' she said, and the last tatters of her old obsession, that oldest desire of all for sheer decency—fell from her, 'then I'll be your mistress Phillip' " (p. 268).

Maggie thinks of the lessons the two have learned: " 'You have learned ordinary personal consideration and I have learned unselfishness—to a degree,' "   and voices what comes closet to "the" theme of *There Is Confusion*. " 'Sometimes I think no matter how one is born, no matter how one acts, there is something out of gear with one somewhere, and that must be changed. Life at its best is a grand corrective' " (p. 267).

Maggie and Phillip do marry, and Maggie nurses him contentedly until his death, using the feminine traits which were so potentially destructive to Peter Bye to become in her relation to Phillip and the grieving Marshall family the nearest thing *There Is Confusion* has to saintly character. But that isn't all. With her worldly experience, her business head, her beauty-shop training, and her new-found freedom from obsession with limiting definitions of propriety and respectability, she sets out to found a chain of Black beauty parlors, a widowed, successful Black business woman.

There Is Confusion essentially depicts its characters' learned distinctions between true and false differences, with much of their initial confusion of values stemming from American race conventions. Several minor motifs are of interest in contributing to this plot pattern. Their contribution lies in increasing alternatives for living choices by testing and bending the habits, customs, expectations of the individual trained within society's norms. As with Fauset's purposeful lack of ranking of the various ways shown by characters in dealing with Black and American identity, there too she places emphasis on tolerance and variety rather than moralistic preaching about what is "right."

Religion, and church-going, for example, are presented in a very practical way in *There Is Confusion*. Organized religion as exemplified by Quakers comes in for some quick satire in the history of the Black and white Bye families. Aaron and Dinah Bye set their slave (and Aaron's son), Joshua free in 1780, "according to the laws of Pennsylvania, which thus allowed the Quakers to salve their consciences without offending their thrifty instincts" (p. 22). Nineteenth century Philadelphia colored society used religious character to measure one's social suitability ("one wasn't 'in' in those old days unless one were, first 'an old citizen,' and, second, unless one were eminently respectable,—almost it might be said God-fearing" [p. 31]); and 1920s New Yorkers, the Marshalls, use church and God or fail to use them as suits their individual temperaments and their periodic needs. Joel Marshall and his wife go to church out of habit, Fauset tells us without judgement; Sylvia goes to please her mother and to show her influence over an otherwise bored Brian; Phillip goes because "he was interested in seeing groups of colored people together"; and Joanna goes only to solo in the choir (p. 73).

When Joanna goes through her most intense experience of unlearning her obsession with art and success—"What did a knowledge of singing, of dancing, of any of the arts amount to without people, without parents, brothers, sisters, lovers to share one's failures, one's triumphs?" (p. 177)—she resorts to prayer of a sort, but more like "the power of positive thinking" than like the prayer of traditional Christianity. " 'If Peter could come back to me now, he'd see how truly I cared about him. God, couldn't you let him come back?' Joanna, who had hardly uttered a prayer outside of 'Now I lay me,' spent most of her thoughts at this time in communion with God—'You Great Power, you great force, you whatever it is that rules things.' Walking, riding, any action at all mechanical she utilized in concentrating on her desire to have everything come right' " (p. 177). Benjamin Mays in *The Negro's God as Reflected in His Literature*, first published in 1938, describes "bewilderment with the implication of a strain of agnosticism with respect to God" in some Black literature, and quotes *Plum Bun* as an example.[17] He could have used *There Is Confusion* as well, for early religious training and probably expectation of traditional belief in her readers did not prevent Jessie Fauset from a quiet but clean sweeping away of religious assumption in both books.

Fauset does use some Biblical motifs, notably the passage "By their fruits ye shall know them," passed down through the generations of the Bye family, penned in a huge old Bible first given "to Joshua and Belle Bye From Aaron and Dinah Bye." Significantly, Aaron does not mention, or claim, his own "fruits"—half-Black Joshua—but Joshua's son Isaiah, when his son Meriwether is born and recorded, writes "By *his* fruits shall ye know *me*" (pp. 24, 29), claiming not only responsibility for his own life but for what he leaves. Peter Bye repeats Isaiah at the end of *There Is Confusion* when his own son Meriwether is born (p. 290). The great Bible and its inscriptions serve to trace Bye history and tie together Peter's discoveries about himself and his heritage in the novel, but Fauset seems to be also suggesting a new teaching in this motif—that one's inheritance is not class or wealth, but struggle and perhaps strength, responsiblity as well as freedom.

Fauset believes strongly in the power of art to effect change in people bound by trained prejudice and discrimination. In *There Is Confusion* the point is subtly made. After a concert, Brian and Joanna mention it. " 'My collar's wringing wet, and I never thought of it. Wonderful how music can make people forget.' 'Even color,' said Joanna thoughtfully. 'Did you see that white woman next to me edge away when I sat down? But when she heard me humming after it was over, she leaned over and asked me if I knew the words' " (p. 77). Joanna agrees with the Frenchman Bertully that "if there's anything that will break down prejudice it will be equality or perhaps even superiority on the part of colored people in the arts" (p. 97). That Fauset holds such a faith would come as no surprise to a new reader accustomed to post-1920s partial fulfillment of it, but that she evidently also believed that the Black contribution to art would be founded on Black folk materials would surprise a new reader of *There Is Confusion* if his/her previous judgements of her work had been based on critical and historical summaries.

Nowhere in the book does Fauset make the statement directly that folk material should be brought to center-front as inspiration for Black art, but Joanna Marshall's break-through American stage success is an outcome of her hard work and training *and* her having picked up one day in the middle of Sixty-third Street a dance game of a "band of colored children."

> "Say little Missy, won't you marry me?
> Sissy in the barn, join in the weddin',
> Sissy in the barn, join in the weddin',
> Sweetest l'il couple I ever did see.
>   Barn! Barn!
> Arms all around me!
>   Barn!" (pp. 47-48)

Joanna interestingly has not learned the dance as a child, perhaps because of her mostly-white schooling, perhaps because of her class, but she picks up the spirit and the form, goes home and teaches the dance song to her friends, brothers and sisters, eventually performs it at a Nursery School benefit, and is ultimately remembered for that performance by Miss Sharples, who brings her into "The Dance of the Nations" (pp. 49-50, 111-12, 229).

During her tryout for the part of "Black America" in that "Dance of the Nations," Joanna stops. " 'If I could only have some real children, ... colored children. Are there any around here?'

'About five thousand down there in Minetta Lane,' Francis [the pianist] told her gravely. 'Want me to get you some?' . . . He and Miss Rosen disappeared and were back in fifteen minutes with ten colored children, of every type and shade, black and brown and yellow, some with stiff pigtails and others with bobbed curling locks. Most of them knew the game already" (p.229). Joanna gets the part—" 'America's got some foolish prejudices, but we'll try her with a sensation and you'll be all of that' "—and so do the children—" 'I suppose you'll need them' " (p. 230). Thus indirectly Fauset appears to be saying that for real Black artistic excellence and impact a combination of ingredients is best: the stuff of the masses of children on the street, the traditionally trained skill of an artist. One must be open to and recognize both ingredients.

A final secondary theme in *There Is Confusion*, contributing, as do the reconsideration of religious belief and the acceptance of artistic folk materials, to the broadening of alternatives for living, and also ignored by commentaries on Fauset, is the role of women, including particular reference to Black women, in American society. Fauset's exploration of women's roles centers around marriage and career, and includes evidence both of molding and discrimination from without, and self-limiting habits and expectations within.

Implicitly in the novel Fauset shows us that in youth and early maturity, women customarily expect to marry, but have very limited notions about marriage; women repress their intelligence and independence in order to not intimidate the men they expect to marry; women avoid careers or work at them frivolously, again in expectation of making a full career of marriage; women lack information and means for dealing with developing sexual desire. Marriage, Fauset shows, means adjustment to realities, adjustment of life style, some change in career if a career has been pursued, frequent economic dependence which prevents divorce. The societal double jeopardy of the Black woman includes double difficulty in pursuing a career, and resulting vulnerability to being used by men, particularly white men. Even in making marriage a career, the Black woman has the disadvantage of the paucity of successful Black men. Fauset uses primarily the differing characters and lives of Joanna Marshall and Maggie Ellersley to display women's social role and, importantly, to display as well means of bending or expanding that role.

Maggie in her growing years sees men and marriage as "one avenue of escape" from the disreputable attachments and the pain of poverty. Men "were stronger than women, they made money." But one must be sure of the money. "Maggie did not want to wash and iron, to go through the dreary existence which had been her mother's when her father was living; he had run on the road. Suppose, just suppose, there were some colored men who were fortunate and successful, who had enough to eat, who could give their wives help. . . . There were colored doctors and lawyers somewhere. Their very titles connoted prosperity" (pp. 58, 59). When Henderson Neal proposes, she lowers her sights a bit and settles for money. "Marriage with Neal was not what she wanted, but it represented to her security, a home for herself and her mother, freedom from all the little nagging worries that beset the woman who fights her own way through the world" (p. 90). Maggie's pre-marriage experience in business, working for Joanna's father in his catering business, and her night school beauty shop training are thus undertaken of necessity, not desire. All unforeseen in her pre-marriage notions of what her life would be, however, the experience and the training enable her economically to divorce Neal when she finds it mentally obligatory to do so, and enable her to carry on her life with independence and dignity when she is widowed by Phillip's death.

Joanna, in contrast, with her career always before her, does little serious thinking about love or marriage in her early years. " 'Love is a wonderful, rare thing, very beautiful, very sweet, but you can do without it,' " she tells Peter. When he replies " 'Not much you can't . . . You have to found your life on love, then you can do all these other things,' " she retorts only with down-to-earth realism. " 'Don't talk like a silly, Peter. You know perfectly well that for a woman love usually means a household of children, the getting of a thousand meals, picking up laundry, no time to herself for meditation, or reading' " (p. 95).

Fauset explains Joanna's resistance to tugs of love at age nineteen as "due partly to her hard unripeness, partly to her deliberate self-training" (p. 103). Joanna knows what she wants and works for it, but ultimately her late-blooming sexuality throws her plans into some confusion. With Peter in the park one night, her moony mind is first filled with "a series of little detached pictures. She saw a glittering stage, Peter, herself, some little children" · (p. 101). As the years of Peter's medical training in Philadelphia go by, "it was hard for her, too, much harder than Peter knew, or than she realized. for she was beginning to feel the tug of passion at her heart strings" (p. 146), Fauset writes discreetly. When Peter renounces Joanna and announces his engagement to Maggie, Joanna in her self-condemning loss is frustrated to the point of illness. "For the first time in her life she saw the importance of human relationships" (pp. 176-77). "She was feeling the pull of awakened and unsatisfied passion. It is doubtful if she could have thus analyzed it, for she had rather deliberately withheld her attention from the basic facts of life. 'Plenty of time for that,' she told herself gayly, a little proud perhaps of a virginal fastidiousness which kept her ignorant as well as innocent. . . . And now Peter was gone—and his departure had opened up this sea, this bottomless pit of torment. . . . 'This is being grown up,' she told herself through endless midnight watches" (pp. 180-81).

Joanna's career helps her even with the physical pain of unfulfilled passion, however, and in this Fauset adds to her gentle but thorough promotion of careers for women in *There Is Confusion*. The benefits are not just economic, as pointed out clearly with Maggie, but psychological as well.

> Very often she found herself vaguely glad that she had her work. Without it, what would she have done? What *did* girls do while they waited for their young men? Heavens, how awful to be sitting around listlessly from day to day, waiting, waiting! Anything was better than that, even pounding a typewriter in a box of an office. It was this lack of interest and purpose on the part of girls which brought about so many hasty marriages which terminated in—no, not poverty—mediocrity. Joanna hated the word; with her visual mind she saw it embodied in broken chairs, cold gravy, dingy linen, sticky children. She would never mind poverty half so much; she would contrive somehow to climb out of that. But ordinary tame mediocrity! (p. 146)

Fauset has cleverly reversed the customary roles of sons and daughters in *There Is Confusion*. Father Joel, looking for the urge for greatness in his sons, is surprised by it in his daughter, Joanna; and Alec and Phillip, the Marshall sons, only begin to be interested in worthwhile careers and hard work toward them after living with their younger sister's ambitions over the years.

Other women in the book briefly present variations of Maggie's and Joanna's pre-marriage anticipations and frustrations. Sylvia prefers domestic work and marries Brian unquestioningly, only after he is secure in a Harvard degree; nevertheless even she has a home-developed but marketable skill in dressmaking, which could support her in widowhood or divorce. Peter's Aunt Susan Graves has made the unusual decision of remaining unmarried after three offers, even though "in those days the position of old maid had its decided disadvantages—few people if any gave her the benefit of the doubt that she might have remained single from choice" (p. 37). The demeanors of the feminine young women of the "old Philadelphia families" whom Peter meets while in medical school contrast pleasantly for him, painfully for Fauset, with Joanna's "intent and serious air," her "queenliness," her "faint condescension" which made men "afraid" of her (pp. 75, 131). The Philadelphia girls are "pretty, nicely dressed," with "apparent lack of aspiration. They seemed to be pretty well satisfied with being girls," Peter finds. "A few were able to live at home, many sewed, a number of others taught. There was no talk of art, of fame, of preparation for the future among them." When Peter mentions his observations to one of the girls, she replies very directly: " 'Well, of course we want to get married, and we're not spoiling our chances by being highbrows' " (p. 107).

Peter's worst self is attracted to this "friendly shallowness," just as it is later exaggerated by Maggie's feminine role-play. One imagines that his knowledge of Joanna is what makes him even aware of the feminine role being a pose. When Maggie takes his arm and plays the dependent, helpless, deferring part, "it was singularly pleasing and yet puzzling to Peter. Joanna now was just as likely to cross the street as not, without waiting for a guiding hand, a protecting arm. If she had once visited a locality she knew quite as much about getting away from it as her escort. But Maggie was helpless, dependent. Strange when they were all growing up together he could have said she was quite as independent in her way as Joanna, and she was decidedly capable in her hair-dressing work" (p. 190).

While Fauset does put down as foolish women's pretense of dependence, of helplessness, of ignorance which gets men to lead them across streets, there are conventional manners between the sexes which she does support. She is careful to show, however, that these manners, even where traditional, are based on mutual consideration and not blind custom. When the orphaned Peter first comes to live with Susan Graves, she observed that "he had lacked finish, that fine courtliness of manner . . . , a knowledge of that delicacy, that attention to trifles which, once gained by a man, give him passport everywhere." Miss Susan had noticed

> the boy's tendency to let her carry bundles, to look after even the heavier household duties. It had never occurred to him if the weather were cold or stormy, to offer to go errands for her. . . . Now the Marshall boys were fine gentlemen. Joel had made them so by teaching, as well as by his attitude toward their mother and sisters. Joanna and Sylvia, particularly Sylvia, helped the boys out with an occasional stitch, an occasional sewing on of a button. When Alexander was getting ready for college, and was working at nights to help with his expenses, Sylvia used to arrange sandwiches and milk for him when he came in late. And Joanna had recopied his chemistry and history notes. These were only kind trivialities, but the boys treated their sisters like queens (p. 52).

Fauset moves from exploring pre-marriage manners between the sexes and expectation of marriage to some exposure of the real thing. Maggie's marriage to Henderson Neal "did not in reality prove as interesting and picturesque as she in common with most girls conceived it to be," but Maggie is ever-practical—"marriage was marriage, and she must make the best of it. Neal was still kind, almost fatherly, very generous, clean, and, as far as she could see, had no bad habits. . . . Certainly he made plenty of money" (p. 118). It is only her discovery of his gambling life that forces her to leave him; even that discovery she sees in a different way after the purging of her obsession with respectability (p. 256). Marriage is not magic, but another of those human relationships to be worked at and struggled with.

Joanna's and Peter's marriage is in many ways the culmination of themes and concerns in *There Is Confusion*. Both have been rid of their obsessions before marriage—Joanna has had her success and has found it hollow; Peter has gotten past his "color-conscious-ness" and hatred of whites. They have gained maturity independent of one another, have passed first passion, but are steady in the know-ledge of much-tested love. Even at that, their marriage requires radical adjustments. Joanna "surprised herself by the pleasure which came to her out of what she had always considered the ordinary things of life," and "rarely regretted leaving the stage," but "still, as her mentality was essentially creative, she found herself more and more impelled toward the expression of the intense appreciation of living which welled up within her." She sings in churches, does some concerts, makes one brief tour, but finds primary creative and intellectual activity in composition and in taking up "that most fascinating of all the sciences—harmony" (pp. 290-91). Peter, in marriage, "had to undergo a complete metamorphosis. . . . At his father's death and during his young manhood he had been absolutely without a notion of the responsibilities which the most average man expects to take upon himself" (p. 291). Though *There Is Confusion* ends in this happy marriage, the courtship of tribulations leading to it and the touch of realism in Joanna's career adjustments and Peter's adjustments to responsibility, make marraige as denouement less trifling than it can often be for fictional women characters.

Both Maggie and Joanna have faced the extra disability of their color on top of their sex. Maggie's lack of a secure family and social position, and her necessary working have subjected her to male contacts and assumptions of her sexual availability. She is in the sub-way, for example, returning home from her work with Joel Mar-shall's catering establishment when she first realizes her love for Phillip Marshall; she thinks of him; she unconsciously smiles. "A white man sitting opposite mistook the smile and leaned forward, leering a little" (p. 81). Joanna's difficulty has been more occupa-tional. In her search for dancing work, one theatrical trust manager tells her directly: " 'We'll try a colored man in a white company but we won't try a colored woman' " (p. 275). She grasps the impact of double discrimination at a party of primarily white and successful artists. She is "not much interested" in the men, for "it was women who had the real difficulties to overcome, disabilities of sex and of tradition." She recognizes that some of these successful white wo-men have overcome poverty and responsibilities, and feels "a little

ashamed" at being "so outstripped" until she discovers the "solution." "These women had not been compelled to endure her long,
heartrending struggle against color. Those who had had means had
been able to plunge immediately into the sea of preparation; they
had had their choice of teachers; as soon as they were equipped they
had been able to approach the guardians of literary and artistic
portals. . . . Sometimes she felt like a battle-scarred veteran among
these successful, happy, chattering people, who, no matter how
seriously, how deeply they took their success, yet never regarded it
with the same degree of wonder, almost of awe with which she
regarded hers" (p. 235).

Jessie Fauset's first novel is not very interesting for its form,
which contains many distracting weaknesses, but it is interesting for
its content. The intent of the book is not to push and praise the
Black middle class; that group is in fact subject to the same probing
of character and choice as is applied by Fauset to non-middle class
characters. When a careful reader overlooks weaknesses in form of
There Is Confusion and sees that the usual summation of Fauset's
intent to promote the Black middle class is in error, that reader will
make some surprising discoveries about Jessie Fauset's novel. Roles
of women are explored. American racial discrimination is exposed.
Free will is displayed. Religion and Black art are freed from conventional assumptions, not bound more tightly. Fauset's first novel is
a first discussion in American literature of several elements of American life seen from an educated Black woman's perspective. By taking
the traditional *Bildungsroman* and family novel patterns and adapt-
ing them to study the peculiar confusion, learning, and ultimate
understanding of American Blacks, Fauset has revealed insight into
the human experience.

As though disturbed by those who mis-read into *There Is
Confusion* the limited and erroneous idea that her purpose was to
promote the Black middle class, Jessie Fauset subtitles her 1929
novel, *Plum Bun*, "A Novel Without a Moral," inviting readers to
sample story and characters without assuming behind them a scold-
ing, prescriptive schoolteacher. The improved formal characteristics
of the second book aid in the intent to clarify theme. Fauset corrects
the most glaring weaknesses of her first novel by narrowing the

number of important characters to one, with the variety of other
characters, Black and white, seen through the maturing perspective
of this controlling character, Angela Murray, and by making time
span and time transitions in *Plum Bun* shorter and smoother than
they were in *There Is Confusion*. Angela's parents' life stories are
told but briefly, and her early youth, with its sources of her later
rebellion and eventual return, is told of efficiently and effectively in
several scenes and events at the beginning of the novel. But Fauset
also goes beyond mere elimination of faulty style in *Plum Bun* to
some positive formal strengths. The external world is described in
more detail in *Plum Bun* than it is in *There Is Confusion*, and is used
with plot to reveal change in Angela's perception. Figurative language
is both more original and more devised for particular ends in the
second book. Finally, the nursery rhyme for formal division and the
fairy tale motifs for coherence are subtly and meaningfully used.

Change in themes between the two novels is made in emphasis,
not idea. The Murray family is not as well-situated financially as were
the Marshalls of *There Is Confusion*, so that the theme of the importance of family, of roots, of enduring relationships, is more carefully made separate from the social and economic class of the characters. Middle-class Negroes and "highbrows" both come in for some
criticism in *Plum Bun*, as in the previous novel. The exposure of
American racial discrimination continues in the second book, but
gathers around the peculiar ironies of discrimination against the
"Black" who by all appearances is white. Again, as in *There Is
Confusion*, emphasis is not on documenting discrimination, however,
but on the various ways characters develop for dealing with their
historical, biological, psychological, and economic realities. In
Plum Bun the psychology of Angela Murray as a light-skinned mulatto who decides to "pass" is fully explored—sources for her actions
in her early life, her decision to pass, what she learns thereby, her
decision to reveal her racial background, the results of the revelation. "Life is a corrective" in both books. In *Plum Bun*, however,
concentration on the growing character of Angela makes a *Bildungsroman* in which this theme is less simple, and more fully developed.

As in *There Is Confusion*, among secondary themes religion in
Plum Bun is shown as of varying meaning and comfort to various

characters at various times, without overt judgement by Fauset as to the "truth" or "goodness" of any one view. Angela herself is as little affected by religious belief as if it did not exist in her youthful or maturing world. In showing again implicitly that Black art is best based partly on Black folk materials, Fauset makes Angela the painter do her best work with portraits of Hettie Daniels, an old Black servant, and "Fourteenth Street types," whom she observes upon her arrival in New York. Finally, in centering on Angela Murray, Fauset explores more fully in *Plum Bun* than she did with the variety of male and female characters in *There Is Confusion,* the limiting roles and habits of women, as well as some cracking of the roles. Exemplification of some of these themes as they are portrayed in *Plum Bun* will be made together with the following emphasis on positive formal characteristics in the book.

Angela Murray's perception dominates *Plum Bun* from first to last. The settings in the external world are described at each point in the book as they are seen from Angela's current mental state. The opening description of Philadelphia's Opal Street, "no jewel of the first water. . .; merely an imitation," with its lack of allure or mystery or sparkle or pretention, is Opal Street as seen by "the restless despair of youth," embodied in young Angela. She has "no high purpose in life," except "to know light, pleasure, gaiety and freedom."[18] Her vision of the street is not at all that of her parents, to whom their little house on Opal Street understandably "represented the *ne plus ultra* of ambition" (p. 12), after their pre-marriage poor and homeless years of service as coachman and maid. Nor does Angela's view agree with that of her younger sister Virginia, whose innocence, seeming helplessness and devotion to teaching are signs of her simple, home-loving nature.

But the house on Opal Street, to that part of Angela Murray looking to the possibilities in the future life, is seen as small, confining, restrictive. It contains "six boxes called by courtesy, rooms—a 'parlour,' a midget of a dining room, a larger kitchen and, above, a front bedroom seemingly large only because it extends for the full width of the house, a mere shadow of a bathroom, and another back bedroom with windows whose possibilities are spoiled by their outlook on sad and diminutive back-yards" (p. 11). Angela envisions entrapment in the setting—of chains made "by duty, by poverty, by weakness or by colour" (p. 13). With the aim of her life being happiness and freedom, Angela is determined to find, instead of cramped Opal Street, "paths which lead to broad thoroughfares, large bright houses, delicate niceties of existence" (p. 12).

Virginia's unsophisticated insight into what makes a home serves as foil to her sister Angela's vision of material happiness. In this small house on the narrow street, Virginia finds "golden sanctity" and "sweet glory" in the household events of a Sunday—making breakfast muffins, church preparation, hymn singing. "Father, mother and children, well-dressed, well-fed, united, going to church on a beautiful Sunday morning; there was an immense cosmic rightness about all this which she sensed rather than realized. She envied no one the incident of finer clothes or a larger home; this unity was the core of happiness. . . . When she grew up she meant to live the same kind of life; she would marry a man exactly like her father and she would conduct her home exactly as did her mother" (p. 22). In this twelve-year-old sense of the rightness of things, culminated in a final hymn sing in the parlor, Virginia predicts the transformation of Angela which is the plot of *Plum Bun*. "They would always be together, her father and mother and she and Angela; . . . there were her parents, arm in arm, and she and—but tonight and other nights she could not see Angela. . . . And then quite suddenly Angela was there again, but a different Angela, not quite the same as in the beginning of the picture" (p. 26).

Philadelphia, Pennsylvania, through which city the diminutive Opal Street threads, is only a larger confinement to Angela. Teenage and young adult conversations in a Murray house bursting with Angela's and Virginia's friends move frequently to the lack of opportunity in the city. And when Angela thinks during her New York sojourn of the possibility of having to return to Philadelphia to live in order to be once again near Virginia, her recall of confinement is intense: "But Philadelphia with its traditions of liberty and its actual economic and social slavery, its iniquitous school system, its prejudiced theatres, its limited offering of occupation! A great, searing hatred arose in her for the huge, slumbering leviathan of a city which had hardly moved a muscle in the last fifty years" (p. 263).

After the death of Virginia's and Angela's parents, and Angela's decisions to sell her half of their house inheritance, to leave Opal Street, Philadelphia, and to "pass" in New York City, she thrills to the new expansiveness she feels just sitting on Fourteenth Street in the new, larger city. "Fourteenth Street is a river, impersonally flowing, broad-bosomed, with strange and devious craft covering its expanse. . . . Fourteenth Street was the rendezvous of life itself" (p. 87). Living but temporarily on "the crest of a wave of excitement and satisfaction which," she thought, "would never wane, never break, never be spent," she was "getting acquainted with life in her own way without restrictions or restraint; she was young, she was temporarily independent, she was intelligent, she was white" (pp. 87-88).

Angela sees the wreckage of other lives' crafts all around her, but her identity with these wrecks when she arrives in New York is purely objective from her viewpoint at the top of the crest. "It was Spring, and the Square was full of rusty specimens of mankind who sat on the benches, as did Angela herself, for hours at a stretch, as though they thought the invigorating air and the mellow sun would work some magical burgeoning on their garments such as was worked on the trees. . . . 'I am seeing life,' thought Angela, 'this is the way people live.' . . . 'A great picture!' she thought. 'I'll make a great picture of these people some day' " (p. 89).

Fauset quietly reminds the reader that Angela must be looked at as she looks at these "types," that no frail human vessel rides the crest for long, that the longer the journey seeking adventure or seeking treasure or seeking harbor, the more the furrows that must be also navigated. As the reader sees Fourteenth Street of New York City through Angela's recently-arrived perception, Fauset probes the psychology of temporary surety. "She was at once almost irreconcilably too concentrated and too objective. Her living during these days was so intense, so almost solidified, as though her desire to live as she did and she herself were so one and the same thing that it would have been practically impossible for another onlooker like herself to insert the point of his discrimination into her firm panoply of satisfaction" (p. 90).

Angela's first visit to Harlem, close after her arrival in New

York, allows the reader again to see something of her naivete and her uninitiated youth in the objective, impersonal, uninvolved interest she reflects.

> Unquestionably there was something very fascinating, even terrible, about this stream of life,—it seemed to her to run thicker, more turgidly than that safe, sublimated existence in which her new friends had their being. It was deeper, more mightily moving even than the torrent of Fourteenth Street. Undoubtedly just as these people,—for she already saw them objectively, doubly so, once with her natural remoteness and once with the remoteness of her new estate,—just as these people could suffer more than others, just so they could enjoy themselves more (p. 97).

At a later Harlem lecture by Dr. Van Meier, a thinly disguised W. E. B. DuBois, Angela's picture of the people around her reveals her distance and lack of similar suffering by its being expressed in terms of art objects. "Here and there a sprinkling of white faces showed up plainly, startlingly distinct patterns against a back-ground of patient, softly stolid black faces; faces beaten and fashioned by life into a mold of steady, rock-like endurance, of unshakable, un-conquered faith. . . . Angela saw a man, bronze, not very tall but built with a beautiful symmetrical completeness, cross the platform and sit in the tall, deep chair next to the table of the presiding officer. He sat with a curious immobility, gazing straight before him like a statue of an East Indian idol" (p. 219).

The months and years go by and Angela changes. She first tries to trap the rich white Roger Fielding into marriage, and then falls prey to her own sexuality and against her will begins an affair with him. During the affair she tries to make the best of her disap-pointment in his conventional male behaviour, but Roger reads her efforts as a further attempt to entrap. Finally she makes a life with-out him, refusing even his resulting offer of marriage. During these events, her longings for wealth, for adventure, for gaiety are replaced by longings for roots, for enduring friendships, for doing better art work. Those changes are shown partly in her later, revised, more sensitive views of Fourteenth Street and Harlem.

> New York, it appeared, had two visages. It could offer an aspect radiant

with promise or a countenance lowering and forbidding. With its flattering possibilities it could elevate to the seventh heaven, or lower to the depths of hell with its crushing negations. And loneliness! Loneliness such as that offered by the great, noisy city could never be imagined. To realize it one would have to experience it. . . . She remembered the people in Union Square on whom she had spied so blithely when she had first come to New York. Then she had thought of them as being "down and out," mere idlers, good for nothing. It had not occurred to her that their chief disaster might be loneliness. Her office was on Twenty-third Street and often at the noon-hour she walked down to the dingy Square and looked again on the sprawling, half-recumbent, dejected figures. And between them and herself she was able to detect a terrifying relationship (pp. 241-42).

Even behind the elegant fronts New York presents, Angela now finds lurking the horrors of homelessness, negation, loneliness, confinement.

The street, like many others in New York, possessed the pseudo elegance and impressiveness which comes from an equipment of brown stone houses with their massive fronts, their ostentatious regularity and simplicity, but a second glance revealed its down-at-heel condition; gaping windows disclosed the pitiful smallness of the rooms that crouched behind the pretentious outsides. There was something faintly humorous, ironical, about being cooped up in these deceptive palaces; according to one's temperament one might laugh or weep at the thought of how these structures, the product of human energy could yet cramp, imprison, even ruin the very activity which had created them (pp. 278-79).

It is appropriate that Angela finds her way back to Opal Street in Philadelphia before the novel's culmination. Just prior to her trip to France, where she goes to paint, she spends a day travelling back to find not the house she left but the essence of home that she had not recognized in her parents' or Virginia's lives because she had not felt the need for it in her own. The house, as she approaches it, is still tiny, yet "how full of secrets, of knowledge, of joy, of despair, suffering, futility. . . . Presently she went up and put her hand on the red brick, wondering blindly if in some way the insensate thing might not communicate with her through touch" (p. 364). You can't go home again, of course, and Angela is rudely made to acknowledge that fact of life when the current occupant of the little Opal Street house chases her away, slams the door, and pulls the blinds, muttering "poor white trash" (p. 365). But Matthew Henson, an old friend, still lives nearby; he sees her and asks her in to his comparable house "across the way." "They ate the meal in the little dark cool dining room . . . but somehow its smallness was no longer irksome; rather it seemed a tiny island of protection reared out of and against an encroaching sea of troubles." Angela voices her thought and the changed vision of life which frames the book. " 'I was thinking what a little haven a house like this could be, what it must have meant to my mother. Funny how I almost pounded down the walls once upon a time trying to get away. Now I can't think of anything more marvellous than having such a place as this, here, there, anywhere, to return to' " (p. 368).

Angela goes back to Opal Street near the end of *Plum Bun*, and Opal Street has changed because she has changed, but Angela Murray doesn't settle down in a little loving house with a loving husband even with the touches of realistic adjustment to marriage, children and home that are seen in *There Is Confusion*. Angela's mature understanding of life and living, of pain, of commitment, of responsibility, and of joy does not depend on setting, on material goods, or on conventional culminations. She is reunited with Anthony Cross, whose commitment to Virginia had made Angela believe him lost to herself, on Christmas Day in Paris. The tear-jerking ending, however, is somewhat deceptive, for Angela's resolutions have come previously and on her own, in her own way. She is doing fine without Anthony; having him is simply an added joy—a plum in the bun, so to speak, a bit of frosting on the staff of life.

Careless selectivity in citing passages from *Plum Bun*, and failure by readers in discerning the dominant and changing perception of Angela Murray as the control over point of view in the novel, have led to misreading. There has, simply, been too little faith in Fauset's stylistic and formal sophistication. Most commonly, the book is summarized, as by Hugh Gloster and Arthur Davis, as dealing principally or almost entirely with the "passing" theme.[19] Davis reveals some of his misunderstanding of form in *Plum Bun*, by adding that Fauset's depiction of "Greenwich Village and of Harlem are severely limited and fail to do justice to life in either section."

Angela, he says, is a "puppet" rather than "a personality,"[20] and one can understand this conclusion when one sees Davis failing to see that everything in the book is Angela—that Greenwich Village and Harlem are not objective realities in *Plum Bun*, but Angela Murray's perceptions, and thereby the reader's map of Angela Murray's thought and feeling and changing views.

The wide setting for Angela's activity—Philadelphia, New York, Philadelphia again—in the way it is used by Fauset to show Angela's state of mind, is supplemented throughout *Plum Bun* by a use of small external detail to reveal inner states, a device unfortunately not fully exploited in the earlier *There Is Confusion*. In one instance of such reverberating use of the small detail, Fauset shows Angela invited to the apartment of a fellow art student, Paulette Lister, soon after her arrival in New York. Paulette's dinner conversation and apartment reveal a not unadmirable self-defined personal feminist, but only after the reader is given a quick glimpse of how radically new this life and this kind of free thought is to the previously protected Angela. " 'Perhaps you'd like to wash your hands?' called Paulette. 'There's a bathroom down the corridor there, you can't miss it. You may have some of my favorite lotion if you want .it—up there on the shelf.' Angela washed her hands and looked up for the lotion. Her eyes opened wide in amazement. Beside the bottle stood a man's shaving mug and brush and a case of razors" (p. 104). Detail of clothing is also used more obviously to reveal something beyond the clothing than was such detail in *There Is Confusion*. For example, the sexual passion which Angela hopes to induce in Roger Fielding on their first date, but which ultimately burns out of control in herself as well, is nicely suggested in her choice of dress for the evening. "Her dress was flame-colour . . . of a plain, rather heavy beautiful glowing silk. The neck was high in back and girlishly modest in front. . . . Thus she gave the effect of a flame herself; intense and opaque at the heart where her dress gleamed and shone, transparent and fragile where her white warm neck and face rose into the tenuous shadow of her hair. Her appearance excited herself" (p. 123).

Even in small physical gestures, Fauset in *Plum Bun* makes description of the external count for what it reveals beyond itself.

When Roger suspects and resents Angela's attempt to keep their affair one of devotion to one another, and then destroys her wish to end it smoothly and politely, she evaluates this finished experience of her life. "The departure of Roger himself—she shut her hand and opened it—meant nothing" (p. 234). In the shut and opened hand are held Angela's understanding of her affair, and by her own extension, understanding of men's attempted use of women through the ages. " 'You knew perfectly well what you were letting yourself in for.' The phrase had the quality of a cosmic echo; perhaps men had been saying it to women since the beginning of time. Doubtless their biblical equivalent were the last words uttered by Abraham to Hagar before she fared forth into the wilderness." "But she had grown too much into the habit of deliberately ordering her life . . . to let herself be sickened, utterly prostrated by what had befallen her. Roger, her companion, had gone. . . . Thank God she had taken nothing from Roger; she had not sold herself, only bestowed that self foolishly, unworthily" (pp. 233, 235). There are no moral condemnations, no morbid guilt feelings; only new understanding of human relationships, confining sex roles. "She shut her hand and opened it."

Fauset makes repeated and competent use of various conventional images in *Plum Bun*—light and dark, cold and warmth, the revolving seasons of the year, the sea. Figurative language is more widely and originally used in this second novel than it was in her first. One less conventional image pattern used figuratively in the novel to reinforce plot and theme involves chance and gamesmanship.

In her youth, Angela Murray sees her life as determined by chance. Biological accident gives Angela her mother's light skin, Virginia her father's dark complexion. Chance, again, gives the two light-skinned Murrays recreational preference for shopping and having tea out in the fanciest of Philadelphia's stores and hotels and the two dark-skinned Murrays a preference for adventuring in the narrow streets of old Philadelphia. Chance plus a bit of innocent negligence on the part of the mother, Mattie Murray, leads the young Angela to the conclusion that "the great rewards of life—riches, glamour, pleasure—are for white-skinned people only" (p. 17).

Youthful Angela and her mother standing in the portico of the Walton Hotel after an afternoon of browsing in exclusive shops, suddenly see Junius Murray and his daugher Virginia pass by in the Saturday throng. The mother makes no attempt to stop them. Angela "saw her mother's face change—with trepidation she thought. She remarked: 'It's a good thing Papa didn't see us, you'd have had to speak to him, wouldn't you?' But her mother, giving her a distracted glance, made no reply" (p. 18).

Angela does not hear her mother's later confession to Junius, her " 'I don't believe I'll ever let myself be quite as silly as that again' " (p. 19). Nor does she recognize in her youth that her mother "plays" white only when no principle or harm to others is involved. Even Mattie's unhesitating fall into her dark husband's arms after he has been called to the white hospital where she has been taken ill from the street does not change Angela's picture of how to be happy. "Certain fortuitous endowments, great physical beauty, unusual strength, a certain unswerving singleness of mind,—gifts bestowed quite blindly and disproportionately by the forces which control life,—these were the qualities which contributed toward a glowing and pleasant existence" (p. 12). Angela's story in *Plum Bun* is the overcoming of the mistaken early belief that happiness is riches and comfort and pleasure—"freedom"—and that "duty, poverty . . . weakness or . . . color" are the chance chains of entrapment that keep one from that happiness.

Chance can of course work against one as easily as for one. Angela finds that even when she is free, white, and twenty-one, life does not give her unmitigated joy and comfort. In her bad moments she imagines and then begins to work on a painting of life as vicious chance. She sketches "a mass of lightly indicated figures passing apparently in review before the tall, cloaked form of a woman, thin to emaciation, her hands on her bony hips, slightly bent forward, laughing uproariously yet with a certain chilling malevolence" (p. 282). The figure in Angela's imagination and growing on her canvas laughs most heartily when the late-discovered love of Angela and Anthony Cross is frustrated by an entanglement of problems stemming from their both having "passed," and from Angela's having cut her sister to avoid discovery of that passing. " 'God!' " Anthony says, raising his arms and "beating the void like a madman. 'You in your foolishness, I in my carelessness . . . and life sitting back laughing, splitting her sides at the joke of it' " (p. 300). As Angela leaves Anthony's room, the painting seems to come to life in the form of Anthony's roommate, Sanchez. "Halfway down the black staircase she met the heedless Sanchez, tall, sallow, thin, glancing at her curiously with a slightly amused smile. . . . Something in his attitude made her think of her unfinished sketch of life. Hysterical, beside herself, she rushed down the remaining steps afraid to look around lest she should see the thin dark figure in pursuit, lest her ears should catch the expansion of that faint smile into a guffaw, uproarious, menacing" (p. 308).

Angela comes near enough to understand, but never submits to, the "blind passivity" of absolute religious faith or "an acceptance of things as they are," both stemming, she believes, from beaten and harried submission of the self to chance. "She would never be able to understand a force which gave one the imagination to point a great desire, the tenacity to cling to it, the emotionalism to spend on its possible relaization but which would then with a careless sweep of the hand wipe out the picture which the creature of its own endowment had created" (p. 311). In fact Angela matures beyond the simplistic attributing of good or evil to chance by the conclusion of *Plum Bun*. Images of chance are replaced by summations of her new understanding of herself, her new independence, and of her growing artistic discipline.

Closely allied to images of chance in the novel are images of gamesmanship, verging on war, centering appropriately on men's and women's roles. Chance gives a woman the weapons of pale skin or beauty or nerve, the immature Angela believes, but knowing how to play the game determines the size of one's winnings. She envisages the game, her chances, the rewards when she arrives in New York. With power of the "certain kind" belonging to women, she would establish a salon where "real, alive, free and untrammeled people" would "come and pour themselves out to her sympathy and magnetism." But to do this, she would need money, influence, even protection. "Perhaps it would be better to marry . . . a white man. . . . She knew that men had a better time of it than women, coloured men than coloured women, white men than white women. . . . It would be fun, great fun to capture power and protection in addition to the freedom and independence which she had so long coveted and which now lay in her hand" (pp. 88-89). To Angela at this stage of the game, race is "a handicap which if guessed at would have been disabling as a game leg or an atrophied body," yet "she had dared enter the lists" (p. 209). Leaving Virginia, even denying her when necessary, going after Roger for his wealth, these Angela sees now as courageous. The fine line between courage and stupidity, between determination to win and disregard for the welfare of oneself and others is as difficult to discern in life as in the fanaticism of sport or battle.

Angela's mother has taught her no rules for the contest she is about to enter, since Mattie Murray was one of the "blessed among women," permitted to be her "normal self" in not "having to play a game" (p. 147). So Angela goes to Martha Burden, one of her new artist friends, with a direct question: " 'How do you get a proposal from the ones you want,—the,—the interesting ones?' " Martha's rules are not unusual; it is just unusual to see them spelled out so explicitly. First, the women must always appear to like the man less than he likes her, whether so or not. Second, she must make him want her. Third, she musn't "give." With a "febrile light" in her eyes, Martha expounds. " 'It is a game, and the hardest game in the world for a woman, but the most fascinating; the hardest in which to strike a happy medium. You see, you have to be careful not to withhold too much and yet to give very little. If we don't give enough we lose them. If we give too much we lose ourselves' " (p. 146).

Entering fully into a game or a war means replacing the laws of living with the rules of battle. Conventional morality, childhood teaching are conveniently set aside for the duration. Angela's early training begins to have for her not the impact of truth, but the usefulness of practicality as she fights for marriage to Roger, while he insists on a "love-nest." "Finally her attitude reduced itself to this: she would have none of the relationship which Roger urged so insistently, not because according to all the training she had ever received, it was unlawful, but because viewed in the light of the great battle she was waging for pleasure, protection, power, it was inexpedient" (p. 201).

Inexpedient though it be, Angela submits to Roger Fielding one dark and rainy night in the coziness of her apartment in an ellipsis on page 204 of *Plum Bun*. Once at this stage, the game takes on new rules. The center of her life must be Roger. "For a while his wishes, his pleasure were the end and aim of her existence; she told herself with a slight tendency toward self-mockery that this was the explanation of being, of her being; that men had other aims, other uses but that the sole excuse for being a woman was to be just that,—a woman" (p. 205). Choice becomes dependence. "For the first time in her knowledge, her whole life was hinging on the words, the moods, the actions of someone else" (p. 213). And when she no longer feels "the old, heady desire to feel herself completely his, to claim him as completely hers," when he has "lost his charm for her" (p. 225), she blames herself and tries to make the best of it. "Because of this mingling of shame and reproach she found herself consciously striving to keep their relations on the highest plane possible in the circumstances" (p. 226). Now consciously making work of devoting herself to Roger, Angela runs up against "unexpected barriers"—Roger resents the "possessing interest. He wanted no claims upon him, he acknowledged none." Again Angela concludes that "in some way she must be at fault," and she tries harder (p. 228).

It is over a small, inadvertent revelation of Roger's limited notions of sex roles that the break-up of the affair comes. Angela has called Roger's home, leaving messages with a servant when Roger is "not at home." Roger explodes. " 'I can't have women calling me up all hours of the day, making me ridiculous in the eyes of my servants.' " Surprised, bewildered, Angela replies reasonably, " 'But you call me whenever you feel like it.' " " 'Of course I do, that's different. I'm a man' " (p. 230). Angela, as has been seen, is unfamiliar with sex roles governing courtship, but has learned by rote Martha Burden's rules for getting the right proposal, and has acted on them. In her affair she has returned to developing her own instinctive rules—rules which fall into a conventional female pattern of early dependence, later disillusionment and resulting self-blame. The small issue of telephone protocol allows her to consciously recognize the primacy of her own feelings and belief over the benefits of following rules and tactics of playing an eternal game for the slight return of possible economic security. "The conversation about the telephone left an effect all out of proportion to its actual importance; it represented for her the apparently unbridgeable difference between the sexes; everything was for men, but even the slightest privilege was to be denied to a woman unless the man chose to grant it. At least there were men who felt like that; not all men, she felt sure, could tolerate such an obviously unjust status" (p. 231).

In refusing an apartment and money from Roger, Angela has maintained enough independence to free her from him now. The game and battle imagery which threads through the portion of *Plum Bun* leading up to the affair, but which disappears while Angela is discovering her own rules in the relationship, reappears briefly in her reordering of her life, her rejection of games. "She was sick of men and their babyish, faithless ways, she did not care enough for Roger to play a game for him" (p. 232). When Roger, thinking she is "playing" hard-to-get, later predictably returns, this time with an offer of marriage, he discovers her new determination. " 'I'd never be able to trust you again and I'm sick of secrets and playing games with human relationships. I'm going to take my friendships straight hereafter' " (p. 324). Her recognition and rejection of thorough-going sex-role games has increased Angela's understanding of herself, of men, and of marriage. "Her sum total of the knowledge of life had been increased; she saw men with a different eye, was able to differentiate between the half dozen young men in her office (p. 247). Angela's "true" differences substitute for society's false ones. One of the signs that Anthony Cross is the man for her is that he is not upset by her departing from social convention to visit him at his apartment, and by her showing him her affection and love.

Looking carefully at game and battle imagery in *Plum Bun* helps expose some of the rather skillfully disguised feminist critique of male and female roles operating in the book. When one turns more specifically to the disguise itself, one finds that Fauset has placed the heaviest concealment in her formal use of nursery rhyme and fairy tale; indeed, the disguise is perhaps too heavy, for it has been heretofore essentially unpenetrated by critics of the novel. Early reviews which held much praise of the book yet objected to the coincidence of the plot. The *New Republic* reviewer (10 April 1929) praised the subject matter and the "convincing, sympathetic" character of Angela—her desires, her negative deceptions, her *carpe diem* philosophy—but deplored the "melodramatic, unreal" story line. The *New York Times* review shows understanding of the dominant point of view of Angela: " 'Plum Bun' is told from the inside looking out, with a simple fidelity to character which has nothing to do with race or creed or color. . . . Her people are individuals first and members of an oppressed race afterward." But this primarily positive review makes brief negative assessment of plot: "Even if there had been a moral it could hardly have survived the highly coincidental character of the story's solution."[21] The *Saturday Review* (6 April 1929) finds that the "twisting, decidedly miraculous course of the plot, the sentimentality," obscure the strengths of book, which lie in its comparison of the white and Negro races.

Helpful in leading a reader to an understanding of what Jessie Fauset was apparently trying to accomplish with the plot line of *Plum Bun* is an article by Francis Gaines written in 1926, three years before the novel, in the *South Atlantic Quarterly*. Gaines points out that American literary romance frequently substitutes for the social gradation lacking in American life a racial difference for the "general tragedy of caste." The romance thus becomes "a literature which essays dramatization of one of the most delicate and most dogged of our social problems." "Fundamentally. . . . American romances are interested in the racial bar sinister as it thwarts the course of true love."

Gaines describes and cites examples of American literary solutions to the racial bar to romance, including failure of the romance to materialize; fleeing of the American environment, as in William Dean Howell's *An Imperative Duty*; sudden death, marriage and slow horror, as in Kate Chopin's "Désirée's Baby." But the most common solution, the most popular plot, Gaines says, "is the device by which the author extends complications into the very nadir of hopelessness and then effects a swift denouement by revealing that the assumption is false, the identification does not exist."[22] Jessie Fauset clearly satirizes this customary romantic plot line in *Plum Bun*.

The Epigraph of *There Is Confusion* is from Tennyson; that of *Plum Bun* is the nursery rhyme: To market, to market

To buy a Plum Bun;
Home again, Home again,
Market is done.

The pattern of the romance as Nathaniel Hawthorne developed it in *The House of the Seven Gables*, departure and return, or isolation to communion, is thus put into child's verse. In his Preface to that romance, Hawthorne described his perceived latitudes and limits. The romance, "while it sins unpardonably, so far as it may swerve aside from the truth of the human heart—has fairly a right to present that truth under circumstances, to a great extent, of the writer's own choosing or creation."[23]

By adopting the freedoms of the American romance for formal structure, Fauset is able to accomplish a whole series of aims in *Plum Bun*. Her potential unsophisticated audience, with whom she had undoubtedly become very familiar in her editing work, could be entertained and intrigued by the complications of the plot, while sophisticated literary critics would perceive and enjoy the intentional satire of romantic racial theme. Racial and sexual questions could be turned on their heads to inspire new insight into stereotypical assumptions, without the author being accused of writing "only" as a Black or as a woman or as a middle class promoter. American assumptions about American liberties and American wealth could be examined quietly from an uncustomary view, without the author being accused of preaching or moralizing. The problem was, and has remained, that Fauset's readers have not perceived the intent through the disguise, have not for the most part assumed conscious formal structure on Fauset's part. More recent summations of Fauset's novels thus concur with the early reviews in assessing plot and overall form. David Littlejohn dismisses all her "vapidly genteel lace-curtain romances" as not rising "above the stuffy, tiny-minded circulating-library norm"[24] and Robert Bone finds that "in spite of an admirable persistence, her novels are uniformly sophomoric, trivial, and dull."[25] Picking out the elements of nursery-rhyme form, and fairy-tale motif will hopefully aid in a more accurate and just reading of Fauset's intent and accomplishment in *Plum Bun*.

The poem "To Market, to Market" is used to divide *Plum Bun* into five sections. The first section of six chapters, "Home," describes the Murray family life, Opal Street and Philadelphia, the death of the parents, and Angela's decision to leave town and to "pass." The seven chapters of the second section, "Market," open with Angela's arrival in New York, and conclude with Virginia's arrival there. "Plum Bun," the third section, is devoted to Angela's affair with Roger Fielding. The five chapters of this center section are introduced by the only chapter in the book which breaks up a regular chronological plot line. The narration of Roger's love-nest proposition is delayed and told in flash-back as the opening portion of "Plum Bun." "Home Again," the fourth section, consisting of six chapters, is the longest section of the book, and is spent exploring Angela's attempts to establish meaningful and lasting relationships with carefully evaluated men and women in her life. Finally, "Market is Done," the shortest section, made up of three chapters, includes Angela's winning of the painting prize of the trip to France, her unplanned revelation of her race mixture made in response to reporters' badgering of the Black Miss Powell, and her final Paris reunion with Anthony Cross.

"Home" in *Plum Bun* is thus first of all childhood and parents' love, and when those are gone, is full acceptance and understanding of one's separate identity before one's full communion with others. The Market is the mistaken dream—wealth if one is poor; white if one is Black. The Plum Bun is the center of irony and discovery. To a poor Black woman, American culture says the Plum Bun is to marry a rich white man. But the bun is stale, Angela discovers; Roger's sexist and racist stereotypes fail to nourish love. The plum is like a poison apple—eat it, fall asleep, lose your identity. Market is done when courageous self-definition is made precisely against society's false values of race, sex, and wealth.

The movement from Home to Market and back to Home newly understood and defined in *Plum Bun* is corroborated by the fairy tale motif, which moves from illusion to reality. The story opens tale-style. "In one of these houses dwelt a father, a mother, and two daughters" (p. 11). In the second section of the book, when Angela first samples the market wares of white wealth in New York City,

"she [sees] her life rounding out like a fairy tale. Poor, coloured—
coloured in America; unknown, a nobody! And here at her hand was
the forward thrust shadow of love and great wealth" (p. 132). Dining out with Roger Fielding, Angela tells him that the food odor is
really "aroma," the mineral water "nectar," and the food "ambro-
sia" or "viands." Even when her dream world is cracked by Roger's
sudden rush to another table to "put a spoke in the wheel of those
"coons"! . . . Coming in here spoiling white people's appetites' "
(p. 134), Angela responds with "triumph" at her exemption from
mortal law. "Life would never cheat her as it had cheated that colored girl this evening. . . . She was free, free to taste life in all its full-
ness and sweetness" (p. 137). Angela sees the setting for her fairy
tale life in fairy tale terms. The Arch of Fifth Avenue in Springtime
New York seems to her "a gateway to paradise"; pots of gold
"doubtless" gleam at the ends of New York's long deep streets; and
"on the short crosswise streets the April sun stream[s] in splendid
banners of deep golden light" (p. 139). Her determination not to
see Roger again after the racial incident in the restaurant is weakened by Cinderella-like contrasting notions of happiness. "She
thought of the little, dark, shabby house, of the made-over dresses
and turned coats. And then she saw Roger and his wealth and his
golden recklessness, his golden keys which could open the doors to
beauty and ease and—decency!" (p. 143).

The "Plum Bun" section brings not Angela's ideas of beauty,
ease and decency, but Roger's offer couched in "cheap current"
phrases. " 'I'm asking you to live in my house, to live for me; to be
my girl; to keep a love-nest where I and only I may come.' " "So
this was her castle, her fortress of protection, her refuge," Angela
thinks in shock (p. 184). If only there were a fairy tale solution;
"if only she could be a girl in a book and when he finally did ask for
her hand, she would be able to tell him that she was going to marry
someone else, someone twice as eligible, twice as handsome, twice
as wealthy" (p. 185). Even when Angela enters into the affair, it is
her tale-dominated picture of life that determines her expectations.
"Of all possible *affaires du coeur* this must in semblance, at any rate,
be the ultimate desideratum, the finest flower of chivalry and devotion" (p. 227). By the end of the "Plum Bun" section, by the end of
the affair, Angela's illusions are dispelled. Gone are the days when

"she dreamed that she alone of all people in the world was exempt from ordinary law" (p. 234). "The radiance which had so bathed every moment of her existence was fading gently, inexorably into the 'light of common day' " (p. 238).

The fairy tale motif largely and appropriately disappears in the final two sections of *Plum Bun*, where Angela is working out her own life and its relation to others on real, honest, permanent bases. The romantic story line is retained, with, however, the twist of subtle satire. Race as the "bar sinister" to American romance has traditionally of course used realization of color to mean horror, danger, defeat, flight. In *Plum Bun* it is the revelation of color in Anthony Cross and in Angela, who have been passing without one another's knowledge, that makes their American romance possible. The twists go further, becoming a veritable tornado of destruction and rebuilding. Anthony's father was killed by a Southern white mob after his white South American wife repelled a white would-be lover, the reasoning being that any Black man who didn't teach his wife her proper position in relation to a white man deserved death. Anthony understandably has resolved to never love or marry a white person. Less understandably, Anthony's widowed mother has refused to have anything to do with Black men. " 'She believes that we, particularly the dark ones, are cursed, otherwise why should we be so abused, so hounded' " (p. 292). In this psychology Anthony's mother resembles the narrator of James Weldon Johnson's 1912 *Autobiography of an Ex-Coloured Man*, who goes white forever after witnessing a lynching, full of "shame at being identified with a people that would with impunity be treated worse than animals."[26] If America wants to see how race gets in the way of love, Fauset seems to say, I'll show more of the warped and twisted human relationships than any white romancer ever suspected.

Superficially, resolution in the plot of *Plum Bun* is "miraculous" and "coincidental" and "melodramatic." But under this surface story line, Fauset re-emphasizes her themes. Virginia has accidentally wandered into Anthony's room the night of her arrival in New York, and her eventual engagement to him is the strongest barrier to Angela's and Anthony's love. Coincidence, yes, but Virginia is wandering precisely because Angela had in the afternoon put being white before being sister. Each sister finds the man loved at the end of the book—Virginia has Matthew Henson, her first choice; Angela has Anthony. Miraculous and melodramatic maybe, but as has already been seen, this happiness for Angela comes only out of her independent development of identity. Fauset takes liberty with her story line, as does the Hawthorne romance, but she also remains true to the truth of the human heart.

Plum Bun is Jessie Fauset's most successful and least understood novel. It is not, as superficial readers have jumped to conclude, a novel about "passing." Rather, it is a carefully constructed Black American *Bildungsroman* in which racial difference is used for the societal barrier perceived by the growing character as first absolute and finally as a false distinction of value to be overcome, ignored, and replaced.[27] In American society, where class does not loom as the unalterable state which is reasonably imposed upon the character of a British novel, unchangeable skin color and the American discrimination which surrounds it are an ingenious and penetrating substitution.

Fauset not only uses the *Bildungsroman* pattern, substituting race for class, but she also makes use of the freedoms of the American romance in order to tell a story with appeal for unsophisticated audiences, and perhaps also in order to indulge her own confessed attraction to the romantic and the sentimental. While she uses the plot freedom of the romance, however, she satirizes traditionally romantic assumption in American literature, particularly in regard to race and sex.

Black blood is customarily a "bar sinister" to American romance. Angela Murray sees it in just that way at the beginning of *Plum Bun*; her romantic ideal of adventure and love points directly toward being white and marrying white as well as rich. The Prince of her false ideals is rich, white Roger Fielding. While she believes in the American fairy-tale romance, marriage with Roger eludes her. It is only when skin color, money, and marriage are seen by Angela in a true transformed light that Roger arrives at her door with his marriage offer; he is, of course, no longer a Prince to Angela, for he represents none of her new and true ideals.

Angela's real Prince, the person who fits her mature and self-developed ideals, is Anthony Cross. Throughout *Plum Bun* Cross lingers in the background under a triple disguise—he is poor, he is Black, but he looks white. The novel concludes romantically with Angela and Anthony united, but importantly, that uniting with a single other loved person is not Angela's goal or the author's goal. Angela has by the end of the book found several people whose balanced value systems coincide with her own evolved morality. These are the people who see her off for France after the revelation of her race has been made, the people who have passed the crucial test of seeing beyond the racial bar. The formation of this select group has also meant that total identification with one person by marriage is no longer a primary need for Angela. Racial and sexual and monetary conventions and rules and deceits were the bonds that bound young Angela Murray. During the course of *Plum Bun* they unobtrusively disintegrate to be replaced by hard work, independence of thought, honesty in human relationships.

Fauset's first two novels define her concerns in content and her skills with form. One must overlook some of the distracting formal weaknesses of *There Is Confusion* in order to perceive the range and insight of Jessie Fauset's thinking. One must remember her literary sophistication as shown in her *Crisis* book reviews, her letters, her essays, her college record in order to perceive the subtle formal development of many of the same thoughts in *Plum Bun*. Close study of both books reveals thought, sensitivity, tolerance, and skill heretofore not suspected, not assumed, or not admitted in the longer fiction of Jessie Redmon Fauset.

Notes

[1]Jessie Fauset to Zona Gale, 14 August 1924, Portage Public Library, Portage, Wisconsin.

[2]Jessie Fauset, *There Is Confusion* (1924; rpt. New York: AMS Press, 1974), p. 41. Subsequent references to this book will be indicated by page number in the text.

[3]Benjamin Brawley, *The Negro Genius* (New York: Dodd, Mead, 1937), p. 222.

[4][Review of *There Is Confusion*], *New York Times Book Section*, 13 April 1924, p. 9.

[5]George Schuyler [Review of *There Is Confusion*], *The Messenger*, 6 (May 1924), 145.

[6]Time transitions are blunt in *Nigger Heaven*, as they are in *There Is Confusion*. Use of the historical perspective is even more blunt and unincorporated into narration in *Nigger Heaven* than it is in Fauset's novel. For example, at one point Mary plunges into a regular lecture on Black history in conversation with Byron (pp. 122-23). Carl Van Vechten, *Nigger Heaven* (1926; rpt. New York: Harper and Row, 1971).

[7]Hugh Gloster, *Negro Voices in American Fiction* (1948; rpt. New York: Russell and Russell, 1965), pp. 138, 139.

[8]Wallace Thurman, "Negro Artists and the Negro," *New Republic*, 52, 31 August 1927, 39.

[9]Arthur Davis, *From the Dark Tower: Afro-American Writers 1900-1960* (Washington, D. C.: Howard University Press, 1974), p. 90.

[10]Nick Aaron Ford, *Black Insights* (Waltham, Massachusetts: Ginn and Company, 1971), p. 59.

[11]Sterling Brown, *The Negro in American Fiction* (1937; rpt. New York Atheneum, 1969), p. 142.

[12]Davis, pp. 92-93.

[13]Addison Gayle, *The Way of the New World: The Black Novel in America* (Garden City, New York: Anchor, 1976), pp. 139, 140, 142, 144, 148, 149.

[14]Lee R. Edwards and Arlyn Diamond, *American Voices, American Women* (New York: Avon, 1973), p. 383.

[15]Roseann Pope Bell, "*The Crisis* and *Opportunity* Magazines: Reflections of a Black Culture, 1920-1930," Diss. Emory University 1974, p. 213.

[16]Kenny Williams, *They Also Spoke: An Essay on Negro Literature in America, 1787-1930* (Nashville, Tennessee: Townsend Press, 1970), p. 269.

[17]Benjamin Mays, *The Negro's God as Reflected in His Literature* (1938; rpt. New York: Atheneum, 1969), pp. 308, 309.

[18]Jessie Fauset, *Plum Bun* (New York: Frederick A. Stokes, 1929), pp. 11, 12, 13. Subsequent references to this book will be indicated by page number in the text.

[19]Gloster, p. 134 and Davis , p. 93.

[20]Davis, p. 93.

[21]" 'White' Negroes" [Review of *Plum Bun*], *New York Times*, 3 March 1929, p. 8.

[22]Francis Gaines, "The Racial Bar Sinister in American Romance," 25, *South Atlantic Quarterly* (October 1926), pp. 396, 397, 399-400.

[23]Nathaniel Hawthorne, "Preface," *House of the Seven Gables* (New York: Norton and Company, 1967), p. 1.

[24]David Littlejohn, *Black on White* (New York: Grossman, 1966), pp. 49-50.

[25]Robert Bone, *The Negro Novel in America*, rev. ed. (New Haven, Connecticut: Yale University Press, 1966), p. 101.

[26]James Weldon Johnson, *The Autobiography of an Ex-Colored Man*, in *Three Negro Classics* (New York: Avon, 1965), p. 499.

27The discussion of a character's developing distinction of true and false differences is indebted to Gary Davis, "Henry Fielding and the Play of Difference," unpublished manuscript.

The Drama of Black Life:

The Chinaberry Tree *and* Comedy: American Style

Jessie Fauset's last two novels contain some distinguishable departures from the content and form of her first two. The departures in form of *The Chinaberry Tree*, 1931, and *Comedy: American Style*, 1933, are more significant in showing what Fauset attempted to do than in showing what she accomplished, for the last two novels are in many ways a weakening and scattering of the formal strengths of *Plum Bun* and a return to some of the stylistic detractions of *There Is Confusion*. Fauset herself, according to her half-brother, Arthur Huff Fauset, preferred *There Is Confusion* and *Plum Bun* to the later two novels (Letter to author, 10 January 1976).

Such weakening and scattering in these last two of her novels, as compared to *Plum Bun*, does by no means lead a careful reader to the conclusion that the two books are not worth consideration. The material which Fauset uses in the two books—"the homelife of the colored American who is not being pressed too hard by the Furies of Prejudice, Ignorance, and Economic Injustice"[1]—and the concentration on action within the Negro race between Black people rather than on what occurs between Black and white, are welcome and useful and insightful departures from typical Black and white early 1930's American fiction. Fauset's sympathetic but critical depiction of the psychology of the middle-class American Black and the ambitious Black has of course been ignored, misread, misinterpreted in many of the critical evaluations made of the period and of *The Chinaberry Tree* and *Comedy: American Style* as it has been with her first two novels. It is important to look carefully at these final long works in order to make clear discovery of what central ideas emerge and what formal attempts are made to encompass the ideas.

Early reviews of *The Chinaberry Tree* were for the most part more perceptive than later criticism of the book has been. One early reviewer of the book discovered what seems clearly to be the key to what otherwise appears as stuffy propriety and materialistic concentration on goods and services. Gerald Sykes in the *Nation* praises the novel highly, saying it is one of those rarest of things, a book under-advertised, of value unperceived even by its publisher. The key to *The Chinaberry Tree*, Sykes says, is the longing of Laurentine Strange for respectability, and in Fauset's understanding of the need and desire of an illegitimate child of a rich white Southern man and a Black servant, she achieves exceptional insight into character. "The passion which animates [Laurentine] is closely allied to the passion which animates the book. What does the illegitimate mulatto grow up to want? Respectability." Laurentine's longing for respectability explains "the striking gentility of certain passages, as well as the exceptional importance attached to small material comforts that most white people would take for granted," Sykes says.[2] In *The Chinaberry Tree*, Fauset sympathetically explores this urge toward "normality," and "decency," and "respectability" in her middle class characters, but she also unobtrusively redefines the terms, suggesting as she goes that both the society which makes judgements of character on limited conventional definitions and the characters who accept society's judgements need reform.

The small New Jersey community of Red Brook provides the social setting for exploration of values. White townspeople appear only in one scene in the book, primarily as onlookers at a community skating party where their presence is used to keep young Black men in line. ("Reverend Simmons came up. 'Now boys, boys don't start nothin'. Too many white folk here for that. We don't want this kind of thing closed to us.' "[3]) It is Black Red Brook society which has over the years ostracized Aunt Sal, lover of the deceased Colonel Halloway, and their daughter Laurentine for no other reason than that Aunt Sal and Colonel Halloway were not married. Laurentine has grown up over-sensitive to what an unwitting small playmate once called her "bad blood," and seeks to overcome the past by marriage to a respectable man. "Oh God, you know all I want is a chance to show them how decent I am' " (p. 36).[4]

Melissa Paul has come from Philadelphia to live with her aunt and cousin, not knowing that her mother Judy had left Red Brook after a much talked-about affair with her best friend's husband, a Mr. Forten. Part of Melissa's young confidence of bearing and attitude comes from mistaken assurance of her legitimacy. When introduced in Red Brook as Judge Strange's daughter, she retorts, " 'But I am Melissa Paul. . . . My father was John Paul of Philadelphia. My mother married after she left here. And now she's married again and living in Chicago.' " The "double marriage" seems to Melissa to "bolster her conventional superiority to Aunt Sal and Laurentine" (p. 27). Young Malory Forten, sent away to school after his father's affair with Judy Strange, returns to Red Brook and conducts a secret courtship with Melissa Paul. Their conventional ideals match. "That curious strain in her which so insisted on conventionality" finds Malory's manners, his figure, his dress vastly satisfying. Malory, at age twenty, has "definitely fixed" views. "He believed in the church. . . . He believed in family, in the Republican party, in moderate wealth, a small family, rather definite place for women" (p. 131). In Melissa Paul and Malory Forten Fauset has deliberately chosen the most convention-bound characters to spring her most unconventional surprise on, for the two are just before their marriage found to be half-brother and half-sister.

Against the longings for "respectability," "decency," and "normality" as defined by Laurentine, Melissa, and Malory comes the redeeming redefinition of the terms by three other characters: Aunt Sal, Dr. Stephen Denleigh, and Asshur Lane. Aunt Sal's view of the affair of her life she keeps to herself; it is not the scornful view of Red Brook or the shamed view of Laurentine. "Oh, she had known happiness, terrible devastating happiness, 'Happiness like fiah,' she had told herself more than once. It had been a special kind of happiness which many other people would have mistaken for suffering, pain and disgrace. 'But it suited me,' she thought." Yet Aunt Sal understands Laurentine's longings and she suppresses her wilful, "wayward" heart to seek safe normality for her daughter—

"because safe and normal ways were the only ways Laurentine understood" (p. 168).

It is not from her subdued mother but from Dr. Stephen Denleigh that Laurentine's views are changed during the course of the book. Denleigh's successful courting of Laurentine is done only through his successful purging of her notions about the meaning of her birth and her mother's affair. With a pale face she "confesses" to him what he already knows and finds without significance. " 'I'm . . . not only illegitimate . . . but the child of a connection that all America frowns on' " (p. 121). "He frowned. . . . 'What bosh to talk to a physician! Biology transcends society! . . . I mean to say the facts of life, birth and death are more important than the rules of living, marriage, law, the sanction of church or man' " (p. 121). Similarly, Denleigh sees past the social illegality of Aunt Sal's liaison with Colonel Halloway. " 'As I see it, the two of them were defying, not the laws of God, nor the laws of man speaking universally. Simply the laws of a certain section of America.' " " 'This was a true love match, the kind you read about' " (p. 160).

The third of the revisionist philosophers of the book is the youngest and most saintly of the group. Asshur Lane is Melissa's high school beau almost from the time of her arrival in Red Brook. When he leaves to go South to Tuskegee Institute, during which absence she falls in love with Malory Forten, he impresses upon her two remembrances. First he enjoins her to be "good," "almost stupid good," and second he promises that if ever she is in trouble, he will come (p. 74). Asshur sees the legal marriage bond for what it is—pointless if no more than legal; needless it only repeats what exists in the loyalty of one person to another. When Melissa raises the specter of the Aunt Sal and Colonel Halloway relationship before him—" 'But Asshur they weren't married' "—he "almost shouted at her: ' Well what of it?' " (p. 73). The memory of Asshur's perception and loyalty contrasts with Malory's conventional concern for propriety when Melissa worries over telling Malory about the Colonel Halloway and Aunt Sal affair. "She wouldn't have been afraid to tell Asshur. . . . Asshur cared for her, for her only. No amount of scandal, no degree of misbehavior connected with her relatives, no libel circulated about herself would change Asshur"

(p. 212). Asshur's loyalty and goodness frame the story line; he returns when Melissa has been felled by the discovery of love for her half-brother. "It was Asshur who restored them. He it was, who with his nice, keen sense of values unperturbed by the world's standards of weights and measures, brought them healing" (p. 336).

Against Red Brook's limited ideas of decency and respectability and the resultant stultifying early beliefs of Laurentine and Melissa comes Asshur's definition of value and the principle theme of the book. "Life, Death, and Essential Honor were the only matters which greatly concerned him in his simple code. Life was for enjoyment; Death was to be met,—with great dignity,—only when it could be no longer avoided; Honor consisted in downing no man and in refusing to consider oneself downed" (p. 336). The theme of *The Chinaberry Tree* is not "the middle class Negro's abhorrence of miscegenation without the benefit of matrimony,"[5] as one writer has said, but just the opposite—true values of life and death and human relationships as opposed to the limited and limiting false values of society's rules.

The essential formal innovation of Fauset's last two novels is in the use of analogue to drama. Elements of theatrical construction are included implicitly in *The Chinaberry Tree*, explicitly and with less success in *Comedy: American Style*. Jessie Fauset showed great interest in drama in the 1920s in her New York City social life and in her *Crisis* literary editing. In a 1932 interview Fauset named theatre-going as her favorite recreation. "The boast of her life is that she once appeared on the Broadway stage with the French actress, Cecile Sorel. 'You may have noticed me; I was part of the mob in the guillotine scene in DuBarry.' "[6] The 1920s was of course a very active period for Black drama, especially by white authors. But in addition to the highly successful productions of O'Neill's *Emperor Jones*, Dorothy and DuBose Heyward's *Porgy* in 1927 and Marc Connelly's *The Green Pastures* in 1930, Charles Gilpin and Paul Robeson were widely seen on the stage as actors, and the Negro musical brought Blacks to the fore as writers, producers and performers. Easily the most popular New York show in 1920 and 1921, for example, was *Shuffle Along*, written and produced by Blacks. Fauset's understandable theatrical interest did not, however, lead to the writing of plays. In 1922 a request for a manuscript led Fauset to reply that she had no experience in playwriting and did not dare attempt it.[7] Rather, her interest in and expertise in drama appears to have found its way into her final novels.

The most immediately recognizable analogue in *The China-berry Tree* is to classical Greek mythology, particularly drama. Fauset's "Foreword" to the novel mentions the Muses, the Furies, the dramatic situation posited by being Negro in America. "The elements of the play fall together involuntarily; they are just waiting for Fate the Producer to quicken them into movement,—for Chance the Prompter to intepret them with fidelity" (p. ix). Alain Locke in a 1932 review of the book mentions its analogues in classic literature, adding that the novel's "Negro peculiarities" tend only to give it "deeper tragedy and universality."[8] With more specificity, Joseph Feeney in a 1974 article, "Greek Tragic Patterns in a Black Novel: Jessie Fauset's *The Chinaberry Tree*," lists and exemplifies aspects of Greek tragedy made use of in the novel. Feeney points out the use of the family curse, the feeling that fate rules events, a "tragic inevitability," and recognition scenes. In addition, he refers to some of the "images and verbal touches" which underscore the "Greek tone" —Melissa's dream of the leering comic mask and the meaning of her name, "honey," for example.[9]

It is possible to make additions to Feeney's listing of Greek dramatic elements in the book. Its periodic use of dance suggests both the dignified movement of tragedy, as in Laurentine's skating, and the satyric gaiety of comedy, as in the rhumba and the Lindy hop. The character of Mr. Jonathan Stede, in his sympathetic interest in the action, his advice, comfort, exhortation and warning, is an appealing substitute for the "ideal public" Of the Greek chorus. The seasonal emphasis, the dwelling on winter's lifelessness and Spring's awakening in *The Chinaberry Tree* suggests the origins of Greek drama in the rituals of yearly death and rebirth. Masks of ·comedy and tragedy are found not only in Melissa's high school English class and in her recurring dream, but also in the bodiless heads which appear in summer screen doors. Finally, the Chinaberry itself, sometimes known as "soapberry," contains saponin and is used to make soap, suggesting in an oblique way the cleansing or purging of emotion in tragedy.

To assume, however, that only the Greek dramatic pattern was in Fauset's mind for formal control in *The Chinaberry Tree* would lead one to the mistaken conclusion Feeney reaches in his article. He asks in his final paragraph, "Does *The Chinaberry Tree* succeed as a Greek tragedy?" The answer is of course "No." The role of Fate or of a family curse is "not as strong as for the Greeks." The Greek-like plot line is in the story of Melissa and Malory, thus to Feeney all of Laurentine's story is peripheral to the "central tragedy." (Gerald Sykes in the *Nation* found just the opposite to be true; though the "greater portion" of the story deals with the narrowly avoided incestuous relationship, yet Laurentine is the book's "real heroine.") Finally, Feeney points out that the happy ending, the joining of lovers, the picnic under the Chinaberry Tree are not Greek tragedy. The tragedy which is present in the book, he concludes, is "alloyed with much conventional sentiment."

It hardly seems fair to ask, "Does *The Chinaberry Tree* succeed as Greek tragedy?" For Fauset was not writing a Greek tragedy; in fact, she seems to be in her quiet unobtrusive way gently satirizing the form and its underlying philosophical and religious assumptions while using it to lend impact to her own concerns. For example, when Laurentine discovers that Melissa is running off to marry Malory Forten, "she was like a maenad." " 'Remember if anything has happened, it's all my fault and,—and Stephen, for her own sake, I shall have to kill her' " (pp. 332, 333). Against the somnolent Red Brook setting, the high school kids' Madison Avenue dreams of "dustpans blue as the sky" and "yellow kitchenware" and "individual green ramekins" from "Barton's" for their first home, and the happy ending Fauset puts on the book, Laurentine's Greek anticipation is glaringly, almost humorously out of place in its extremity. Fauset does not intend to say life is just like a Greek tragedy. Rather she is as always pointing out variation between convention and virtue, distinction between fate and choice, inevitability and responsibility. To follow unthinkingly the conventions as developed by Greek artists would be as foreign to Fauset's way as it would be to her to unthinkingly extol 1930s American social habits.

If a rather specific underlying dramatic analogue is sought for the elements of form in *The Chinaberry Tree*, it can probably be found more readily in the socially-restrictive and socially-restorative Shakespearean "festive comedy" than in Greek tragedy or Greek drama. C. L. Barber's *Shakespeare's Festive Comedy: A Study of Dramatic Form and Its Relation to Social Custom* describes art as developing "underlying configurations in the social life of a culture." Many of the elements of social festivity made use of by Shakespeare appear with much the same intent in *The Chinaberry Tree*. The *Bildungsroman* pattern of the young girl discovering true and false differences during the course of her growth experiences as seen in *Plum Bun* becomes in *The Chinaberry Tree* a discovery of true identity, true love, and true value for the social group as well as the individual.

The "saturnalian pattern" which Barber describes as controlling the form of Shakespeare's festive comedy involves statement and counterstatement moving through release to clarification. Clarification is "a heightened awareness of the relation between man and nature—the nature celebrated on holiday," and it "comes with movement between poles of restraint and release in everybody's experience."[10] This pattern is particularly appropriate to Fauset's depiction of Melissa's and Laurentine's early misconceptions about "respectability" and "decency" and their developing understanding of the relationship of society's rules to nature's laws. The peculiar social inhibitions of Black society continuously observed by white judges intensify both the sense of social restriction and the need for saturnalian release.

Many elements of Shakespearean festive comedy used to achieve final clarification, as described by Barber, are present also in *The Chinaberry Tree*. Festivity is bound to increased seasonal awareness. The skating party, Christmas Eve, Easter, the summer picnic under the tree are the festive events of the novel. People are "being tossed about by a force which puts them beside themselves to take them beyond themselves." The force is often love—"a compelling rhythm in man and nature." The festive seasonal events which cross social and class lines are times "when maids might find out who their true love would be by dream or divinations." Melissa's dreams predict both the horror of near-incest with Malory and the assurance of Asshur's true love. The use of moonlight and woods as metamorphic areas where reality and dream merge and meld together is present in *The Chinaberry Tree* as in its Shakespearean analogue. Finally, clowning portions interact imaginatively with the rest of the novel, as in Jonathan Stede's regular expectation of Pentecost in the form of fried onions or other physical treats, suited so well to a novel whose conclusion unites the spiritual, emotional, and physical.[11]

Universal elements of dramatic form which Fauset makes use of in *The Chinaberry Tree* supplement the saturnalian pattern of the book. Elements of costume, make-up and dress, receive some emphasis here as they do in Fauset's previous novels. In *The Chinaberry Tree*, however, the emphasis more appropriately suits the dramatic underpinnings of the book. Setting is dramatically conceived and executed in *The Chinaberry Tree* in a way which is entirely absent from Fauset's other novels, and is tied closely to nature and seasonal change.

It is for the characters who are most bound by conventional social morality and legalistic emphasis on appearances that Fauset makes the most elaborate costume descriptions. Laurentine's expertise in designing and dressmaking is conveyed by extensive description of the clothing she and Melissa don for various occasions. Early in the novel, when Laurentine has hopes of snagging the respectable but ultimately disloyal Phillip Hackett, she stands in front of her mirror speculating on how she will "exercise the spell of her beauty on him." The beauty is only skin and clothing deep.

> Her slender, well-moulded figure showed to every advantage in a dress of green developed in silk and wool, its uneven hem-line reaching in places to her ankle. Her stockings of tan and her dainty yet sturdy, slender shoes of brown and tan snakeskin afforded just the necessary contrast. . . . Her black, waving hair parted smoothly in the middle and drawn to the conventional flat knot in the nape of her neck gave her a slightly foreign look which was accentuated by her long, black, oval ear-rings. . . . The bell rang, and, pulling on her tiny, smart, green felt hat, she got hastily into her green cloth coat with its high mink collar (p. 35).

Laurentine adds to dress the "discreet use of discreet scents and powders," but Melissa "was the frank coquette." Piled on her dressing table are "creams, cleansing ones, tissue-building ones . . . , vanishing creams, bleaching creams, tints for darkening the eyelids, tiny brushes for eyelashes, pastes for finger-nails, powders in several tints . . . , strange combs and curling irons" (p. 127). Makeup and all the time-consuming work of making up are ironically an important part of Melissa's youthful innocent appeal.

Fauset does not forget the scenic impact of varied skin color among Black people, especially when variations are emphasized by dress. Melissa is invited to her first high-class teenage party by Kitty Brown, daughter of one of the community's Black doctors. Female dress is again selected for description. "In and out among the uniformity of male attire flashed the girls in their brilliant and gay summer dresses. Cotton was in vogue and the shimmering freshness of organdy and embroidery and lace lent its special charm. Melissa in a thin peacock blue which set off her clear skin and reddish hair was completely satisfied with her own appearance. . . . The other girls beautifully dressed had evidently chosen their colorful gowns with regard to their varying complexions" (p. 105).

At times Fauset's costume descriptions have in totality a distinctly stage-like effect. One such scene includes the introduction of the lounging pajamas designed by Laurentine for Mrs. Ismay, a doctor's wife. "Mrs. Ismay, in her blue pajamas, Laurentine in a deep peach dress, with still deeper tinted lace arranged in the smart, sparse fashion of the day at neck and wrists, Mrs. Brown, Kitt's mother, encased trimly in a cleverly modern black and white gown, were playing bridge with Dr. Ismay" (p. 148).

It is likely that Fauset is here, as in *Plum Bun*, using a device which has the possibility of a dual appeal to a dual audience. The former novel uses the romantic plot line to appeal to an unsophisticated reader while it subtly satirizes romantic American assumptions. *The Chinaberry Tree* uses extensive, dramatic, stagey description of costume and makeup to titilate a susceptible Black female reading audience. Fauset is able to sell to and reach an audience who might not otherwise be tempted by serious fiction. At the same time she uses these dramatic elements to extend and clarify the serious point of the novel. Costume and makeup are used in *The Chinaberry Tree* as are descriptions of food, furniture and other material goods. All reveal the mistaken but understandable desire of the illegitimate daughter and her cousin for respectability. Emphasis on proper appearance is overcompensation, in a sense, for the moral laxity assumed to be characteristic of the Black woman. Significantly, the descriptions of costume disappear after Laurentine and Melissa have been made by Denleigh and Asshur Lane to see that convention is a limited determinant of virtue.

At a crucial point in the plot of the novel, when Malory has brought Melissa to his own home, only to be told by the bodiless head of his sister in the screen door that "No, Malory, she can never come into this house," Melissa runs home to face whatever reality lies beneath costume and makeup. "When she got up to her room she was half fainting, but she dashed to her mirror, pulled all her clothes off, examined minutely her delicate, yellow body. 'Could I have the leprosy, I wonder? Oh God what is it?' " (pp. 326, 327) The final picnic scene under the Chinaberry tree does not include a single word about lace or organdy or snake-skin or silk. Laurentine and Melissa, "like spent swimmers," are thinking not of their dainty bodies encased in exquisite garments, but of "the feel of the solid ground beneath their feet, the grateful monotony of the skies above their heads" (pp. 340-41).

Fauset's changing descriptions of costume and makeup support the theme of *The Chinaberry Tree* and suggest a relationship to the stage, but it is left to another drama element in the book to lend a kind of unity and shape to the novel. That drama element is stage setting, and the specific setting used in *The Chinaberry Tree* is the area of the tree itself. None of Fauset's other novels uses setting as a thematic or unifying principle for the entire book. And none of the other novels makes as full an attempt as is here made to relate an essentially rural landscape, with trees, flowers, grass, ice, snow in near-constant attendance upon action and character development.

The reader is told on the first page of the novel that the Chinaberry Tree was a gift from Colonel Halloway to Aunt Sal. He "had

had it fetched years ago . . . from Alabama." Of the setting that was his legacy to the Black woman he loved—the trim white and green house, the "miniature grounds" full of peonies and crocuses and gladiolas and roses and grapes—what the three women of the book "loved most in that most lovely of places was the Chinaberry Tree" (p. 1). Later the meaning of the tree to the three women is made more specific. "The Chinaberry Tree brought back the past to Aunt Sal; to Laurentine it represented the future; but to fortunate Melissa, it meant now, the happy, happy present" (p. 27).

Aunt Sal sits daily on the hexagonal seat around the tree and remembers "that past which he and she had found so sweet." Laurentine, however, "could not remember any time in her life when . . . [the tree] had not cast its shadow on the side lawn. She had played under it as a child with two exquisite dolls, wondering rather wistfully why the few children in the neighborhood didn't play with her" (p. 2). The beauty of the tree is to Laurentine only a promise of future companionship and love. "Laurentine went out in the chilly night and sat for hours under the Chinaberry Tree. When would the future, which she so clearly envisaged, come?" (p. 13). On the night that Phil Hackett deserts her, not appearing for the date which she expects to be a proposal, she looks out hopefully on "the wintry skeleton of the Chinaberry Tree" (p. 57). But the hope dissipates as she waits hour by hour. Finally "she stood by the window looking down as she had earlier in the evening on the icy skeleton of the Chinaberry Tree" (p. 60). The loss and emptiness of winter and of skeleton branches have replaced her hope. "She had never stood under the Chinaberry Tree with Philip Hackett" (p. 61).

As the months pass, the loss of Phil Hackett is somewhat assuaged by the new friendship of Mrs. Ismay. Laurentine's hopes for future happiness again rise and are again attached in her mind to the tree. "She forgot about Phil Hackett, forgot her aching loneliness and her desperate yearnings, she would rise and look out the window, marking idly how the August moonlight went sifting through the thick foliage of the Chinaberry Tree. . . . Some day she would have her own little group over. They would have supper, eat and drink. They would make merry under the Chinaberry Tree" (p. 100). Almost beyond her greatest hopes, she revels finally in the love of

Dr. Denleigh. On a "heavenly" night, "mellow and balmy, yet invigorating," she brings him to her house to sit under the tree. The
"trivial incident had for her the force of a ritual. She had ridden,
walked and talked with Hackett, but she had never sat with him
beneath the Tree" (p. 151). The dream of future happiness is finally
becoming present reality for Laurentine, though she has yet to be
cleansed of her conventional ideas about shame attached to the love
affair represented by the Chinaberry Tree.

Melissa's first sight of the Tree when she arrives to live with
Aunt Sal and Laurentine shows that to her it represents stability and
security and propriety, all in contrast to the disruptive life she has
known with her mother. "Here she would stay, here in this house, in
the shade of this Tree she must and would live . . . far way from her
mother's friends, and the hateful little house, and their disorderly,
ragged precarious life" (p. 16). As Melissa begins socializing in Red
Brook, the tree becomes an accurate forecaster of the man with
whom she will ultimately find happiness. Asshur and Melissa find
comfort and peace and togetherness in their conversations on the
hexagonal seat under the tree. "In the hot early evening of June she
sat under the Chinaberry Tree with Asshur, her weary mind suddenly calm, her hurt heart finding balm" (p. 81). In late June "they were
silent watching the scorching sun's assault on the area beyond which
the thick foliage of the delectable Tree did not extend. Here in this
retreat were rest and cool and shelter" (p. 89). Asshur tells Melissa
he is leaving for Alabama, and "the Chinaberry Tree looked down on
her first real weeping" (p. 92). Even long after Asshur is gone, replaced by Malory, the Tree makes Melissa think of Asshur, just as
she thinks of him in times of trouble and difficulty (p. 180).

Malory Forten and Melissa cannot sit together under the tree,
for their surreptitious courtship does not allow him to visit her.
Out of new distrust Laurentine begrudges young men's visits to
Melissa, and Laurentine's bedroom window overlooks the tree.
Melissa hopes for recovery of the openness and peace she had known
with Asshur under the tree. "Clandestine meetings were no part of
any plan of hers. Laurentine will be all right pretty soon and then
Malory will be coming right here to see me and we'll sit out here and
talk and talk under the Chinaberry Tree. Oh Malory, Malory!' "

(p. 109). When Malory makes a secret visit to Melissa in the kitchen of the snug house on Christmas Eve, he sees the skeleton of the tree for the first time, "with here and there a leaf fluttering in the chilly night," and he brings her out to sit on the snowy seat. " 'Why this place is too good to be true; isn't it really just the right place for a lover—and his lass?' " (pp. 192, 195) But Melissa's anticipation of sitting under the tree with Malory did not include the unease she feels as the event comes to pass. Only "beyond the radius of the Chinaberry Tree" does her "uneasiness" leave her, and "her old admiration" for Malory surge up (p. 196). Malory and Melissa never do sit openly, freely, and peacefully under the tree. When their clandestine meetings take place late at night in a garden swing on the far border of Aunt Sal's property, Malory, "with his sure sense of values," knows that "the Chinaberry Tree was the place where they really should foregather" (p. 258). But when they do silently move toward the tree, Laurentine sees them (p. 267).

Laurentine and Melissa, the first consciously, the second un-consciously, make their choices of male companion by relating the men they know to the tree. The resolution of the book occurs also under the Chinaberry tree. Aunt Sal, to whom the tree represented the past, is once again "free to think of her dead lover. . . . She had always been willing to pay the Piper. Now, with Laurentine safe and satisfied, she was at liberty to recall the Piper's tune" (p. 340). Laurentine has found the happiness that the tree promised in the future only by going through some present changes herself. And Melissa has found that the future she had rejected with Asshur is now her salvation in the present under the tree. A kind of pantheist-ic God surrounds the group and "the Chinaberry Tree became a temple" (p. 341).

Throughout *The Chinaberry Tree* the tree is at center stage, with characters beginning their actions under it, then moving away from it, then coming back under it again for denouement. Showing change of fortune and change of season in first its thick foliage and then its skeleton frame and then its foliage and shelter again, it reminds one of the tree or the bouquet of flowers in August Strind-berg's *A Dream Play*. Hugh Gloster has said that *The Chinaberry Tree* is "something of a modern analogue to Hawthorne's *The Scarlet*

Letter because of its study of the consequences of "the sins of the fathers."[12] It would seem even more fruitful to compare the Fauset novel to Hawthorne's *The House of the Seven Gables*, for both books use the happy ending to resolve inheritance questions, and use as well the great overhanging tree with its seasonal changes to predict and reflect action. A prop which dominates perception of character and viewer, which anticipates action and choice, and which shields and surrounds and protects, the tree is an appropriate archetypal symbol for Fauset's new definitions of virtue and respectability. The Tree of Life representing true love after the fall befits the novel's theme. The miscegenational affair of Colonel Halloway and Aunt Sal becomes in the tree a legacy of devotion, love, loyalty, and virtue that exists directly opposed to society's opinions.

It must be admitted, however, that despite the appropriateness of the tree as symbol, and despite the pleasing unity and shape that the tree gives the novel, it is somewhat overdone and obvious as a literary device. Perhaps part of the reason for a kind of awkwardness with use of the tree as well as with description of the other outdoor settings in *The Chinaberry Tree* is Fauset's own urban upbringing and later life. She has neither the unity with trees and flowers and animals likely in one who was raised close to nature, or the specificity of detail and insightfulness of figurative description of one tremendously interested in the natural world. One cannot help but feel in reading *The Chinaberry Tree* that its extensive use of the natural world, so unusual in Fauset's work, was imposed upon her real interests as something necessary to the book but not delightful to her.

Richard Wright once tried to define what he called "perspective" in answer to the question of what a Black writer should write. "Perspective," he said, is "that part of a poem, novel or play which a writer never puts directly on paper. It is that fixed point in intellectual space where a writer stands to view the struggles, hopes, and sufferings of his people. There are times when he may stand too close and the result is a blurred vision. Or he may stand too far away and the result is a neglect of important things."[13] Though such judgements approach the uncomfortably subjective, one has the feeling in reading *The Chinaberry Tree* that Fauset never gets the accurate perspective—she vacillates between standing too far away and standing too close.

There are several probable reasons for her third novel's falling short of Fauset's achievement in *Plum Bun*. All but the first eighty pages of *The Chinaberry Tree* was written during the summer of 1931 in a park on Riverside Drive after an 8:00 a.m. French class at Columbia University. "Never would I have got my novel done in such good season if it hadn't been for taking that French course and being thereby forced to get up early every day," Fauset told an interviewer in 1932. The story of the book, however, was a true one which Fauset had heard when she was fifteen, and one which she had always intended to write. Since she had worked it out in her mind over the years, she said, "when I came to the mechanical process of writing, I could do so in a straight-forward manner almost without revision."[14] That the story was heard by Fauset when she was fifteen, which would have made it the year 1897, and that the book was written essentially without revisions between the press of two academic years' teaching duties at De Witt Clinton High School in New York City, help explain some of the divided feeling of *The Chinaberry Tree*.

The book has a simultaneous time-sense of about 1930 and about 1895. Modern touches are sprinkled liberally throughout the book. Several characters light up cigarettes; even a female character, Gertrude Brown, comes home from college and courageously lights up before her father. Stephen Denleigh rides around in a "shiny tricky little dark blue sports model" of a Ford (p. 118). He battles traffic on the way to and from New York City and comes home exhausted. Malory, "in spite of his fondness for words and literature . . . liked slang, believing that it had about it an exactness, an appositeness that nothing, no other form of expression, equalled" (p. 288). Melissa has a fondness for gangster movies. Yet the touches of modernity do not quite put one in the modern world in *The Chinaberry Tree*. The community skating party, the horse and sleigh rides, the walks in the woods, the political manipulation, the style in which the book is written all put one in the world of 1897, when Fauset first heard the story.

The Chinaberry Tree suffers somewhat from intrusive, unincorporated incidents which are explained partly by its method of composition. Writing "in a straightforward manner, almost without revision," Fauset says that she nevertheless makes "certain interpolations that I put into the original story. For instance, the incident that happened to Dr. Denleigh and Laurentine at the restaurant in Pelham happened, almost exactly as it is described, to my husband and me last summer while I was writing my novel."[15] The trip to New York City by Denleigh, Laurentine and Mrs. Ismay seems to have no function in *The Chinaberry Tree* except to make opportunity for the incorporation of the restaurant incident. The incident itself, in which an immigrant waiter is rude to the Black customers, raises many questions and thoughts which it is clearly not Fauset's conscious intention to introduce into the novel. The interpolated restaurant incident is a portion of *The Chinaberry Tree* which Richard Wright would probably label "blurry" from too close a proximity of the author.

In addition to story source and method of composition, there are other possible explanations for some of the weaknesses of *The Chinaberry Tree* which it is only fair to keep in mind. By the time of Fauset's third novel the height of the Harlem Renaissance period was over and the Great Depression was on. With decline in popularity and decline in income the Black writer found it ever more difficult to publish. Fauset wanted very much to support herself by her writing; she looked "wistfully to the day" when she would be able to devote a year or two to a novel, " 'just to see what I really could do if I had my full time and energy to devote to my work.' " In 1932 she "confesses" to studying issues of the *Saturday Evening Post* "in a candid effort to analyze and isolate the germs of popular writing."[16] To no avail. She continues teaching year after year, not able by time for artistry or knack for popularity to make her living by writing.

Having to be aware of a white audience which could publish and buy her work, and a Black audience whose respect was essential to her legitimacy as a Black writer was probably an irreconcilable split for Fauset at this time more so than in the 1920s. She was sensitive to changing racial attitudes. The question of "passing," for example, was becoming passé. Whereas Blacks once sought beauty in the white race, "now they are discovering it among themselves," Fauset observed in the early thirties, "and are becoming satisfied to stay within theselves. As enlightenment spreads, the taboo against intermarriage increases."[17] There were new questions and possibilities here to exploit but there was never enough time or energy. *The Chinaberry Tree* seems to be at once a retreat to a safer, surer set of beliefs and problems, and an attempt to deal with some of the questions being raised by Blacks by 1930—the relationship between the urban and the rural Black, for example, and the impact of new urbanism on an essentially rural people.

The Chinaberry Tree is an intriguing, if flawed, novel. To sum up its impact, it is useful to return to Gerald Sykes' perceptive review of the work. Sykes perceives in Jessie Fauset "pride, the pride of a genuine aristocrat." Aristocratic pride in the author leads to some over-elegance in the writing, but it also makes Fauset "such a remarkable psychologist." However many the artistic errors, she has "a rare understanding of people and their motives." Every moment of *The Chinaberry Tree* "speaks of yearning. That is why, once it is seen as a whole, even the faults are charming, for the story they tell is poignant and beautiful, too."[18] Fauset in 1931 wrote with her usual modesty to Zona Gale that *The Chinaberry Tree* "is a rather simple though dramatic story of life confined almost completely to colored people. No controversial material whatever."[19] Miscegenation, incest, ideal love without marriage could not have been completely uncontroversial for Fauset's readers. Her achievement in *The Chinaberry Tree* is to deal seriously and insightfully with some significant social and personal concerns while also telling a suspenseful, entertaining story that is not without beauty.

Comedy: American Style zeroes in on the ironies of American Black life with more directness and less sentimentality than any of Jessie Fauset's novels. This last of her longer published works takes most of the major and minor thematic elements of her first novel and intensifies them in various ways. White racial discrimination faced by Northern urban Blacks in *There Is Confusion* is essentially internalized into the Black characters themselves in *Comedy: American Style*. The range of characters and actions possible given the realities of discrimination is narrowed historically and by introducing fewer characters in the final novel than in the first one. Limited alternatives available to women generally and to Black women particularly as shown in *There Is Confusion* become in *Comedy: American Style* a concentration on the powers wrought by mistaken, misled mothers. Fauset in the final novel includes new 1930s slants on the race issue, slants stemming from insights gained through the controversies of the Harlem Renaissance period. The dominant theme which emerges from these exploratory themes is not so different in the final book as compared to the first. Both novels place emphasis on the importance of human relationships and the attaining of happiness through those relationships; life and the plot of the two novels are a working out of this understanding of essentials. Where the final novel does finally differ from the first, however, is in its unstinting depiction of the characters who fail to attain true understanding as well as of characters who succeed.

The meaning of race discrimination for Fauset was frequently expressed in terms of its being a burden added to the ordinary trials of living. "Life is hard for everyone, but to ordinary difficulties are added intangible difficulties in the case of the Negro. For him life is very uncertain. He's never sure what sort of break he may get. . . . It would seem that my people are cut off from advantages exactly in proportion to their color."[20] This statement from a Fauset interview differs only in emphasis from the understanding of American life that Teresa Cary of *Comedy: American Style* gains as a college student. "In that moment she saw brightly and clearly one fundamental cause for the lagging of colored people in America. This senseless prejudice, this silly scorn, this unwelcome patronage, this tardiness on the part of her country to acknowledge the rights of its citizens. . . . all these combined into a crushing load under which a black man must struggle to get himself upright before he could even attempt the ordinary business of life."[21] The irony of Teresa's life is that no white person destroys it for her, at least directly. No white person keeps Teresa from marrying the man she loves. No white person denies her the career which seems later to be her only possible source of happiness. No white person pushes her into a senseless hateful marriage with a man she grows to despise. No white person forces her beautiful, talented, much-loved younger brother to commit suicide. All these destructive acts come not from a white American, but from Teresa's own Black mother, Olivia Blanchard Cary.

In the character Olivia Cary Fauset has achieved "the most penetrating study of color mania in American fiction," a successful "analysis of psychopathic Aryanism," according to Hugh Gloster.[22] Though critics would often have one believe otherwise about the customary class of Jessie Fauset's fictional characters, Olivia Cary is her only central character who comes from the highest class of Black women. Elise McDougald in 1925 described four groups of Black women. At the bottom is a large group of women in domestic service or working casually, dependent upon a fluctuating economy. Just above that group are the "many" in trades and industry, and above that "a most active and progressive group": those in business and the professions. At the top is "a very small leisure group—the wives and daughters of men who are in business and the professions and in a few well-paid personal service occupations.[23] Significantly, Fauset's most caustic criticism of a Black character is of Olivia ("blanched") Cary, a woman of this essentially parasitic class and life style.

All of Olivia's motivations are from her desire to be white, her hatred of Black. Superficially she justifies her actions in relation to her marriage, her social life, and her children by saying that it is for their own good. Sending away one of young Teresa's dark-skinned friends, she tells her, " 'You don't understand these things yet, Teresa. But you will when you're older . . . and you'll be grateful to me. I just don't want you to have Marise and people like that around because I don't want you to grow up among folks who live the life that most colored people have to live . . . , narrow and stultified and stupid. Always pushed in the background . . . out of everything. Looked down upon and despised!' " In action, though, Olivia Cary does nothing in the best interests of her family. She is indeed a deceived character who is never in the course of the book undeceived.

Fauset is not totally convincing in explaining what kind of sources such color mania as Olivia Cary's is likely to have. Early in the book the reader learns a great deal about her mother, Janet Blanchard, who is very class-conscious but not at all color-conscious (p. 14), so family heredity or environment is not passed off as the source. We learn that Olivia was a very odd child from babyhood on in not displaying any evidence of affection for other humans, including her parents (pp. 5, 7). Added to this incapacity for love are two simple experiences. First, as a small child she is called " 'you nasty little nigger' " by another child. Second, when Janet Blanchard is widowed, she moves to a New England milltown where she is not known and settles near an Italian community. Olivia is one day called "that little Italian girl" by a teacher, and from the resulting realization that she can be white, as far as anyone knows, stems Olivia's life-long determination to "pass," to marry light and have "passable" children, to get them to marry white.

If the delineation of sources for Olivia's mania is weak, the depicition of the negative power she wields over the lives of her husband and children is not. Two things only get in the way of Olivia's plans and form the conflicts in the plot line. First, the man she marries, Dr. Christopher Cary, while light enough to "pass" does not care to, and continually frustrates Olivia's pretenses of being white by bringing home obviously colored friends and by doctoring colored patients. Through his sensible efforts of accepting his racial inheritance and of teaching them of Black history and biography, the older two children, Christopher and Teresa, are raised free of their mother's dominating concern. The second barrier to Olivia's goals is even more difficult to overcome. Olivia anticipates the birth of her children happily only because she expects them to be white. Her third child, she tells big Christopher, would be a boy. " 'He'll be the handsomest and most attractive of us all. And I'll name him after myself. An Oliver for your Christopher' " (p. 40). Olivia has a long convalescence from the third birth, and does not see the baby until he is a month old. "Olivia sat up, arms outstretched to receive him. Her baby! Her eyes stretched wide to behold every fraction of his tiny person. But the expectant smile faded as completely as though an unseen hand had wiped it off . . . 'That's not my baby!' " Olivia's third child is just as she predicted: the handsomest and most attractive of them all, and named Oliver after her. He is also, like Olivia's father, obviously Negro.

The pathological extent of Olivia's fixed idea is shown in her treatment of Oliver. He is exceptionally attractive, personable, intelligent and loving—but his mother can't stand him. She pretends she does not know him when he runs up to her on the streetcorner where she is talking to her white lady friends. She sends him away for long periods to live with his two sets of grandparents. Ultimately, she dresses him up as a Filipino servant to wait on her white guests. Family and friends keep Oliver from knowledge of the reason for his mother's disgust, but he accidentally discovers the reason in a letter she has written her husband from France. " 'If you and Chris would come and settle down over here we could all be as white as we look ... if it just weren't for Oliver. I know you don't like me to talk about this ... but really, Chris, Oliver and his unfortunate color has certainly been a mill-stone around our necks all our lives' " (p. 221). Others can understand and scorn Olivia's madness, but when Teresa fails him, too, young Oliver has no defenses against rejection by his mother of the one thing about himself he cannot change. He shoots himself.

Teresa by some subtle deceit puts up a good fight against her mother's absolute requirement that she act as white as she looks. While away from her mother she is able to create her own life. Sent to an all-white prep school, she fails to tell her mother when the school becomes integrated by a girl named Alicia who becomes Teresa's good friend. Alicia's father is a judge in Chicago. Olivia's social and racial ambitions allow Teresa to vacation at Alicia's home; Olivia of course doesn't know that the family is Black. In Chicago Teresa meets and falls in love with a dark handsome mulatto named Henry Bates, and the two make secret marriage plans for a year and a half while Henry finishes school. Olivia foils the plans on the very day of their elopement by accidental discovery of them together on the street, but it is not her current and vehement opposition that separates the lovers. Instead, the treacherous lack of racial birthright and assurance that has been Teresa's upbringing betrays her at the crucial moment of the interview between Bates, her mother, and herself. When Henry turns to her—" 'Well, Teresa, how do you feel about it?' "—she replies, " 'You know how I feel ... But Henry, perhaps there is something to Mother's point of view.' She was surprised herself at the words issuing from her lips ... 'I was thinking, I was wondering. . . . You're Spanish, you know. Couldn't you use it most of the time and . . . and pass for a Mexican?' " (p. 143)

Teresa loses Henry Bates, and realizes her mother's power over her. "For twenty-one years, almost a third of her allotted span, she had yielded to her mother's obsession. She would probably yield again . . . for the breakdown in her resistance showed clearly how completely her inner self was under her mother's domination' " (pp. 148-49). Teresa is right. Her late-sprouted plans to become a professional French tutor for a while appear to have strength to raise her out of the smothering muck of her mother's power, but the growth is false, without sustaining roots. Her mother decides she is to marry the provincial, money-hungry, lower-echelon Professor at the University of Toulouse, Aristide Pailleron—who is white. Teresa acquiesces and slowly dies in everything but body.

Three of the Cary family are destroyed by color mania. Oliver dies physically. Teresa dies mentally, emotionally. Olivia lives on in isolation and poverty. Only young and old Christopher overcome and survive, with much intermittent pain. Sterling Brown has written that in *Comedy: American Style* "the intraracial color snobbishness and the latent self-hatred of anti-Negro Negroes could be glimpsed,"[24] but Fauset actually goes much further than a "glimpse." In its picture of American race discrimination *Comedy: American Style* is thorough in showing a certain kind of Black prejudice against Black. The thinking reader must of course look beyond that portrayal to sources in the society, probably to conclude with Kenny Williams that "Fauset ultimately does not blame her characters for their own weaknesses, rather she blames American society which so emphasized the differences between the two races that these characters become victimized by it."[25] But within the novel itself, concentration is on what internalization of race discrimination does to the Black character and the Black family.

Having said that there is much direct negative criticism of color-struck Blacks and indirect negative criticism of prejudiced whites in *Comedy: American Style*, one must then go on to point out that it is not in Fauset's nature here or elsewhere to write pure protest fiction. She presents alternative solutions to race relations in the United States in characters contrasted to Olivia Cary and in quick but perceptive references to positive traits of Black culture and history.

Christopher Cary, Sr. is a quiet antidote to his wife's disease. Christopher Cary, Jr. is able to resist his mother's domination in a way that his less aggressive sister finds impossible. But it is in a woman outside the family that the primary contrast to Olivia Cary is given. Phebe Grant is a very light skinned Black; in fact she is blond and blue-eyed. Her light skin and hair come from her runaway white father—she is illegitimate. Her mother is of the lowest class of Black women, having marginal employment and income with a white family. Phebe herself by her responsibility and cleverness rises from seamstress with that white family to shop-owning modiste. More significantly, Phebe plays no games with her racial inheritance. As a school girl, when the teacher asks her what race she belongs to, she replies, " 'I belong to the black or Negro race.' " The teacher giggles and asks again. " 'I belong to the black or Negro race' " says Phebe again (p. 35). In direct contrast to Olivia Cary's schoolgirl choice, Phebe makes clear her race mixture and her race preference.

Phebe is offered the prize Olivia craves for her daughter— marriage to a rich white man, Llewellyn Nash. As soon as she dis- covers Nash's intentions, Phebe, however, tells him of her racial mixture. Nash can marry a poor girl, a shop girl, an illegitimate girl, but he cannot marry a girl of invisible Black blood, though he does offer Phebe a permanent mistress-ship in his life. Phebe sends back the proposition and its envelope—a huge floral box full of paper money. Again in direct contrast to Olivia, Phebe refuses a life based on deceit, no matter how attractive its other foundations.

As a final contrast to Olivia, Phebe is absolutely loyal, though severely tested. She marries Christopher Cary long after the real love of her life, Nicholas Campbell, has left her and has married her friend Marise. In *Comedy: American Style* as in *There Is Confusion* Fauset spends some time depicting the trials of marriage even for responsible, mature, de-romanticized adults such as Christopher and Phebe. Phebe is still working in her Philadelphia shop. She is nursing

Christopher, Sr. back into health. She is the sounding board for the complaints of her mother about Olivia, since the two extended families are living together in the rooming house which Phebe had originally purchased for her mother and herself. Phebe is coming home from work exhausted; her husband is coming home from his infant medical practice exhausted; and their life in their bedroom once they get there is not thrilling.

Nicholas contacts Phebe from New York, with a pertinent, tempting suggestion, for he is also a bit disillusioned with married life. The temptation is carefully great, and Phebe's yielding very near when her loyalty to Chris is reasserted. "A sick distaste invaded her. Standing where she had dismounted from the cab, she too in her turn surveyed the house. Nicholas would be on the sixth floor awaiting her. The large staring windows regarded her with weary cynicism. 'So here you are too' they seemed to signal her. In that moment she saw her husband's tall, shabby figure walking slowly, wearily up the path that led to their house. She saw his fatigued face shadowed with responsibility, marred with lines that had come too early. As in a mirror she beheld that glance of trust which seemed to say: 'I'm too tired, Phebe, to tell you of my love. But you know it and I trust you' " (pp. 311-12).

Phebe triumphs over temptation and is rewarded upon her return to Philadelphia by Chris, Jr.'s new attentions, Chris Sr.'s healthy demeanor, and Olivia's recent and permanent absence. For these struggling characters—Chris Jr., Chris Sr., and Phebe—there is a kind of happy ending, at least a temporary victory over their trials and an increased strength from having overcome. There is no easy way of dealing successfully with life or race in America, Fauset reminds us, but there are alternatives to Olivia Cary's imitation white life. Phebe Grant's alternative is acceptance of her inheritance, hard work, unswerving loyalty and honesty.

Jessie Fauset is obviously attuned to an opinion about Black women's possibilities that W. E. B. DuBois expresses in his rather amazing 1920 essay, "The Damnation of Women." He describes the world women are up against. "All womanhood is hampered today because the world on which it is emerging is a world that tries to

worship both virgins and mothers and in the end despises motherhood and despoils virgins." He outlines necessary advances. "The
future woman must have a life work and economic independence.
She must have knowledge. She must have the right of motherhood
at her own discretion." Finally, he dwells on the unique history and
possibility of the Black woman. "I instinctively feel and know that
it is the five million women of my race who really count" as opposed
to Black men. Freedom has been thrust upon them, DuBois says.
They have been expected not to be beautiful, but comptent.[26]
By contrasting parasitic and manipulative Olivia Cary with enter-
prising and faithful Phebe Grant, Fauset creates characters who mirror the negative and positive potential for women's role in society.

It is interesting that Fauset sees the power of the mistaken
mother as so intense in *Comedy: American Style*. Olivia's influence
is of course fully exposed, but Fauset summarizes Dr. Cary's mother's teachings as well. Dr. Cary marries Olivia primarily because she
fits all his mother's dictums on women and wives. " 'A really nice
girl never lets a man know she likes him.' " " 'Never bother with a
woman who runs after you. If she runs after you, she'll run after
other men.' " " 'A good woman comes to her husband entirely ignorant. She learns everything direct from her husband.' " ("The
more completely Chris became acquainted with the elementals of
biology, physiology, and therapeutics, the more he questioned the
wisdom of such ignorance, but he supposed that was just the hard
luck of being a woman.") " 'You can always tell a good woman
because she is so cold' " (p. 27). As in her other novels, Fauset
criticizes the mistaken notions of sexism, but in a less obvious way
than she criticizes racism. Mothers mistaken about race, and mothers
mistaken about sex both wreak havoc in children's lives.

Moreso than in her previous three novels, Fauset in *Comedy:
American Style* presents positive aspects of Black culture that further suggest alternative to white imitation or assimilation. Sprinkled in
the earlier books are brief suggestions of this positive alternative:
Laurentine in *The Chinaberry Tree* feels a oneness in a Black crowd
at the Lafayette Theatre (p. 307); Angela notices the same thing at
the Van Meier lecture in *Plum Bun;* Virginia in that book expresses
the belief that Black people are happier and less selfish than white.

In *Comedy: American Style*, however, the discussion of positive Black culture is wider and more clearly influenced by the many race discussions coming out of the intense Harlem Renaissance period.

In Teresa Cary, Fauset creates a character handicapped by lack of a race identity. "Emotionally, as far as race was concerned, she was a girl without a country. . . . Later in life it occurred to her that she had been deprived of her racial birthright and that that was as great a cause for tears as any indignity that befall a man. . . . She had become, and she would always remain, individual and aloof, never a part of a component whole" (p. 89). Teresa's situation is different than that of a character like Angela Murray in *Plum Bun*, who chooses to "pass." With a mother who tries to make her white and a father who assumes her Blackness, Teresa has no clear identification in her own mind, either to accept or to rebel against. She is the eternal miserable observer, the eternal drifter. Other light-skinned Blacks, with Black identity, carry on the "gesture of whiteness with pride, with amusement, with a sense of perpetrating a huge joke. But to this eighteen-year-old girl the process had already brought misery, embarrassment and the hint of future wretchedness" (p. 90).

Since Fauset spends much of the novel on the unfortunate fate of a character wihout a racial birthright, she must also suggest the characteristics of that birthright. Elsewhere, outside her novels, Fauset has spoken of the Black birthright as being a "spontanaeity of humor, mellow understanding, tolerance, warmth of fellowship that is beautiful." As the race "suffers, so does it rejoice. Target of the slings of fate, it learns the art of interpretation."[27] She has also stated the relevance to American literature of depicting that birthright. "I see sometimes the colored man as the last stronghold of those early American virtures which once we fought so hard to preserve—integrity, pride, indomitableness and a sort of gay hardihood. . . . A pity to let the archives of America build up without a record of the deeds and thoughts of these people, so brave and grave and gay. So I have tried to set them down."[28]

In *Comedy: American Style*, Fauset succinctly explores the Black birthright which Teresa has been denied through insights of various characters. Belief like Olivia's that the white race was created superior is denied by the fact that "there were more unwhite than white people in the world" (p. 206). The slave history of the American Black "had not been a special curse visited upon a special people. . . . It had been a cause to produce an effect, a necessity to permit a certain group of people an opportunity to glimpse and adopt another kind of cilivization" (p. 193). The essence of American Black history is survival.

> "Isn't that the salvation of all us colored people that we just don't play if we know we're going to lose? I know it's the fashion to admire the Indian because he put up such a good fight against the invading pale-face. But where is he now? Mostly dead . . . his relicts herded on reservations, his oil-land maladministered. . . . But you take us . . . "poor colored people" . . . we put up a fight of another kind. . . . We clung to life in the face of the cruelest treatment that the country has ever known. We learned new ways, new idioms of speech, new adjustments to climate and food. We even learnt and adapted new ideals of beauty" (pp. 261-62).

But the time for adoption of "white is beautiful—exclusively" —is past. Teresa thinks of the fallacy of white denial of Black beauty in observing "how earnestly and deliberately Americans every summer exposed themselves on shore and water to the burning sun in order to obtain the effect which, when natural, they affected so to despise" (p. 124). *Comedy: American Style* dwells on the particular beauty of certain shades of Black people. Nicholas Campbell and Henry Bates possess the "same combination of color, recklessness, hair, manner . . . which belongs to one special type of the American Negro of mixed blood, the chesnut brown. And there is no other species of mankind which possess just that same fatalness of charm except perhaps a certain type of Irishman" (p. 93). Dr. Cary agrees with Teresa that " 'your Henry's type [is] the most attractive that the world produces. . . .' He sighed . . . , thinking of some lovely creatures, all bronze and gold and fire, whom he had met in his youth" (p. 145).

Fauset's ideal Black person as suggested in *Comedy: American Style* is the one who has gone through acceptance and respect for racial inheritance to a confident but unchauvinistic awareness of human worth. Young Christopher Cary is described as such a post-Renaissance person. "He was entirely without the slightly self-righteous attitude which characterized so many young colored people of his day and station. Christopher never talked about 'my people,' never mouthed pompous phrases pertaining to 'the good of the race.' He was in this respect the forerunner of the modern young colored man who takes his training as a matter of course for himself primarily and for the race next" (p. 25). Alicia Barrett is another such person. Her "whole attitude said serenely: 'Here I am, the best of my kind, and I am perfectly satisfied with my kind.' Thus she arrived at a *ne plus ultra* at once personally satisfying and completely baffling to all conjectures on superior bloods, racial admixtures, hybridizations and all the sociological and biological generalizations of the day" (p. 83). The ultimate teaching is that which Grandfather Cary tries to give Oliver—"that greatness knew no race, no color; that real worth was the same the world over; that it was immediately recognizable and that it was a mark of genuine manhood to know no false shame" (pp. 193-94). Thus, Fauset tells us, a racial birthright is essential to a healthy emotional development, but exclusive racial identification is not the ideal goal of the mature adult.

One feels the greater difficulty of obtaining happiness and full, honest human relationships in *Comedy: American Style* than in Fauset's previous three novels, though those goals are the same in all four books. In this final novel, there are central characters who don't succeed in reaching those goals. It is not ture, however, that most of the characters "are ultimately frustrated, ill-adjusted and doomed, . . . victims of their own desire to deny their race, and of the cruelty, prejudice and lack of understanding by which they are surrounded."[29] Most of the characters are not doomed, but some of them are. In that realistic assessment of Black life in America Fauset concludes her long fiction.

Turning from thoughts and themes which emerge in Jessie Fauset's last novel to the form which she devised to contain them, one is struck by the singularity of what she attempted in this book, but is disappointed by its lack of full success. The use of dramatic analogue is direct here as it was indirect in *The Chinaberry Tree*. Division of the book is made in terms of elements of a play, with some subtle double entendre. The plan of the book is clever and appropriate to the topics dealt with; the language, however, is not manipulated with the imagination or skill required to create out of that plan a truly excellent novel.

In form, Fauset returns in *Comedy: American Style* to a Table of Contents division such as that used in *Plum Bun*. In this last novel the six divisions are elements of a play: "The Plot," "The Characters," "Teresa's Act," "Oliver's Act," "Phebe's Act," and "Curtain." The first section, "The Plot," deals with Olivia's childhood and young adulthood up to her marriage to Christopher Cary. The label "Plot" suggests that given Olivia's color mania, all else that happens in the book is somehow bound to follow. It also suggests that there is a subversive plan involved in the story. Since the ideal means of social control is to somehow induce the controlling principles into the very hearts and minds of the controlled, one does not have to think very far to discover the double meaning of "plot" as it is used for the first section of *Comedy: American Style*. To the extent that anti-Black feeling can be made part of Black consciousness, white American discrimination is made more efficient. By encouragement of Black hatred by Blacks, as by ignoring crime of Black against Black, the extant power of white dominant society is made ever more secure. Olivia Cary is an important component of such a plan.

The second section of the novel, "The Characters," begins after many years have elapsed. Olivia is well established as the domineering wife and mother of three. Before the section concludes with the good-by party for Teresa, who is off for prep school, controlling characteristics are established for the array of characters from the younger generation by means of some theater-like references. Two settings are contrasted in the young world of Teresa, Phebe, Marise, and Nicholas. The Cary household is cold except occasionally when Olivia is absent. Dark-skinned children are turned away at the door. Marise's home on the other hand is gay, warm, and open to all colors and temperaments. Periodically, Marise's mother sticks her head in the door to remind the children, later the high-schoolers, to be happy. "It seemed so wonderful to . . . [Teresa] that Marise's mother instead of talking of Ambition, or Standing or Racial Superiority should mention only Happiness" (p. 44).

It is in the warm setting of Marise's home that the young people play theatre, adopting roles that predict their futures. Marise dances with a precocious perfection; "she would never be second in any line" (p. 46). Phebe dances not for an audience, as does Marise, but "from a need to express herself"; when she becomes aware of Nicholas' eyes on her, she subsides "blushing and confused." "Nicholas' attention wavered; it wandered to Phebe, flickered once more to Marise and returned again to the little blond girl." As for Teresa, she accepts for costume "only a faded garland of flowers, she would be audience, she said" (pp. 46, 47).

Teresa "the interested and thoughtful spectator" (p. 57) observes the scenic color and action of her going away party, wanting "to etch this picture on her mind" (p. 57). Colors of faces and clothing mingle and contrast—nut-brown and pale lemon skins, "burnt" hair and pale gold hair and dark hair. Christopher and Marise "mysteriously seemed to convert" a waltz "into a ritual." About Nicholas there is "a peculiar faun-like quality that would never be held" (pp. 60, 58). Teresa the onlooker tries to store up the color and movement and gaiety of the moment for future sustenance, for her feeling of impending fate is intense. " 'I feel like a fly in a spider's web. I know I'm going to be caught, and I know I'm going to hang there. I won't have a lot of pain. I'll just live on stupid and dull and unable to stir. Hating everything' " (p. 55).

The next three sections of the novel—"Teresa's Act," "Oliver's Act," and "Phebe's Act"—are devoted to the stories of each of these characters in turn. "Act" in each case refers to the fact that the section belongs to that character, but also appears to refer to the crucial deed each character performs in the race comedy of American life. Teresa submits unwillingly, almost unwittingly, to her mother's debilitating influence in the key interview with the two of them and Henry Bates. Given this act, all the rest of Teresa's acquiescence and slow death follows. Oliver picks up the gun and uses it on himself, but dies with "the light of the declining day athwart his smiling face" (p. 226) Only Phebe's act departs from sad comic irony. She marries carefully and resists the temptation to deviate from the loyalty her careful choice has promised.

Apart from this double meaning suggested by the word "Act," there is little in these three sections of the book that exploits the possibility Fauset has established by means of this formal division. It would seem to be an excellent opportunity to use language suited to the perceptions of each character in turn, but there is no such accommodation made to changing views. The lack of language inventiveness is especially noticeable in "Oliver's Act." Having as central character an intelligent sensitive child whose perspicacity can nevertheless not penetrate the mystery of his mother's disaffection for him, would suggest an excellent chance for delving into that child's perception from the inside out rather than in external summary. But Fauset's writing does not accommodate itself to Oliver's character. Rather, we are told in her usual precise intellectual prose that "because of his mother's indifference, he has known, before he was six years old, three widely different homes. In his childish way he had made contrasts and had long since decided which home—by which at that time he meant environment—he truly preferred" (p. 187).

Fauset does recognize the possibilities of language variants. Teresa Cary admires various qualities of Black English. Henry Bates' imitation of "the soft lingo of the Southern immigrant" appeals to her. " 'Bofe of us has got to get heaps an' heaps mo' education than we has yet, Honey' " (p. 94). So does his "whimsical accent," as in " 'and often.' " "She loved his deliberate negroid inflection from which her mother had so carefully guarded her" (p. 95). But self-consciously, Fauset always points out her awareness of departing from Standard American English. " 'Oh piffle!' said Teresa, happily slangy" (p. 97). The self-conscious inhibition seems to prevent creative and effective use of the language skills Fauset clearly has. Her standardized style comes not from inability to depart from it, but from unwillingness to do so. She thereby loses one potential benefit of the dramatic structure she has chosen to give *Comedy: American Style*—the revelation of character through the character's language.

The possible formal strength of drama analogy is in *Comedy: Amerian Style* also weakened by material which seems stylistically intrusive in that structure. It has been seen that this last Fauset novel explores positive elements of Black American birthright to an extent not evident in the earlier novels. The expository method by which this exploration is made does not, however, fit readily with the overall dramatic structure of the book. Christopher Cary Sr.'s teachings to his children are revealed in a summary form, almost like a direct lecture from the author (p. 39). Oliver's grandfather's teachings on slave history are given in the same undramatic and non-individualized way (p. 193). Other descriptions are developed beyond their dramatic functions. Much time is spent discussing "Old Philadelphia," for example, even though that particular societal syndrome is not crucial to the prime characters of the novel (p. 190). The travel descriptions of Olivia's and Teresa's boat trip to France and their tours of Toulouse and surrounding area serve more to show the range of the author's experience than to develop insight into the characters and their actions (pp. 164, 175). Finally, the many pages spent on Janet Blanchard's life, while interesting as a picture of a remarkable self-educated woman, do little for the central plot of Olivia Blanchard Cary and her effect on the lives which surround her. Fauset's dramatic divisions in *Comedy: American Style* are more superficially imposed upon the book than organically grown out of it.

The final section of this bitter comedy of American life is called "Curtain." Olivia Cary has left the Philadelphia home of the Carys and Phebe's family to go first to Teresa's cottage in Toulouse, where she is kicked out by Aristide, who is enraged because no money has come from this rich American family he thought he had married into. She tries Paris but low funds force her into an isolated, cramped, lonely lifestyle. She tries to maintain her pretenses of grandeur with another woman doing the same thing. " 'I have a daughter too, in Toulouse. She's married to one of the professors at the University there, a brilliant fellow and so charming! My daughter is always writing me to come there and live with them' " (p. 323). Desperate, she writes her husband for funds for the trip home. Delightfully, he writes that he does not have enough money to bring her home, but that he will send her $50 a month so she can stay in Paris. Olivia Blanchard Cary is last seen looking out into the "thin watery sunshine" of the "tangled garden" outside the window of her pension in *la rue Romain*. There sit a mother and son, reading and laughing together. "He was a slender, rather tall lad, but young.

About the age of Oliver in the days when he used to come running up to his mother's room to confide in her about his algebra" (p. 327).

With these lines and no added comment Fauset concludes *Comedy: American Style*. While the contrast between Olivia and the mother and son in the garden is plain, there is no evidence that Olivia sees it or learns from it or regrets any of her past acts. The forced lonely exile in Paris is a culminating irony for both Olivia Cary and for Fauset's picture of the unhumorous ironies of American Black life. Olivia is finally white, with no person and no situation to endanger that status. She has exactly what she wanted—and what she deserved. By making Olivia white and unfree in Paris Fauset has reinforced her dominant theme, evident in all four of her novels. Racial barriers abound, and sexual barriers abound, but beyond all that what really counts for happiness and for fulfillment are human relationships. Paris might be the Black expatriate's dream of the discrimination-free society, and being white might look like a cure-all for the problems of the American Black, but neither is worth dreaming about or sacrificing for if one has failed in the area of relating to other human beings. Jessie Fauset might have some difficulties with form in the modern novel, some stylistic quirks, some shyness of innovation, but her head and her heart, one concludes, are very much in the right places.

Notes

1 Jessie Fauset, "Foreword," *The Chinaberry Tree* (New York: Frederick A. Stokes Comapny, 1931), p. ix.

2 Gerald Sykes, "Amber-Tinted Elegance," *Nation*, 27 July 1932, p. 88.

3 Jessie Fauset, *The Chinaberry Tree* (New York: Frederick A. Stokes Company, 1931), p. 44. Subsequent references to this novel will be indicated

by page number in the text. The conventional moral values of Red Brook's Black community are obviously reactions at least in part to the white community's judgement. One reviewer of *The Chinaberry Tree*, Edwin Burgum in *Opportunity*, March 1932, page 88, points out accurately that "for any race that suffers consciously from surrounding prejudice, the attainment of respectability is the one sort of imitation that can eradicate it." Fauset, however, makes no explicit point of this fact in the novel. White onlooking as a determinant of Black behavior occurs only in the skating scene. Fauset thus either intends to show the inhumane holding to conventional judgement from generation to generation in the Black community as either Blacks' complete internalizing of the dominant society's values, or as a human characteristic to be found everywhere, no matter what the race.

[4]One of the most unfair selective quotations of Fauset by a hostile critic is Paule Marshall's quotation of this line to supposedly show the "flight away from the black brother at the bottom of the heap" and the attempt to prove the mulatto as better than darker skinned Blacks. ("The Negro Women in Literature," *Freedomways*, 1966, p. 22.) The most elementary literary criticism would remind Marshall that this is a character speaking early in a book, and that by the time the book ends, the character's early erroneous assumptions have been turned upside down.

[5]Nick Aaron Ford, ed., *Black Insights* (Waltham, Massachusetts: Ginn & Company, 1971), p. 59.

[6]Marion L. Starkey, "Jessie Fauset," *Southern Workman* (May 1932), p. 220.

[7]Letter from Jessie Fauset to Montgomery Gregory, 29 March 1922. Thomas M. Gregroy Papers, Box 2, Moorland-Spingarn Research Center, Howard University.

[8]Alain Locke, "We Turn to Prose—A Retrospective Review of the Literature of the Negro for 1931," *Opportunity* (February 1932), p. 43.

[9]Joseph J. Feeney, S. J., "Greek Tragic Patterns in a Black Novel; Jessie Fauset's *The Chinaberry Tree*," *CLA Journal* (December 1974), pp. 211-15.

[10]C. L. Barber, *Shakespeare's Festive Comedy: A Study of Dramatic Form and Its Relation to Social Custom* (Princeton, N.J.: Princeton University Press, 1959), pp. 4-5, 8.

[11] These elements of Shakespeare's Festive Comedy are discussed by Barber on pages 79, 129, 9, 123, and 156.

[12] Hugh Gloster, *Negro Voices in American Fiction* (1948; rpt. New York: Russell & Russell, 1965), p. 36.

[13] Richard Wright, "Blueprint for Negro Writing," *New Challenge* (Fall, 1937), p. 61.

[14] Starkey, pp. 218, 219.

[15] *Ibid.*, pp. 219-20.

[16] *Ibid.*, p. 217.

[17] Florence Smith **Vincent**, "There are 20,000 Persons 'Passing' Says Noted Author," *Pittsburgh Courier*, 11 May 1929, Section 2, p. 1.

[18] Sykes, p. 88.

[19] Jessie Fauset to Zona Gale, 20 October 1931, **Zona** Gale Papers, State Historical Society of Wisconsin, Madison, Wisconsin.

[20] Vincent, p. 1.

[21] Jessie Fauset, *Comedy: American Style* (1933; rpt. College Park, Maryland: McGrath Publishing Company, 1969), p. 124. Subsequent references to this novel will be indicated by page number in the text.

[22] Gloster, p. 138.

[23] Elise Johnson McDougald, "The Double Task: The Struggle of Negro Women for Sex and Race Emancipation," *Survey* (1 March 1925), p. 689.

[24] Sterling Brown, "A Century of Negro Portraiture in American Literature," *Massachusetts Review*, VII (Winter, 1966). Reprinted in Jules Chametzky and Sidney Kaplan, eds. *Black and White in American Culture: An Anthology From the Massachusetts Review* (University of Massachusetts Press, 1969), p. 345.

[25] Kenny Williams, *They Also Spoke: An Essay on Negro Literature in America, 1787-1930* (Nashville, Tennessee: Townsend Press, 1970), p. 269.

[26]W. E. B. DuBois, "The Damnation of Women," *Darkwater* (1920; rpt. New York: Schocken, 1969), pp. 163-86.

[27]Vincent, p. 1.

[28]Gwendolyn Cherry, *et. al.*, *Portraits in Color: The Lives of Colorful Negro Women* (New York: Pageant Press, 1962), p. 144.

[29]"The Color Line," *New York Times Book Review*, 19 November 1933, p. 19.

Conclusion

This study of Jessie Redmon Fauset began by saying that at this stage in criticism of her work, it is necessary to consider biographical as well as literary materials. Such dual emphasis is in part a necessary corrective for the many superficial critiques of Fauset's novels which have assumed thematic emphases based on frequently erroneous, misleading, or incomplete knowledge about her life. She was an "Old Philadelphian," such critiques run. She was "established," "comfortable," "protected," "elite." What could be more reasonable than to suppose that she wrote her books to promote and advance the social group to which she was so happily confined? What more needs to be said, once Fauset is thus handily categorized? Why even bother to read the novels carefully, let alone other things she wrote?

In fact, study of Jessie Fauset's life and her work, made without preconceptions about either, results in the emergence of a person and a writer who does not yet appear in Black literature anthologies and histories. Here is a Black woman who set off for Cornell at a time when Black faces were rare and Black women's faces were practically non-existent on America's major college campuses. She went to Cornell not on her daddy's money, but on a hard-won scholarship. She worked her way to a Phi Beta Kappa election. She defied habits and expectations and norms for Black and white women alike by her college career, her subsequent professional career, her financial independence. She joined and worked for the organizaton that was out there all alone in 1910 in working for Black rights—the NAACP. She stayed with its publishing arm, *The Crisis*, as writer, then editor, then writer again, for sixteen years. She saw to it that when Harlem exploded in population and creativity, she was there to take part, to encourage, to enjoy some of the goals toward which she had worked.

A study of Fauset's life reveals the shallowness of the biographical sketches which classify and dismiss her as an "Old Philadelphian" whose family rather than whose achievements gave her a position in society. Such a study also shows to what an extent her own life was a model of the sort she sought to promote for encouragement of the young. Learning of advances gained against great odds—in Jessie Fauset's case racism and sexism—can entertain and inspire as well as correct cumulative misconceptions. The story of Jessie Fauset's life is interesting and revealing in itself.

It is nevertheless for her work that Fauset is most likely to be remembered and studied. Her influence on Black art in the period of the Harlem Renaissance cannot be measured. It can be exposed as it has not been before, and it can be evaluated on the basis of that exposure. Fauset's editorial work can be separated and examined apart from the previously dominating image of W. E. B. DuBois. She can be given credit for the literary achievement and influence of *The Crisis* in the 1920s, the educational impressiveness of the *Brownies' Book*. Her views on language learning, on poverty, on "Black power," tucked into her reviews and articles and essays, can be described as advanced for the time at which they were written, carefully thought-out and informed.

Jessie Fauset's four novels can and must be more closely studied than they have been. The reader and the critic need to come to her work having discarded carelessly made assumptions about her themes and her aims and her achievements or failures. The reader-critic should come with one assumption only: that Jessie Fauset the novelist was educated, sophisticated, widely-read, and deliberate in what she created. Such an assumption will hopefully help a reader perceive some of the formal parallels to other literature, some of the calculated disguise Fauset used in her novels.

Jessie Fauset's primary strengths are strengths of character. Intelligence and curiosity are supplemented by kindness, generosity, graciousness, tolerance. She impresses one as being well-rounded, well-adjusted—traits which made her an excellent literary editor and friend to artists. The same traits might be said to have prevented her from making a greater name for herself in literature, however. She had no dominating passion, no driving opinions which scattered all else before. In comparison with the other female novelist of the Harlem Renaissance period, Nella Larsen, Fauset has a wider scope of interests, a more inclusive range of themes and concerns, but correspondingly a less intense presentation.

The strengths of Fauset's writing are the strengths of her character. Her essays reveal curiosity and sympathy most fully, but the novels, too, leave one with an impression of strength gained through difficulties overcome. Far from promoting a limited notion of "respectability," Fauset's emphasis falls very much on recognizing morality which is at variance with society's codes. American society's restrictive codes frequently center around sex roles and race roles, as Fauset knew very well. Many of the female characters she chose to portray quietly but surely examined those codes, discarded many of them, and created their own. They do not scream or preach while doing so. Fauset's presentation of alternatives to defining "Black American woman" is done in a way which is itself an unobtrusive alternative to dominant opining. Her books, while they also entertain, are more exploratory than dogmatic, more searching than protesting.

The weaknesses of Fauset's writing can be better understood from facts of her life. A kind of self-consciousness seems to prevent her from using in her novels the unusual first person viewpoints, the dialect, or the passion that one finds in some of her short stories and poetry. Her concern for language preciseness leads to her calling attention to "non-standard" English when she slips into it. Those characteristics are not surprising in one who has achieved financial security and prominence primarily through schooling. A scholarship to Cornell would not have been found in 1900 for a woman advocating Black English.

Fauset's awareness of her audience perhaps also prevented her from greater experimentation in form than she engaged in. She was greatly concerned about the education of the young, evidenced in

her teaching and in materials written for *The Crisis* and the *Brownies'
Book*. Fauset's 1912 *Crisis* article on the Montessori Method indicates the beginning of a constant concern in her life. To write what
could edify the young, entertain the unsophisticated, and delight the
literary critic, white or Black, was no small task. In typical unselfishness, Fauset placed creating what was helpful to others before
creating pure art for her own pleasure.

Jessie Fauset and her novels have been much maligned. She
deserves accuracy about her life. Her work deserves exposure and
close study. At the point of humility before the researcher's task
of accuracy and the critic's task of perception, one is moved by the
struggle of living, the vitality of literature. The facts of Jessie Redmon Fauset's life and the truths of her writing are individual. They
are also universal.

Bibliography

I. Books, Articles, Newspaper Sources Found Useful in This Study.
    Bibliographies, Dictionary Catalogues to Library Collections, Research
    Guides, Indexes to Black Literature, Checklists, and Standard Refer-
    ence Works are Not Included, Except Those Which are Cited Directly
    in the Text.

Adams, Russell. *Great Negroes, Past and Present*. Chicago, 1964.

Adoff, Arnold. *The Poetry of Black America: Anthology of the 20th
    Century*. New York: Harper and Row, 1973. Jessie Fauset,
    "Oriflamme," p. 18.

Analytical Guide and Indexes to the Crisis, 1910-1960. Westport,
    Connecticut: Greenwood Press, 1975.

Aptheker, Herbert. "Afro-American Superiority: A Neglected Theme
    in the Literature." *Black Life and Culture in the United States*.
    Ed. R. L. Goldstein. New York: Thomas Y. Crowell, 1971,
    pp. 165-79.

—. *The Annotated Bibliography of the Published Writings of W. E. B.
    DuBois*. Millwood, New York: Kraus-Thompson, 1973.

—, ed. *The Correspondence of W. E. B. DuBois. Vol. I: Selections
    1877-1934*. Amherst: University of Massachusetts Press, 1973.

—, ed. *A Documentary History of the Negro People: The Reconstruc-
    tion Era to 1910*. New York: The Citadel Press, 1951.

—, ed. *A Documentary History of the Negro People: 1910 to 1932*.
    Secaucus, New Jersey; The Citadel Press, 1973.

Baker, Ray Stannard. *Following the Color Line: American Negro Citizenship in the Progressive Era.* 1908; rpt. New York: Harper and Row, 1964.

Barber, C. L. *Shakespeare's Festive Comedy: A Study of Dramatic Form and Its Relation to Social Custom.* Princeton, New Jersey: Princeton University Press, 1959.

Bardolph, Richard. *The Negro Vanguard.* New York: Alfred A. Knopf, Inc., 1959.

Becker, M. L. "The Reader's Guide" [Review of *The Chinaberry Tree*]. *Saturday Review of Literature,* 5 March 1932, p. 577.

Bell, Roseann Pope. "*The Crisis* and *Opportunity* Magazines: Reflections of a Black Culture, 1920-1930." Diss. Emory University, 1974.

Bercovici, Konrad. "Real Negro City Arising in Harlem." *New York World,* 22 September 1924, n. pag.

Berry, Ephraim. "To Market, To Market: The Bookshelf." *Chicago Defender,* 8 June 1929, II, p. 1.

Berry, Faith. "Voice for the Jazz Age, Great Migration, or Black Bourgeoisie." *Black World* (November 1970), pp. 10-16.

B. K. [Review of *Plum Bun*]. *New Republic,* 10 April 1929, p. 235.

Bland, Edward. "Social Forces Shaping the Negro Novel." *Negro Quarterly* (Fall 1942), pp. 241-48.

Bond, Horace Mann. "Negro Leadership Since Washington." *South Atlantic Quarterly* (April 1925), pp. 115-30.

Bone, Robert. *The Negro Novel in America.* Rev. ed. New Haven, Connecticut: Yale University Press, 1966.

Bontemps, Arna. "The Black Renaissance of the Twenties." *Black World* (November 1970), pp. 5-9.

—. ed. *Golden Slippers: An Anthology of Negro Poetry for the Young Reader*. New York: Harper and Row, 1941. Jessie Fauset, "I Think I See Her," p. 165.

—. "The Harlem Renaissance." *Saturday Review of Literature*, 22 March 1947, pp. 12-13, 44.

—, ed. *The Harlem Renaissance Remembered*. New York: Dodd, Mead and Company, 1972.

—. "The Negro Renaissance: Jean Toomer and the Harlem Writers of the 1920's." *Anger and Beyond*. Ed. Herbert Hill. New York: Harper and Row, 1966, pp. 20-36.

—. "Special Collections of Negroana." *Library Quarterly* (July 1944), pp. 187-206.

— and Jack Conroy. *Any Place But Here*. New York: Hill and Wang, 1966.

Braithwaite, William S. "Alain Locke's Relationship to the Negro in American Literature." *Phylon* (Second Quarter 1957), pp. 166-73.

—. "The Novels of Jessie Fauset." *Opportunity* (January 1934), pp. 24-28. Reprinted in Robert Hemenway. *The Black Novelist*. Columbus, Ohio: Charles E. Merrill, 1970, and in Philip Butcher, ed. *The William Stanley Braithwaite Reader*. Ann Arbor, Michigan: The University of Michigan Press, 1972.

—. "Some Contemporary Poets of the Negro Race." *The Crisis* (April 1919), pp. 275-80.

Brawley, Benjamin. "Negro Contemporary Literature." *English Journal* (March 1929), pp. 194-202.

—. *The Negro in Literature and Art in the United States*. New York: Duffield and Green, Inc., 1929.

—. "The Negro Literary Renaissance." *Southern Workman* (April 1927), pp. 177-84.

—. "The Promise of Negro Literature." *The Journal of Negro History*, 19 (1934), pp. 56-59.

—. *The Negro Genius*. New York: Dodd, Mead and Company, 1937.

Brisbane, Robert. *The Black Vanguard*. Valley Forge, Pennsylvania: Judson Press, 1970.

Brown, Jean Collier. "The Negro Woman Worker: 1860-1890." *Black Women in White America*. Ed. Gerda Lerner. New York: Random House, 1973, pp. 430-31.

Brown, Sterling. "A Century of Negro Portraiture in American Literature." *Black and White in American Culture: An Anthology from the Massachusetts Review*. Ed. Jules Chametzky and Sidney Kaplan. Amherst: University of Massachusetts Press, 1969, pp. 333-59.

—. "The Negro Author and His Publisher." *Negro Quarterly* (Spring 1942), pp. 7-20.

—. "Negro Character as Seen by White Authors." *Journal of Negro Education* (January 1933), pp. 180-201.

—. *The Negro in American Fiction* and *The Negro in Poetry and Drama*. 1937; rpt. New York: Atheneum, 1969.

—. "Our Literary Audience." *Opportunity* (February 1930), pp. 42-46, 61.

—, Arthur P. Davis and Ulysses Lee. *The Negro Caravan: Writings by American Negroes*. New York: Citadel Press, 1941. Jessie Fauset, "Color Struck," pp. 189-96.

Burgum, Edwin Berry. [Review of *The Chinaberry Tree*]. *Opportunity* (March 1932), pp. 88-89.

Callis, Henry Arthur, et. al. "The Legacy of W. E. B. DuBois." *Freedomways* (Winter 1965), pp. 17-18.

Calverton, V. F. *An Anthology of American Negro Literature*. New York: Modern Library, 1929. Jessie Fauset, "La Vie C'est La Vie" and from *There Is Confusion*, pp. 92-106; 206.

—. "The Negro's New Belligerant Attitude." *Current History* (September 1929), pp. 1081-88.

Calvin, Floyd. "The Digest." *Pittsburgh Courier*, 5 April 1924, p. 20.

—. "The Digest." *Pittsburgh Courier*, 19 April 1924, p. 20.

—. "Harlem Society Repudiated." *Pittsburgh Courier*, 23 January 1932, p. 2.

Chamberlain, John. "The Negro as Writer." *Bookman* (February 1930), pp. 603-11.

Chapman, Abraham. "The Harlem Renaissance in Literary History." *CLA Journal*, 11 (1967), pp. 38-58.

"Charleston a Hit in Home, Dance Hall, and Ballroom." *Harlem on My Mind*. Ed. Allen Schoener. New York: Random House, 1968, pp. 66-67.

Cherry, Gwendolyn, et. al. *Portraits in Color*. New York: Pageant Press, 1962.

Chesnutt, Charles. "Post-Bellum, Pre-Harlem." *The Crisis* (June 1931), pp. 193-94.

Childress, Alice. "The Negro Woman in American Literature." *Freedomways*, 6 (1966), pp. 14-19; 75-80.

Clarke, John Henrik. *Harlem: Community in Transition*. New York: Citadel Press, 1969.

—. "The Neglected Dimensions of the Harlem Renaissance." *Black World* (November 1970), pp. 118-29.

—. "The Origin and Growth of Afro-American Literature." *Negro Digest* (December 1967), pp. 54-67.

—, Esther Jackson, Ernest Kaiser, J. H. Dell, eds. *Black Titan: W. E. B. DuBois: An Anthology by the Editors of Freedomways.* Boston: Beacon Press, 1970.

Coleman, Horace. "The Black Aesthetic Straitjacket." Paper for the Midwest Modern Language Association Meeting, Fall 1975, Chicago.

"The Color Line." [Review of *Comedy: American Style*]. *New York Times Book Review*, 19 November 1933, p. 19.

Cullen, Countee. *Caroling Dusk: An Anthology of Verse by Negro Poets.* New York: Harper and Brothers, 1927. Jessie Fauset, "Words! Words!" "Touche," "Noblesse Oblige," "La Vie C'est La Vie," "The Return," "Recontre," "Fragment," pp. 65-70.

Culp, D. W., ed. *Twentieth Century Negro Literature or a Cyclopedia of Thought on the Vital Topics Relating to the American Negro by One Hundred of America's Greatest Negroes.* 1902; rpt. New York: Arno Press, 1969.

Cunard, Nancy. *Negro Anthology.* 1934; rpt. New York: Frederick Ungar, 1970.

Dannett, Sylvia. *Profiles of Negro Womanhood. Vol. II: 20th Century.* New York: Negro Heritage Library, 1966.

Davis, Allison. "Our Negro 'Intellectuals.' " *The Crisis* (August 1928), pp. 268-69; 284-86.

Davis, Arthur P. *From the Dark Tower: Afro-American Writers, 1900-1960.* Washington, D. C.: Howard University Press, 1974.

—. "Growing up in The New Negro Renaissance: 1920-1935." *Negro American Literature Forum*, 2 (1966), pp. 53-59.

—, and Saunders Redding. *Cavalcade: Negro American Writing from 1760 to the Present*. Boston: Houghton Mifflin, 1971. Jessie Fauset, "Class," pp. 354-58.

Davis, Elizabeth. *Lifting as They Climb: The National Association of Colored Women*. n. p., 1933.

Davis, Gary. "Henry Fielding and the Play of Difference." Unpublished Manuscript.

Daykin, Walter. "Social Thought in Negro Novels." *Sociology and Social Research* (January-February 1935), pp. 247-52.

DeArmond, Fred. "A Note on the Sociology of Negro Literature." *Opportunity* (December 1925), pp. 369-71.

"The Debut of the Younger School of Negro Writers," *Opportunity* (May 1924), pp. 143-44.

The Delta Journal: Official Publication of Delta Sigma Theta Sorority, 1946.

Detweiler, Frederick G. *The Negro Press, and Its Editors*. 1922; rpt. College Park, Maryland: McGrath Publishing Company, 1968.

Dreer, Herman. *American Literature by Negro Authors*. New York: Macmillan, 1950. Jessie Fauset, "Christmas Time," pp. 255-63.

"The Drop Sinister." *The Crisis* (October 1915), pp. 286-87.

DuBois, W. E. B. "The Browsing Reader." *The Crisis* (March 1929), pp. 125, 138.

—. "Criteria for Negro Art." *The Crisis* (October 1926), pp. 290-97.

—. *Darkwater* 1920; rpt. New York: Schocken Books, 1969.

—. *Dusk of Dawn: An Essay Toward an Autobiography of a Race Concept*. New York: Harcourt, Brace and Company, 1940.

—. "Negro Journalism." *The Crisis* (July 1929), pp. 242-45.

—. *Philadelphia Negro*. Philadelphia, 1899.

—. "Returning Soldiers." *The Crisis* (May 1919), pp. 13-14.

—. "Review: In Abraham's Bosom." *The Crisis* (March 1927), p. 12.

—. "Some High School Teachers of New York City." *The Crisis* (July 1926), pp. 137-40.

—. *Souls of Black Folk*. 1903; rpt. *Three Negro Classics*. New York: Avon, 1965.

—. "The Winds of Time." *Chicago Defender*, 3 November 1945, p. 15.

—, and Alain Locke. "The Younger Literary Movement." *The Crisis* (February 1924), pp. 161-63.

Edwards, Lee and Arlyn Diamond. *American Voices, American Women*. New York: Avon, 1973. Jessie Fauset, from *Plum Bun*, pp. 384-432.

E. D. W. [Review of *There Is Confusion*]. *New Republic*, 9 July 1924, p. 192.

Fauset, Arthur. *For Freedom: A Biographical Story of the American Negro*. Philadelphia: Franklin Publishing and Supply Company, 1927.

Fauset, Jessie Redmon. "After School: A Poem." *Brownies' Book* (January 1920), p. 30.

—. "Again It is September." *The Crisis* (September 1917), p. 248.

—. "As to Books." *The Crisis* (May 1922), pp. 66-68.

—. "At The Zoo. Verses." *Brownies' Book* (March 1920), pp. 85-86.

—. " 'Batouala' is Translated." *The Crisis* (September 1922), pp. 218-19.

—. *The Chinaberry Tree*. New York: Frederick A. Stokes Company, 1931.

—. "Christmas Eve in France," *The Independent* (December 1917), p. 552.

—. *Comedy: American Style*. 1933; rpt. College Park, Maryland: McGrath Publishing Company, 1969.

—. "Cordelia Goes on the War Path. A Story." *Brownies' Book* (May 1921), pp. 148-54.

—. " 'Courage!' He Said." *The Crisis* (November 1929), p. 378.

—. "Dark Algiers The White." *The Crisis* (April 1925; May 1925), pp. 255-58; 16-22.

—. "Dedication." *Brownies' Book* (January 1920), p. 32.

—. "Dilworth Road Revisited." *The Crisis* (August 1922), p. 167.

—. "Double Trouble." *The Crisis* (August 1923; September 1923), pp. 155-59; 205-09.

—. "Douce Sourvenance." *The Crisis* (May 1920), p. 42.

—. "The Easter Idyl. A Poem." *Brownies' Book* (April 1920), pp. 112-13.

—. "The Emancipator of Brazil." *The Crisis* (March 1921), pp. 208-09.

—. "Emmy." *The Crisis* (December 1912; January 1913), pp. 79-87; 134-42.

—. "The Enigma of the Sorbonne." *The Crisis* (March 1925), pp. 216-19.

—. "Episodes in Tangier." *The Metropolitan: A Monthly Review* (January 1935), pp. 8-9.

—. "The Eucalyptus Tree: A Reverie of Rome, the Catacombs, Christianity, and the Moving Beauty of Italy." *The Crisis* (January 1926), pp. 116-17.

—. "Ghosts and Kittens. A Story." *Brownies' Book* (February 1921), pp. 46-51.

—. "The Gift of Laughter." *The New Negro*. Ed. Alain Locke. 1925; rpt. New York: Atheneum, 1969, pp. 161-67.

—. "Henry Ossawa Tanner." *The Crisis* (April 1924), pp. 255-58.

—. "Here's April!" *The Crisis* (April 1924), p. 277.

—. "Impressions of the Second Pan-African Congress." *The Crisis* (November 1921), pp. 12-18.

—, trans. "Joseph and Mary Come to Bethlehem." Tr. from an Old French chanson. *The Crisis* (December 1920), pp. 72-73.

—, trans. "Kirongozi (Essays on Life in the Belgian Congo)." *The Crisis* (March 1924), pp. 208-09

—, trans. "La Question des Noirs aux Etats-Unis by Frank L. Schoell." *The Crisis* (June 1924), pp. 83-86.

—. "La Vie C'Est La Vie." *The Crisis* (July 1922), p. 124.

—. " 'Looking Backward.' " *The Crisis* (January 1922), pp. 125-26.

—. "Mary Elizabeth. A Story." *The Crisis* (December 1919), pp. 51-56.

—. "Merry Christmas to All: A Story." *Brownies' Book* (December 1920), pp. 355-60.

—. "The Montessori Method—Its Possibilities." *The Crisis* (July 1912), pp. 136-38.

—. "My House and a Glimpse of My Life Therein." *The Crisis* (July 1914), pp. 143-45.

—. "Nationalism and Egypt." *The Crisis* (April 1920), pp. 310-16.

—. "The Negro in Art: How Shall He be Portrayed: A Symposium." *The Crisis* (June 1926), p. 71.

—. "The New Books." *The Crisis* (February 1924), pp. 174-77.

—. "New Literature on the Negro." *The Crisis* (June 1920), pp. 78-83.

—. "No End of Books." *The Crisis* (March 1922), pp. 208-10.

—. "Nostalgia." *The Crisis* (August 1921), pp. 154-58.

—. "On The Bookshelf." *The Crisis* (May 1921), pp. 60-64.

—. "Oriflamme." *The Crisis* (January 1920), p. 128.

—. "Our Book Shelf." *The Crisis* (March 1926), pp. 238-39.

—. "Out of the West." *The Crisis* (November 1923), pp. 11-18.

—. "Pastures New." *The Crisis* (September 1920), pp. 224-26.

—. *Plum Bun*. New York: Frederick A. Stokes Company, 1929.

—, trans. "The Pool. A Poem. Amedee Brun." *The Crisis* (September 1921), p. 205.

—. "Rain Fugue." *The Crisis* (August 1924), p. 155.

—. " 'Rank Imposes Obligation.' A Biographical Essay on Martin Robinson Delany." *The Crisis* (November 1926), pp. 9-13.

—. "Recontre." *The Crisis* (January 1924), p. 122.

—. "The Return." *The Crisis* (January 1919), p. 118.

—. trans. "The Return of the Bells. A Story." *Brownies' Book* (April 1920), pp. 99-102.

—. "Rondeau." *The Crisis* (April 1912), p. 252.

—. "Saint-George, Chevalier of France." *The Crisis* (May 1921), pp. 9-12.

—. "The Sleeper Wakes." *The Crisis* (August 1920; September 1920; October 1920), pp. 168-73; 226-29; 267-74.

—. "Some Books for Boys and Girls." *The Crisis* (October 1912), pp. 295-98.

—. "Some Notes on Color." *The World Tomorrow* (March 1922), pp. 76-77. Rpt. Herbert Aptheker, ed. *A Documentary History of the Negro People in the United States: 1910-1932*. Secaucus, New Jersey: The Citadel Press, 1973, pp. 354-58. A condensed version, entitled "Negro View of the Color Problem," is in *Missionary Review* (June 1926), pp. 442-43.

—. "Song for a Lost Comrade (To O. B. J.)." *The Crisis* (November 1922), p. 22.

—. "Spring Songs. Verses." *Brownies' Book* (May 1920), pp. 146-47.

—. "Stars in Alabama." *The Crisis* (January 1928), p. 14.

—. "Sunday Afternoon." *The Crisis* (February 1922), pp. 162-64.

—, trans. "The Sun of Brittany." *The Crisis* (November 1927), p. 303.

—. "The Symbolism of Bert Williams." *The Crisis* (May 1922), pp. 12-15.

—. "In Talladega." *The Crisis* (February 1928), pp. 47-48.

—. "That Story of George Washington." *Brownies' Book* (February 1920), p. 64.

—. *There Is Confusion.* 1924; rpt. New York: AMS Press, 1974.

—. " 'There Was One Time.' A Story of Spring." *The Crisis* (April 1917; May 1917), pp. 272-77; 11-15.

—. "The Thirteenth Biennial of the N. A. C. W." *The Crisis* (October 1922), pp. 257-60.

—. "This Way to the Flea Market." *The Crisis* (February 1925), pp. 161-63.

—. "Three Books." *The Crisis* (December 1920), pp. 62-64.

—, trans. "To a Foreign Maid." *The Crisis* (February 1923), p. 158.

—. "Tracing Shadows." *The Crisis* (September 1915), pp. 247-51.

—, trans. "The Treasures of the Poor." *The Crisis* (December 1917), pp. 63-65.

—. "Turkey Drumsticks. A Thanksgiving Story." *Brownies' Book* (November 1920), pp. 342-46.

—. "Two Christmas Songs, Verses." *Brownies' Book* (December 1920), p. 384.

—. "What Europe Thought of the Pan-African Congress." *The Crisis* (December 1921), pp. 60-69.

—. "What to Read." *The Crisis* (March 1912), pp. 211-12.

—. "What to Read." *The Crisis* (April 1912), pp. 261-62.

—. "What to Read." *The Crisis* (June 1912), pp. 92-93.

—. "What to Read." *The Crisis* (August 1912), p. 183.

—. "What to Read." *The Crisis* (September 1912), pp. 249-50.

—. "What to Read." *The Crisis* (November 1912), p. 38.

—. "What to Read." *The Crisis* (September 1913), p. 248.

—. " '—When Christmas Comes.' " *The Crisis* (December 1922), pp. 61-63.

—. " 'Wings for God's Chillun': The Story of Burghardt DuBois." *The World Tomorrow* (August 1929), pp. 333-36. Published anonymously.

—. "Yarrow Revisited." *The Crisis* (January 1925), pp. 107-09.

—. "The 'Y' Conference at Talladega." *The Crisis* (September 1923), pp. 213-15.

— and Alain Locke. "Notes on the New Books." *The Crisis* (February 1923), pp. 161-65.

Feeney, Joseph J. "Greek Tragic Patterns in a Black Novel: Jessie Fauset's *The Chinaberry Tree*." CLA Journal (December 1974), pp. 211-15.

Fisher, Rudolph. "The Caucasian Storms Harlem." *American Mercury* (August 1927), pp. 393-98.

Flexner, Eleanor. *Century of Struggle: The Woman's Rights Movement in the United States*. New York: Atheneum, 1973.

Ford, Nick Aaron. *The Contemporary Negro Novel, A Study in Race Relations.* Boston: Meador, 1936.

—, ed. *Black Insights.* Waltham, Massachusetts: Ginn and Company, 1971.

Franklin, John Hope. *From Slavery to Freedom.* New York: Alfred A. Knopf, 1974.

Frazier, E. Franklin. "The American Negro's New Leaders." *Current History*, 28 (1928), 56-59.

—. *The Negro Church in America.* New York: Schocken Books, 1964.

—. *The Negro in the United States.* Rev. ed. New York: Macmillan, 1971.

—. "Racial Self-Expression." *Ebony and Topaz.* New York: National Urban League, 1927, pp. 119-21.

Gaines, Francis Pendleton. "The Racial Bar Sinister in American Romance." *South Atlantic Quarterly* (October 1926), pp. 396-402.

Gayle, Addison, ed. *The Black Aesthetic.* New York: Doubleday, 1970.

—. "The Harlem Renaissance: Towards a Black Aesthetic." *Midcontinent American Studies Journal* (Fall 1970), pp. 78-87.

—. *The Way of the New World: The Black Novel in America.* New York: Garden City, New York, 1976.

George, Carol. *Segregated Sabbaths.* New York: Oxford University Press, 1973.

Gilmer, Walter. *Horace Liverright: Publisher of the Twenties.* New York: David Lewis, 1970.

Glicksberg, Charles I. "The Negro Cult of the Primitive." *Antioch Review*, 4 (1944), 47-55.

Gloster, Hugh. *Negro Voices in American Fiction*. 1948; rpt. New York: Russell and Russell, 1965.

"The Greatest Needs of Negro Womanhood: A Symposium." *The Messenger* (September 1927), pp. 272, 285, 288.

Hart, Robert. "Black-White Literary Relations in the Harlem Renaissance." *American Literature* (January 1973), pp. 612-28.

Hartt, Rollin L. "The New Negro: 'When He's Hit, He Hits Back!' " *The Independent* (January 1921), pp. 59-60, 76.

Hawkins, Mason A. "Colored High Schools." *The Crisis* (June 1911), pp. 73-75.

Hawthorne, Nathaniel. "Preface." *The House of the Seven Gables*. New York: Norton and Company, 1967.

Hemenway, Robert. "Introduction: Perceptions of Black America Issue." *Mid-Continent American Studies Journal* (Fall 1970), pp. 7-11.

—. *Zora Neale Hurston*. Urbana, Illinois: University of Illinois, 1977.

Hixson, William B. *Moorfield Storey and the Abolitionist Tradition*. New York: Oxford, 1972.

Hoffman, Frederick. *The Twenties: American Writing in the Postwar Decade*. New York: Viking, 1955.

Huggins, Nathan. *Harlem Renaissance*. New York: Oxford, 1971.

—, ed. *Voices from the Harlem Renaissance*. New York: Oxford, 1976. Jessie Fauset, "Dead Fires," p. 313.

Hughes, Langston. *The Big Sea*. New York: Hill and Wang, 1940.

—. *Fight for Freedom: The Story of the NAACP*. New York: W. W. Norton, 1962.

—. "Harlem Literati in the 20's." *Saturday Review Gallery*. Ed. J. Beatty. New York: Simon and Schuster, 1959, pp. 207-12.

—. "The Negro Artist and the Racial Mountain." *Nation*, 23 June 1926, pp. 692-94.

—. "To Certain Intellectuals." *The Messenger* (February 1925), p. 103.

—. "The Twenties: Harlem and Its Negritude." *African Forum* (Spring 1966), pp. 11-20.

— and Arna Bontemps. *The Poetry of the Negro, 1746-1949*. Garden City, New York: Doubleday, 1949. Jessie Fauset, "Enigma," "La Vie C'Est La Vie," "Dead Fires," "Oblivion," pp. 65-67.

— and Milton Meltzer. *A Pictorial History of the Negro in America*. New York: Crown Publishers, 1963.

International Library of Negro Life and History: The Quest for Equality: From Civil War to Civil Rights. New York: Charles Wesley Publishers Company, 1970.

Isaacs, Harold. *The New World of the Negro American*. New York: Viking, 1963.

Jackson, Augusta. "The Renascence of Negro Literature." M. A. Thesis Altanta University, 1936.

Jackson, George G. "Of Irony in Negro Fiction." *Dissertation Abstracts* University of Michigan, 1953, pp. 388-89.

Jacobs, George W. "Negro Authors Must Eat." *Nation*, 12 June 1929, pp. 710-11.

Jahn, Janheinz. *Neo-African Literature. A History of Black Writing*. New York: Grove Press, 1968.

"Jessie Fauset, Noted Negro Writer, Dies." *Montclair* (*New Jersey*) *Times*, 4 May 1961, p. 6. From Cornell University Deceased Alumni File.

"Jessie Fauset, Novelist, Dies." *Philadelphia Evening Bulletin*, 4 May 1961, p. 25.

"Jessie Fauset, 76, Novelist and Poet." *New York Times*, 4 May 1961.

Johnson, Abby Arthur. "Literary Midwife: Jessie Redmon Fauset and the Harlem Renaissance." *Phylon* (June 1978), pp. 143-53.

Johnson, Charles S. "A Note on the New Literary Movement." *Opportunity* (March 1926), pp. 80-81.

—. "The Rise of the Negro Magazine." *Journal of Negro History* (January 1928), pp. 7-21.

Johnson, James Weldon. *Along This Way*. 1933; rpt. New York: Viking Press, 1967.

—. *Autobiography of an Ex-Colored Man. Three Negro Classics.* New York: Avon, 1965.

—, ed. *The Book of American Negro Poetry*. New York: Harcourt, Brace and World, 1931. Jessie Fauset, "La Vie C'Est La Vie," "Christmas Eve in France," "Dead Fires," "Oriflamme," "Oblivion," pp. 205-08.

—. "Dilemma of the Negro Author." *American Mercury* (December 1928), pp. 477-81.

—. "Negro Authors and White Publishers." *The Crisis* (July 1929), pp. 228-29.

—. "Race Prejudice and the Negro Artist." *Harpers* (November 1928), pp. 769-76.

Kaiser, Ernest. "The Literature of Harlem." *Freedomways*, 3 (1963) 276-91.

Keller, Frances. "The Harlem Literary Renaissance." *North American Review* (May 1968), pp. 29-34.

Kellogg, Charles. *NAACP: A History of the National Association for the Advancement of Colored People. I: 1909-1920*. Baltimore, Maryland: Johns Hopkins Press, 1967.

Kerlin, Robert T. *Negro Poets and Their Poems*. Rev. ed. Washington, D. C.: Associated Publishers, 1935. Jessie Fauset, "Oriflamme," p. 162.

—. *The Voice of the Negro*. 1920; rpt. New York: Arno Press, 1968.

Larsen, Nella. *Passing*. New York: Alfred A. Knopf, 1929.

—. *Quicksand*. 1928; rpt. New York: Negro Universities Press, 1969.

Lash, John S. "The Race Consciousness of the American Negro Author." *Social Forces* (October 1949), pp. 24-34.

"Lecturers for the Summer School." *Tuskegee Messenger*, 25 June 1927, p. 8.

Lemons, J. Stanley. "Black Stereotypes as Reflected in Popular Culture, 1880-1920." *American Literature* (Spring 1977), pp. 102-116.

Lerner, Gerda, ed. *Black Women in White America: A Documentary History*. New York: Random House, 1973.

Littlejohn, David. *Black on White*. New York: Grossman, 1966.

Locke, Alain. "Black Truth and Black Beauty." *Opportunity* (January 1933), pp. 14-18.

—. "Both Sides of the Color Line" [Review of *Plum Bun*]. *Survey*, 1 June 1929, pp. 325-26.

—, ed. *The New Negro: An Interpretation.* 1925; rpt. New York: Atheneum, 1969.

—. "The Saving Grace of Realism: Retrospective Review of the Negro Literature of 1933." *Opportunity* (January 1934), pp. 8-11, 30.

—. "Self-Criticism: The Third Dimension in Culture." *Phylon*, 11 (1950), 391-94.

—. "We Turn to Prose: A Retrospective Review of the Literature of the Negro for 1931." *Opportunity* (February 1932), pp. 40-44.

Logan, Rayford. *The Betrayal of the Negro: From Rutherford Hayes to Woodrow Wilson.* Rev. ed. New York: Collier, 1965.

—. *W. E. B. DuBois: A Profile.* New York: Hill and Wang, 1971.

Lomax, Michael L. "Fantasies of Affirmation: The 1920's Novel of Negro Life." *CLA Journal* (December 1972), pp. 232-46.

Malec, Michael. "Some Observations on the Content of *Crisis*, 1932-1962." *Phylon*, 28 (1967), pp. 161-67.

Marshall, Paule. "The Negro Woman in Literature." *Freedomways*, 6 (1966), 20-25.

Mays, Benjamin. The Negro's God as Reflected in his Literature. 1938; rpt. New York: Athemeum, 1969.

McDougald, Elise Johsnon. "The Double Task: The Struggle of Negro Women for Sex and Race Emanicipation." *Survey*, 1 March 1925, pp. 689-91.

McKay, Claude. *A Long Way From Home.* Intro. St. Clair Drake. 1937; rpt. New York: Harcourt, Brace and World, 1970.

Mencken, H. L. "Burrs Under the Saddle: The Colored Brother." *Montgomery Advertiser*, 18 July 1927, n. pag. (In Mary Church

Terrell Papers, Manuscript Division, Library of Congress.)

"Miss Jessie Fauset Addresses Summer School Teachers." *The Tuskegee Student* (July 1923), p. 3.

Muraskin, William. "An Alienated Elite: Short Stories in *The Crisis*, 1910-1950." *Journal of Black Studies*, 1 (1971), 282-305.

NAACP Annual Report for 1919 (January 1920).

"The New Books" [Review of *Plum Bun*]. *Saturday Review of Literature*, 6 April 1929, p. 866.

Nussbaum, Anna, ed. *Afrika Singt: Eine Ausless Neuer Afro-Amerikanischer Lyrik*. Wien: F. G. Speideische Verlagsbuchhandlung, 1929. Jessie Fauset, "Erleuchtung," pp. 126-27.

"One Hundred and Ten Delegates to the Pan-African Congress by Countries." *The Crisis* (December 1921), pp. 68-69.

Ottley, Roi. "How Colored is Harlem?" *New World A-Coming*. Boston: Houghton Mifflin, 1943, pp. 40-58.

Ovington, Mary White. *Half a Man: The Status of the Negro in New York*. New York: Longmans, Green and Company, 1911.

—. *Portraits in Color*. Freeport, New York: Books for Libraries, 1972.

—. *The Walls Came Tumbling Down*. New York: Harcourt, Brace, 1947.

Park, Robert E. "Negro Race Consciousness as Reflected in Race Literature." *American Review* (September-October 1923), pp. 505-16.

Payne, Daniel. *History of the African Methodist Episcopal Church*. 1891; rpt. New York: Johnson Reprint Company, 1968.

"Poets." *Ebony* (February 1941), p. 41.

Porter, Edna. *Double Blossoms*. New York: Lewis Copeland Company, 1931. Jessie Fauset, " 'Courage!' He Said," pp. 39-40.

Pratt, Annis. "Archetypal Theory and Women's Fiction: 1688-1975." Paper for Women's Caucus for the Modern Languages Panel: "The Theory of Feminist Literary Critics," San Francisco, California, 27 December 1975.

—. "The New Feminist Criticism." *College English* (May 1971), pp. 872-78.

Pritchard, Myron T. and Mary White Ovington. *The Upward Path*. New York: Harcourt Brace & Howe, 1920. Jessie Fauset, "The Rondeau," p. 120.

Proctor Samuel D. "Survival Techniques and the Black Middle Class." *Black Life and Culture in the United States*. Ed. R. L. Goldstein. New York: Thomas Y. Crowell, 1971, pp. 280-94.

Record, Wilson. "Negro Intellectual Leadership in the NAACP, 1910-1940." *Phylon* (Second Quarter 1956), pp. 375-89.

Reddick, L. D. "Publishers are Awful." *Negro Quarterly* (Summer 1942), pp. 187-89.

Redding, Saunders. "The Negro Author: His Publisher, His Public, and His Purse." *Publishers. Weekly*, 24 March 1945, pp. 1284-88.

—. "Problems of the Negro Writer." *Black and White in American Culture: An Anthology from the Massachusetts Review*. Ed. Jules Chametzky and Sidney Kaplan. Amherst: University of Massachusetts Press, 1969, pp. 360-71.

Reedy, Sidney. "The Negro Magazine: A Critical Study of its Educational Significance." *Journal of Negro Education* (October 1934), pp. 598-604.

[Review of *The Chinaberry Tree*]. *Booklist* (February 1932), pp. 259-60.

[Review of *The Chinaberry Tree*]. *Saturday Review of Literature*, 6 February 1932, p. 511.

[Review of *The Chinaberry Tree*]. *The Times Literary Supplement*, 23 June 1932, p. 466.

[Review of *The Chinaberry Tree*]. *Wisconsin Library Bulletin* (March 1932), p. 90.

[Review of *Comedy: American Style*]. *Booklist* (December 1933), p. 120.

[Review of *Comedy: American Style*]. *Nation*, 3 January 1934, p. 26.

[Review of *Plum Bun*]. *Booklist* (May 1929), pp. 321-22.

[Review of *Plum Bun*]. *The Times Literary Supplement*, 29 November 1928, p. 939.

[Review of *Plum Bun*]. *Wisconsin Library Bulletin* (March 1929), p. 102.

[Review of *There Is Confusion*]. *Booklist* (July 1924), p. 378.

[Review of *There Is Confusion*]. *Literary Digest International Book Review* (June 1924), pp. 555-56.

[Review of *There Is Confusion*]. *New York Times Book Section*, 13 April 1924, pp. 9, 16.

[Review of *There Is Confusion*]. *The Times Literary Supplement*, 4 December 1924, p. 828.

[Review of *There Is Confusion*]. *Wisconsin Library Bulletin* (October 1924), p. 212.

Robinson, Carrie C. "A Study of Literary Subject Matter of *The Crisis.*" M. A. Thesis Fisk University, 1934.

Rowell, Charles. "A Bibliography of Bibliographies for the Study of Black American Literature and Folklore." *Black Experience, A Southern University Journal* (June 1969), pp. 95-111.

Rudwick, Elliott. *W. E. B. DuBois: Propagandist of the Negro Protest.* New York: Atheneum, 1969.

—. "W. E. B. DuBois in the role of *Crisis* Editor." *Journal of Negro History* (July 1958), pp. 214-40.

Rush, Theresa and Arata Myers. *Black American Writers Past and Present: A Biographical and Bibliographical Dictionary.* Metuchen, New Jersey: The Scarecrow Press, 1975.

Schoener, Allan, ed. *Harlem on my Mind.* New York: Random House, 1968.

Schuyler, George. "Ballad of Negro Artists." *The Messenger* (August 1926), p. 239.

—. *Black No More.* 1931: rpt. New York: Negro Universities Press, 1969.

—. "The Negro Art Hokum." *Nation,* 16 June 1926, pp. 662-63.

—. [Review of *There Is Confusion*]. *The Messenger* (May 1924), pp. 145-46.

—. "The Van Vechten Revolution." *Phylon,* 11 (1950), 362-68.

Showalter, Elaine. "Literary Criticism." *Signs: Journal of Women in Culture and Society* (Winter 1975), pp. 435-60.

Singh, Amritjit. *The Novels of the Harlem Renaissance: Twelve Black Writers 1923-1933.* University Park, Pennsylvania: Pennsylvania State University Press, 1976.

Sinnette, Elinor. " 'The Brownies' Book': A Pioneer Publication for Children." *Freedomways* (Winter 1965), pp. 133-42.

Smith, Beverly. "Population Rises Steadily: Illness Takes Heavy Toll; Unemployment and Low Wages Result from Race Prejudice." *New York Herald Tribune*, 10 February 1930. In Allan Schoener, ed. *Harlem on my Mind*. New York: Random House, 1968.

Smith, Charles Spencer. *A History of the African Methodist Episcopal Church*. 1891; rpt. New York: Johnson Reprint Corporation, 1968.

Snelson, Floyd. "Van Vechtens Desert 'Gay Spots' of Harlem; Nite Life to Miss Em." *Pittsburgh Courier*, 23 January 1932, p. 4.

"Speaking of Books.' [Review of *Plum Bun*]. *Outlook and Independent*, 13 March 1929, p. 430.

St. James, Warren D. *The National Association for the Advancement of Colored People: A Case Study in Pressure Groups*. New York: Exposition Press, 1958.

Starkey, Marion L. "Jessie Fauset." *Southern Workman* (May 1932), pp. 217-20.

Stribling, Thomas S. *Birthright*. New York: The Century Company, 1921.

Sykes, Gerald. "Amber-Tinted Elegance" [Review of *The Chinaberry Tree*]. *Nation*, 27 July 1932, p. 88.

Tatham, Campbell. "Double Order: The Spectrum of Black Aesthetics." *Mid-continent American Studies Journal* (Fall 1970), pp. 88-100.

Terrell, Mary Church. "What It Means to be Colored in the Capital of the United States." *Black Women in White America*. Ed. Gerda Lerner. New York: Random House, 1973, pp. 378-382.

Rpt. from *The Independent* (January 1907), pp. 181-86.

Thurman, Wallace, et. al, eds. *Fire!!* (November 1926): rpt. New York: Negro Universities Press, 1970.

—. "Negro Artists and the Negro." *New Republic*, 31 August 1927, pp. 37-39.

—. "Negro Poets and Their Poetry." *Bookman* (July 1928), pp. 255-61.

Turner, E. R. *The Negro in Pennsylvania*. 1911; rpt. New York: Arno Press, 1969.

The Tuskegee *Institute Bulletin* (June 1927).

Van Doren, Carl. "The Younger Generation of Negro Writers." *Opportunity* (May 1924), pp. 144-45.

—. "The Roving Critic: The Negro Renaissance." *Century* (March 1926), pp. 635-37.

Van Vechten, Carl. *Nigger Heaven*. 1926; rpt. New York: Harper, 1971.

Vincent, Florence Smith. "There are 20,000 Persons 'Passing' Says Noted Author." *Pittsburgh Courier*, 11 May 1929, II, p. 1.

Waldron, Edward. "Walter White and the Harlem Renaissance: Letters from 1924-1927." *CLA Journal* (June 1973), pp. 438-57.

Walrond, Eric, "The New Negro Faces America." *Current History* (February 1923), pp. 786-88.

Walters, Ronald. "The Negro Press and the Image of Success, 1920-1931." *Midcontinent American Studies Journal* (Fall 1970), pp. 36-55.

Waring, Nora. "Books." *The Crisis* (July 1926), p. 142.

White, Newman Ivey and Walter Clinton Jackson, eds. *An Anthology of Verse by American Negroes*. 1924; rpt. Durham, North Carolina: Moore Publishing Comapny, 1968. Jessie Fauset, "Oriflamme," p. 194.

" 'White' Negroes" [Review of *Plum Bun*]. *New York Times*, 3 March 1929, p. 8.

Williams, Kenny. *They Also Spoke*. Nashville Tennessee: Townsend Press, 1970.

Wintz, Gary DeCordova. "Black Writers in 'Nigger Heaven': The Harlem Renaissance." Diss. Kansas State University, 1974.

Wolters, Raymond. *Negroes and the Great Depression: The Problem of Economic Recovery*. Westport, Connecticut: Greenwood Publishing Company, 1970.

Wright, J. C. "The New Dunbar High School, Washington, D. C." *The Crisis* (March 1917), pp. 220-22.

Wright, Richard. "Blueprint for Negro Writing." *New Challenge* (Fall 1937), pp. 53-65.

Wright, Richard R. Jr. *The Negro in Pennsylvania: A Study in Economic History*. 1912; rpt. New York: Arno Press, 1969.

Yellin, Jean Fagan. "An Index of Literary Materials in *The Crisis*, 1910-1934: Articles, Belles-Lettres, and Book Reviews." *CLA Journal*, 14 (1971), 197-234; 452-465.

II.   Letters and other materials from the following sources which
      were of use in this study:

Amistad Research Center, Dillard University, Countee Cullen Papers
      B. F. Seldon to Jessie Fauset, n.d.
      John H. Patton to Jessie Fauset, 8 February 1920
      Harry E. Davis to Jessie Fauset, 27 December 1923
      Jessie Fauset to Countee Cullen,
                        1 May 1923
                        20 July 1923
                        30 August 1923
                        n. d. October 1925
                        4 November 1925
                        n. d. 1926
                        25 May 1927
                        25 January 1932
      Jessie Fauset to Ida Cullen,
                        11 March 1946
                        14 May 1946
                        24 September 1949
                        26 June 1950
                        2 August 1951
                        20 June 1953
      Manuscript, "La Vie C'est La Vie," signed "To my friend Countee Cullen,
          J. F."

Bryn Mawr College Archives, M. Carey Thomas Office Files, letter-
      books, 1897-1925.

Collection of American Literature, Beinecke Rare Book and Man-
      uscript Library, Yale University, James Weldon Johnson Mem-
      orial Collection
      Jessie Fauset to Harold Jackman,
                        21 December 1924
                        3 December 1933 (Postmark)
                        13 May 1934
                        18 November 1936
                        15 September 1939
                        21 September 1939
                        5 October 1939
                        19 January 1942

Jessie Fauset to Mrs. James Weldon Johnson,
                        19 January 1925
                        1 June 1921
                        29 June 1938
Manuscript, "The Crescent Moon"

Cornell University Archives
    Vital Statistics Card
    Ben F. Stambaugh to Professor L. Coles
    "Information About Cornell Alumnae for the Federation of Cornell
        Women's Clubs"
    1905 Cornellian

Fisk University Library, Nashville, Tennessee, Jean Toomer Collection
    Jessie Fauset to Jean Toomer,
                        17 February 1922
                        24 February 1922
                        14 April 1922

Library of Congress, Manuscript Division
    Harmon Foundation Files
    Mary Church Terrell Papers

NAACP Files, including
    Mary White Ovington to Jessie Fauset,
                        3 November 1923
                        5 November 1923
    Jessie Fauset to Mary White Ovington,
                        6 November 1923
                        8 November 1923
    Jessie Fauset to Arthur Spingarn, 18 March 1922

Moorland-Spingarn Research Center, Howard University
    Jessie Fauset to Arthur Spingarn,
                        n. d.
                        20 January 1923
                        21 February 1923
                        25 October 1923
                        8 November 1923
                        11 February 1924

25 February 1924
3 March 1924
26 January 1926
28 March 1928
8 August 1928
Jessie Fauset to Mr. and Mrs. Arthur Spingarn, 10 February 1925
Jessie Fauset to Mrs. Spingarn,
            n. d.
            5 December 1925
Jessie Fauset to Montgomery Gregory,
            12 December 1921
            29 March 1922
Jessie Fauset to Joel Spingarn,
            12 February 1913
            9 October 1913
            18 October 1913
            24 October 1913
            26 April 1923
Mary Childs Nerney to Joel Spingarn, 6 January 1916
Jessie Fauset to Archibald Grimke, 11 April 1905
Jessie Fauset to Alain Locke, 9 January 1933

Portage Public Library, Portage, Wisconsin
Jessie Fauset to Zona Gale,
            14 August 1924
            20 October 1931

The State Historical Society of Wisconsin, Madison, Wisconsin,
Archives Division, Zona Gale Papers
Jessie Fauset to Zona Gale,
            22 October 1931
            25 October 1931

University of Massachusetts, Amherst, Massachusetts, the W. E. B.
DuBois Papers
W. E. B. DuBois to Jessie Fauset,
            12 June 1918
            13 November 1924
            4 December 1924
            6 March 1925
            11 March 1925

                        6 April 1925
                        10 September 1925
                        29 March 1926
                        7 April 1926
                        12 April 1926
                        14 April 1926
Jessie Fauset to W. E. B. DuBois,
                        25 February 1918
                        31 March 1926
                        7 April 1926
                        14 April 1926
                        27 April 1926

Letters to the Author from the Following:
    Alexander, Sadie T. M., 30 January 1976
    Aptheker, Herbert, 25 February 1976
    Dzwonkoski, Peter, 19 February 1976
    Elliott, Hamilton, 19 February 1976
    Fauset, Arthur Huff, 26 December 1975
                        n. d. January 1976
                        10 January 1976
                        26 January 1976
                        25 February 1976
                        24 March 1976
    Fletcher, Juanita D., 5 January 1976
    Lane, David A., 29 March 1976
    Malval, Fritz, 27 October 1975
    Reed, Gertrude, 11 August 1976
    Reed, Vincent, 16 March 1976
    Shepherd, Barbara, 17 February 1976
    Smith, Elsie B., 7 March 1976
    Westlake, Neda, 19 January 1976

Miscellaneous
    Last Will and Testamentary of Jessie F. Harris, Register of Wills, City Hall,
        Philadelphia, Pennsylvania
    Death Certificate, Department of Health, Vital Statistics, Commonwealth
        of Pennsylvania
    Birth Certificate, State of New Jersey
    Interviews, Arthur Huff Fauset, 1 April 1976
                William Zeitz, 1 April 1976
    Reminiscences of George Schuyler and W. E. B. DuBois, The Columbia
        Oral History Collection, Columbia University

Index

Jessie Redmon Fauset,
Black American Writer

Composed in IBM Electronic Selectric Composer *Journal Roman* and printed offset by Cushing-Malloy, Incorporated, Ann Arbor, Michigan. The paper on which the book is printed is the Northwest Paper Company's *Caslon;* the book was sewn and bound by Edward Dekker & Sons, Grand Rapids, Michigan.

Jessie Redmon Fauset, Black American Writer is a Trenowyth book, the scholarly publishing division of The Whitston Publishing Company.

This edition consists of 750 casebound copies.